# EXPORT MANAGEMENT

# EXPORT MANAGEMENT

## An International Context

### edited by
### Michael R. Czinkota
### George Tesar

PRAEGER

PRAEGER SPECIAL STUDIES • PRAEGER SCIENTIFIC

382.6
E 962

Library of Congress Cataloging in Publication Data
Main Entry under title:

Export management.

    Includes bibliographical references and index.
    1. Export marketing—Addresses, essays, lectures.
I. Czinkota, Michael R.  II. Tesar, George.
HF1009.5.E933      658.8′48      81-17817
ISBN 0-03-060331-5      AACR2

Published in 1982 by Praeger Publishers
CBS Educational and Professional Publishing
a Division of CBS Inc.
521 Fifth Avenue, New York, New York 10175 U.S.A.

Printed in the United States of America

# PREFACE

The management of export operations of firms is a relatively unexplored area in international marketing. Yet it is one of the areas that can contribute much to the growth of firms and to the stimulation of an economy. An increasing number of researchers, managers, and government administrators are therefore interested in learning how various types of firms manage export operations.

Some reasons for this increase in interest are that managers desire to learn from their counterparts how the successful export operations are managed in order to improve their own performance, and government administrators wish to understand how export operations are managed in order to further and promote exports. Researchers are also increasingly paying more attention to the involvement of firms in export operations and their management of these activities as a dimension of international marketing.

Although basic components of exporting are well established in the area of international trade, empirical studies have not systematically examined the internal factors that contribute to the motivation of individual firms to get involved in export operations. More specifically, few studies focus directly on the management aspects of export operations and their integration into the overall management functions. This problem exists partly because relatively little research has been directed toward the identification, integration, and development of the export function as part of overall management. Since export management is an integral part of the company's internal operations, an examination of export operations should result in the development of a conceptual framework in which those operations can take place.

Since export concerns are common to most nations, no one country has a monopoly on export problems and solutions. In spite of the commonalities, however, export research has tended, particularly in the United States, to be carried out in an ethnocentric fashion. It is the purpose of this volume to provide the reader with an international view of export management. To accomplish this cross-fertilization of ideas, a group of prominent scholars in the area of exporting met in Washington, D.C., during May and June 1981 for an International Symposium on Exporting, which was sponsored by Georgetown University and the Organization of American States. The chapters in this volume represent papers that were presented at this meeting. It is hoped that by showing the same concern from different socioeconomic aspects, the reader will be able to more fully understand the issues and complexities of export management.

This volume consists of four parts. In Part I, studies are presented that discuss the underlying behavioral factors that motivate export activities of smaller-sized firms and investigate characteristics common to these firms. Part II presents findings that concern the export activities of multinational corporations. Part III contains studies that deal with issues of export planning and strategy. Part IV represents an evaluation of the current state of export research as perceived by the participants in the export symposium.

Michael R. Czinkota
Co-Chairman
International Symposium on Exporting

# ACKNOWLEDGMENTS

The International Symposium on Exporting, at which the contributions to this volume were presented, was cosponsored by Georgetown University and the Organization of American States. Dean Ronald L. Smith of the Georgetown University School of Business Administration provided encouragement and financial support. Don Shay of Management Analysis Center, Inc. and Sea-Land Industries, Inc. provided financial assistance. Renato Tovar and Jane Mohan of the Organization of American States aided in the many details of the conference. Elizabeth Chant assisted with the review correspondence. Julie Ruth served as conference coordinator. Our thanks go to all of them.

We are deeply grateful to the members of the Review Panel who scrutinized and evaluated more than 60 papers. These members were: Nizamettin Aydin, Ohio University; Warren Bilkey, University of Wisconsin; Peter Buckley, University of Bradford; Tamer Cavusgil, University of Wisconsin, Whitewater; Bernardo Gluch, Organization of American States; Wesley Johnston, The Ohio State University; Pat Joynt, Norwegian School of Management; Bernard LaLonde, The Ohio State University; Eloy Mestre, Organization of American States; Jane Mohan, Organization of American States; Lars Otterbeck, Stockholm School of Economics; David Ricks, University of South Carolina; Elyette Roux, University of Marseille; Helmut Soldner, University of Augsburg; Jesse Tarleton, College of William and Mary; Lawrence Welch, Norwegian School of Management; Finn Wiedersheim-Paul, Uppsala University; and Nicholas Williamson, Georgia State University.

# CONTENTS

ix

# LIST OF TABLES

## LIST OF FIGURES

# PART I
## EXPORT BEHAVIOR
## AND CHARACTERISTICS OF
## SMALL-SIZED FIRMS

Part I consists of eight contributions, all of which discuss the underlying behavioral factors and characteristics of smaller-sized exporting firms in different socioeconomic climates. Wesley Johnston and Michael Czinkota examine managerial motivations as determinants of industrial export behavior by investigating the frequency of proactive and reactive motivations of exporting firms. Initial and current motivations are measured, allowing an analysis of changes in motivations for the firms surveyed. Stan Reid focuses on elements of export behavior by presenting a conceptual framework for investigating the relationships between different measures of firm size and their effect on export activities. Mary Brooks and Philip Rosson compare various dimensions of exporting and nonexporting Canadian firms, paying particular attention to the issues of profitability and motivation. Pat Joynt compares the export behavior of Norwegian and U.S. firms. His results suggest that the traditional approaches to the study of export operations are not consistent with the outcome of his research. Ernest Ogram focuses on the development of profiles of exporting and nonexporting manufacturing firms in Georgia. George Tesar and Jesse Tarleton replicate a previous empirical study of U.S. exporters for validation purposes and to provide a basis for the development of a conceptual and theoretical foundation for export operations, export development, and export stimulation. Gérard Garnier compares the behavior of exporting and nonexporting Canadian firms in two industries, with particular focus on the personality of the entrepreneur, and provides a model for the export process. Erdener Kaynak and Lois Stevenson study the export orientation of manufacturers in Nova Scotia, with particular focus on actual and perceived obstacles to export marketing.

# 1

## MANAGERIAL MOTIVATIONS AS DETERMINANTS OF INDUSTRIAL EXPORT BEHAVIOR

Wesley J. Johnston
Michael R. Czinkota

The United States is becoming increasingly concerned with its export performance. Growing deficits in the balance of trade and continuing import pressures will probably continue to keep this interest at a high level, since in the long run any imbalance between outflow activities (exports) and inflow activities (imports) must be corrected. Although this correction can take on many different forms, such as gold or capital transfers, the least painful and therefore probably the most desirable form is the stimulation of exports by U.S. firms while reducing or holding constant the level of imports.

In response to this export stimulation need, the U.S. government has instituted or strengthened a variety of different programs aimed at export promotion. Currently, however, all these programs seem to have two common shortcomings: lack of information as to what services are needed by whom and scarce financial resources. These shortcomings exist because of a general lack of knowledge about the export development process and have resulted in a less than precise targeting of export assistance and in the ineffective use of existing resources (Weil, 1978). In an effort to understand and explain the export activities of domestic firms, researchers have concentrated a great deal of effort in finding industry and firm determinants of export activity. One goal of their research has been the isolation of specific structural characteristics capable of discriminating between firms that export and those that do not. These efforts, however, have not seen a payoff proportional to input and have to date been able to conclusively identify only technology and product variables as important structural factors contributing to export activities of firms (Reid, 1980). Perhaps this lack of success in explaining export activities of firms is a result of the insufficient emphasis that has been placed on the role of managerial motivation in the export decision. The purpose of this research is to investigate various managerial motivations for exporting and their correlates. It is hoped that the recognition and understanding of these motivations can be useful to groups and institutions concerned with export promotion by aiding them in appealing to these motivations and, through these appeals, increase the export activities of firms.

## BACKGROUND

Differences in the motivations of a firm's management seem to result in varying needs for export promotion. Bilkey and Tesar (1977) found that management's perception of the firm's competitive advantages plays a major role in the exploration of the feasibility of exporting. In measuring the quality of management, these authors also found that firms who initially obtained their own first export order had better and more dynamic managements when compared to firms whose initial order was unsolicited.

Pavord and Bogart (1975) distinguished firms that actively seek exports and those that do not, leading them to a framework of firms whose exporting efforts are characterized by no activity, passive activity, minor activity, and aggressive activity. The authors found that significant differences existed between seekers and nonseekers of export opportunities in regard to the severity of exporting problems.

Wiedersheim-Paul et al. (1978) distinguished three groups of firms: active, passive, and domestic. The authors then analyzed these groups on the dimensions of: willingness to start exporting, information collection activity, and information transmission activity. Factors that were seen as major causes for an increase in the willingness to export were new decision makers or changes in management's attitudes and external changes. An increase in the economic advantages of exporting through export promotion was seen by the authors as unlikely to affect the attitudes of decision makers who perform more passive activities and have less positive attitudes toward exporting.

Favorable expectations of exporting by management and the aspirations of management for the firm were also identified as major factors contributing to the differentiation of firms and their export behavior in an Automatic Interaction Detector Analysis carried out by Cavusgil et al. (1979). In a more recent study (Cavusgil and Nevin, 1981), export marketing behavior of firms was found to be related to expectations of management, level of commitment to export marketing, differential firm advantages, and the strength of managerial aspirations. These results support the belief that reluctance of firms to export may be largely attributable to a lack of determination or motivation to export by management.

Underlying all these studies seems to be the finding that the managerial attitudes held by a firm's management play a major role in the firm's progress in exporting and in its needs for assistance. Major distinctions of management attitudes seem to be active versus passive and aggressive versus not aggressive.

AN INVESTIGATION

This investigation of the motivational framework of firms was carried out in five phases:

- The identification and description of motivational factors
- The development of a rank order of importance for these motivational factors
- The determination of the extent to which firms are unidimensional in their motivation
- The determination of the stability of motivations over time
- The determination of the explanatory power that motivational factors have in differentiating among firms

The identification and description of motivational factors was carried out by aggregating the exporting literature as it related to these factors. Main works used here were by Bilkey and Tesar (1977) and Pavord and Bogart (1975). Subsequently, these motivations were augmented through findings of personal interviews with business executives. All sources indicated that motivations could be categorized into two groups. One category contained motivations that were the result of reactive behavior to environmental or outside change, while the other category of motivations contained active or aggressive behavior based on a firm's internal situation. Table 1.1 gives an overview of the motivations that were found to exist. These motivations are presented with their definitions and separated into "proactive" and "reactive" categories.

In order to carry out the further steps of the research process, primary data were collected. To avoid biases due to advantages or disadvantages in exporting for firms based on natural resources, it was decided to sample only industries that were not tied down to a specific market location by the nature of their production process (Stobaugh, 1974). Biases that result from tax and duty restrictions

## TABLE 1.1

Possible Export Motivations for Smaller-Sized U.S. Manufacturers

| Type | Motivation | Definition |
|------|-----------|-----------|
| Proactive | Exclusive information | Knowledge about foreign customers, marketplaces, or market situations that is not widely shared by other firms |
| | Managerial urge | Desire, drive, enthusiasm of management toward exporting |
| | Unique products | Product type of one firm that is not widely available from international competitors |
| | Profit advantage | Higher profitability of international sales when compared to domestic sales |
| | Marketing advantage | Specialized marketing knowledge distinguishing firm from its competitors |
| | Technological advantage | Knowledge of a specialized technology that is not widely available internationally |
| | DISC | Tax benefits obtained through the formation of a Domestic International Sales Corporation |
| Reactive | Competitive pressures | Fear of loss from foreign markets resulting from international activities of competing firms |
| | Overproduction | Existence of inventories that are significantly above desired levels |
| | Declining domestic sales | Continuous reduction of the firm's U.S. sales or its U.S. market share |
| | Excess capacity | Underutilization of existing equipment |
| | Saturated domestic market | Contraction of total domestic sales market volume |
| | Proximity to ports | Physical closeness to international shipping facilities |

imposed by foreign governments were reduced by focusing exclusively on industrial goods and excluding consumer goods, which are much more often subject to such government-imposed trade distortions. To insure that the industries examined had some export potential, three industries were selected from a list of industries with strong future export potential as predicted by the U.S. Department of Commerce. These industries were materials handling equipment manufacturers (SIC* 353), avionic and aviation support manufacturers (SIC 372), and industrial instruments manufacturers (SIC 382). Finally, since information from the Department of Commerce has indicated that it was mainly smaller-sized firms who did not export and who thus were the target of export promotion activities (Department of Commerce, n.d.) only firms under $50 million in annual sales were included in this study.

All these considerations then provided a selection framework for the universe of concern based on the following criteria that had to be met by firms for inclusion in this study:

- Small- and medium-sized firms (below $50 million in annual sales volume)
- Operating within a footloose industry (not tied by location of natural resources)
- Manufacturing industrial goods (SIC 353, 372, 382)
- Identified as having strong export potential.

By using the Dun and Bradstreet Million Dollar Directory and Middle Market Directory, 1,004 firms were identified for inclusion in the study.

The study data were collected through a mail questionnaire that had been pretested extensively for clarity, difficulty, and response. The overall response rate to the questionnaire was within the range normally found in mail surveys without incentives. Out of the 1,004 questionnaires mailed, 301 were returned for an overall response rate of 30 percent, 181 of which were fully usable for purpose of this particular analysis. To test for nonresponse bias the Wilcoxon Distribution Free Rank Sum Test was used (Hollander and Wolfe, 1973). Using sales volume, which was available for all firms, as the basis of comparison, nonrespondents were compared with the responses received. Similarities between nonrespondents and respondents were accepted at the .004 level. Therefore, it would appear that the responses received are representative of the

---

*Standard Industrial Classification.

entire group of firms surveyed and that no response bias existed in terms of firm size. While no response bias appears to exist with respect to firm size, other biases may exist. Since the analysis was confined to exporting firms and excluded firms in the consumer goods industry, one should exercise caution when generalizing the results of this study.

In order to determine the relative importance of the motivational factors, firms were asked to indicate whether or not they were motivated in their exporting effort by a particular factor. The rank order of main factors, that is, factors that motivated more than one-third of the firms, is shown in Table 1.2. It is interesting to note that while motivations were fairly widely distributed, profit advantage and unique products clearly were mentioned most often. Also of the seven factors in this main group, six were proactive in nature, and only one (competitive pressures) was reactive. Tables 1.3 to 1.5 depict the distribution of the factors that currently motivate the export activities of firms.

TABLE 1.2

Main Factors Motivating the Exporting Effort

| Rank | Motivational Factors | Percentage of Firms Motivated by a Factor |
|------|----------------------|-------------------------------------------|
| 1 | Profit advantage | 65 |
| 2 | Unique products | 62 |
| 3 | Technological advantage | 53 |
| 4 | Managerial urge | 44 |
| 5 | DISC | 36 |
| 6 | Competitive pressures | 35 |
| 7 | Marketing advantage | 34 |

As can be seen, most firms were motivated at least by some proactive factors, while many were not motivated at all by reactive motivations. The overall motivational score, which was determined by scoring each proactive motivation as +1 and each reactive motivation as -1,* indicated that only 15 firms had an entirely negative,

---

*It should be kept in mind here that the plus and minus notations are used for reasons of convenience and do not indicate a judgment of the firm's management.

## TABLE 1.3

### Distribution of Current Proactive Motivations among Firms

| Number of Proactive Motivations | Number of Firms | Frequency (percent) |
|:---:|:---:|:---:|
| 0 | 2 | 1.1 |
| 1 | 27 | 14.9 |
| 2 | 40 | 22.1 |
| 3 | 42 | 23.2 |
| 4 | 39 | 21.5 |
| 5 | 17 | 9.4 |
| 6 | 11 | 6.1 |
| 7 | 3 | 1.7 |
|  | 181 | 100.0 |

## TABLE 1.4

### Distribution of Current Reactive Motivations among Firms

| Number of Reactive Motivations | Number of Firms | Frequency (percent) |
|:---:|:---:|:---:|
| 0 | 71 | 39.2 |
| 1 | 54 | 29.8 |
| 2 | 33 | 18.2 |
| 3 | 15 | 8.3 |
| 4 | 7 | 3.9 |
| 5 | 0 | 0.0 |
| 6 | 1 | 0.6 |
|  | 181 | 100.0 |

## TABLE 1.5

### Summary Distribution of Current Motivational Factors among Firms

| Motivation Score* | Number of Firms | Frequency (percent) |
|---|---|---|
| -3 | 1 | 0.6 |
| -2 | 5 | 2.8 |
| -1 | 9 | 5.0 |
| 0 | 20 | 11.0 |
| 1 | 42 | 23.2 |
| 2 | 37 | 20.4 |
| 3 | 29 | 16.0 |
| 4 | 17 | 9.4 |
| 5 | 14 | 7.7 |
| 6 | 6 | 3.3 |
| 7 | 1 | 0.6 |
| | 181 | 100.0 |

*With each proactive motivation scoring +1 and each reactive motivation scoring -1.

that is, reactive motivation. In arriving at the "motivational score" for firms an equal weight was assigned to each motivational factor. While it may be questionable as to whether each motivational factor would have exactly the same degree of influence in precipitating export activities, this scale does provide measurement of exporting motivations as will be discussed later. Again it can be seen that firms are mainly motivated by proactive factors. A comparison of initial and current motivations, which is depicted in Table 1.6, shows that the mainly proactive motivation of firms also holds true for the initial exporting effort. It also shows that, over time, both firms that have been reactive and proactive tend to be less extreme in their motivations.

In order to determine whether firms generally are unidimensional in their motivation, that is, whether firms that are proactive score only on proactive factors and vice versa, a cross-tabulation was carried out. Table 7.1 presents the results of this analysis, which indicated that 108 out of the 181 firms (60 percent) were motivated by both proactive and reactive factors. This was particularly true for firms that were motivated by only a few proactive factors, that is, they were mainly the ones who also were motivated by some reactive factors. Firms that were highly motivated by proactive factors or highly motivated by reactive factors tended not to be motivated by the opposing factor group. This result indicates that firms that are motivated only by a few factors in their exporting effort tend not to be unidimensional in the direction of their motivations.

TABLE 1.6

Summary Distribution of Initial Motivational
Factors among Firms

| Motivation Score* | Number of Firms | Frequency* (percent) |
|---|---|---|
| -3 | 2 | 1.1 |
| -2 | 3 | 1.7 |
| -1 | 10 | 5.5 |
| 0 | 19 | 10.5 |
| 1 | 52 | 28.7 |
| 2 | 31 | 17.1 |
| 3 | 32 | 17.7 |
| 4 | 22 | 12.2 |
| 5 | 5 | 2.8 |
| 6 | 4 | 2.2 |
| 7 | 1 | 0.6 |

*With each proactive motivation scoring +1 and each reactive motivation scoring -1.

In order to measure the stability of motivations for exporting over time, firms were asked in the questionnaire to indicate which motivations initially stimulated their export activities, and which factors were currently motivating their export activities. By comparing the two responses, which had been requested in two separate sections of the questionnaire, an analysis of shifts in motivation over time was made possible. Since only overall motivational scores were compared, only shifts in the motivational score sums were observed. The results are shown in Table 1.8. This analysis indicated that only 69 firms (38 percent) had remained stable in their

TABLE 1.7

Cross-Tabulation of Current Proactive and Reactive
Motivational Factors among Firms
(percent of firms)

| Reactive | Proactive | | | | | | | | Row Totals* |
|---|---|---|---|---|---|---|---|---|---|
| | 0 | 1 | 2 | 3 | 4 | 5 | 6 | 7 | |
| 0 | 0.0 | 8.3 | 7.7 | 9.9 | 6.1 | 5.0 | 2.2 | 0.6 | 39.2 |
| 1 | 0.6 | 3.9 | 7.2 | 6.6 | 5.5 | 2.2 | 2.8 | 1.1 | 29.8 |
| 2 | 0.0 | 2.2 | 5.5 | 3.3 | 5.5 | 0.6 | 1.1 | 0.0 | 18.2 |
| 3 | 0.6 | 0.6 | 0.6 | 1.7 | 3.9 | 1.1 | 0.0 | 0.0 | 8.3 |
| 4 | 0.0 | 0.0 | 1.7 | 1.7 | 0.0 | 0.6 | 0.0 | 0.0 | 3.9 |
| 5 | 0.0 | 0.0 | 0.0 | 0.0 | 0.0 | 0.0 | 0.0 | 0.0 | 0.0 |
| 6 | 0.0 | 0.0 | 0.0 | 0.0 | 0.6 | 0.0 | 0.0 | 0.0 | 0.6 |
| Column totals | 1.1 | 14.9 | 22.1 | 23.2 | 21.5 | 9.4 | 6.1 | 1.7 | 100.0 |

*Columns may not add due to rounding.

## TABLE 1.8

### Shifts in the Motivations of Firms over Time
(number of firms)

| Motivational score of current export effort | Motivational Score of Initial Export Effort | | | | | | | | | | | Row Totals |
|---|---|---|---|---|---|---|---|---|---|---|---|---|
| | -3 | -2 | -1 | 0 | 1 | 2 | 3 | 4 | 5 | 6 | 7 | |
| -3 | 0 | 1 | 0 | 0 | 0 | 0 | 0 | 0 | 0 | 0 | 0 | 1 |
| -2 | 1 | 1 | 0 | 2 | 1 | 0 | 0 | 0 | 0 | 0 | 0 | 5 |
| -1 | 0 | 0 | 3 | 1 | 2 | 2 | 0 | 0 | 1 | 0 | 0 | 9 |
| 0 | 0 | 0 | 2 | 8 | 3 | 4 | 3 | 0 | 0 | 0 | 0 | 20 |
| 1 | 0 | 0 | 2 | 3 | 26 | 7 | 1 | 3 | 0 | 0 | 0 | 42 |
| 2 | 1 | 1 | 1 | 4 | 11 | 9 | 8 | 2 | 0 | 0 | 0 | 37 |
| 3 | 0 | 0 | 2 | 0 | 4 | 5 | 13 | 4 | 1 | 0 | 0 | 29 |
| 4 | 0 | 0 | 0 | 0 | 3 | 2 | 4 | 6 | 2 | 0 | 0 | 17 |
| 5 | 0 | 0 | 0 | 1 | 1 | 1 | 2 | 5 | 1 | 3 | 0 | 14 |
| 6 | 0 | 0 | 0 | 0 | 1 | 1 | 1 | 2 | 0 | 1 | 0 | 6 |
| 7 | 0 | 0 | 0 | 0 | 0 | 0 | 0 | 0 | 0 | 0 | 1 | 1 |
| Column totals | 2 | 3 | 10 | 19 | 52 | 31 | 32 | 22 | 5 | 4 | 1 | 181 |

motivation to export from the time of their initial exporting effort
to the time of the current export effort. Of the firms, 61 (34 percent) indicated that they had become more proactively motivated,
while 51 firms (28 percent) indicated that over time they had become more motivated by reactive factors. Of these shifts, however, only 30 (27 percent) involved a shift of two factors or more,
and only 14 (13 percent) involved a shift of three factors or more.
It seems, therefore, that while motivational factors vary over time
in the extent of their impact on the firm's exporting effort, this
variation occurs mainly within a rather narrow limit.

Finally, this study investigated the explanatory power of motivational factors in differentiating among firms. This investigation
enabled the researchers to engage in an interesting methodological
comparison. In a previous study (Czinkota, 1980) the impact of
motivational factors had already been explored with the same data
set. In that study, firms had been grouped into categories based on
their overall motivational score for current export motivation.
Scoring proactive motivations as +1 and reactive motivations as -1,
firms were categorized as reactive if their overall motivational
score was negative, as proactive if their overall motivational score
was positive, and as situational if their overall motivational score
was zero (this type of scoring also has been used in other studies).
With the help of analysis of variance, firms in these three categories
were then compared to each other on the basis of their scores for
different exporting issues ranging from advertising to service considerations, with each issue having been evaluated as to its importance, the problem it posed, the value it represented to the customer, the likelihood of its being improved internally, and the likelihood of the issue being improved through the assistance of an outside group. Using the Duncan test, this analysis resulted in 12 significant differences among categories out of a total of 100 possible
differences. The present study analyzed the same issue by correlating the motivational factor scores with the exporting variables,
using the Pearson Correlation Coefficient. Rather than using the
motivational factors as categorical data, they now were treated as
continuous variables. Table 1.9 shows that 19 correlations were
now found to be significant at the .05 level or higher. While this
result is, from an overall perspective, still less than dramatic, it
indicates that the new approach to the data in constructing a motivational scale improved the results by more than 50 percent. The
categorization of firms as proactive, reactive, or situational therefore seems less useful since it prevented a large amount of valuable
information from being recognized. Further research could extend
the "motivational scale" approach by allowing for different weights
for each managerial motivation toward exporting.

TABLE 1.9

Variables Significantly Correlating with
Export Motivation Scale

| Variable* | Correlation | p< |
|---|---|---|
| Sales volume | +.19 | .01 |
| Importance of financing | -.16 | .02 |
| Importance of funds transfer | -.14 | .04 |
| Importance of providing repair service | +.14 | .04 |
| Problem of obtaining financial information | -.17 | .02 |
| Problem of funds transfer | -.17 | .02 |
| Value to customer of | | |
| Nonproduct variables | +.18 | .02 |
| Advertising | +.16 | .03 |
| Distribution coordination | -.15 | .04 |
| Financing | -.19 | .02 |
| Improvement in external change of information on | | |
| Business practices | -.15 | .04 |
| Communication | -.25 | .01 |
| Transport rate determination | -.17 | .02 |
| Distribution coordination | -.15 | .04 |
| Financing | -.20 | .01 |
| Pricing internationally | -.15 | .04 |
| Providing parts availability | -.17 | .02 |
| Providing repair service | -.19 | .02 |
| Providing technical advice | -.17 | .03 |

*With the exception of sales volume, which was measured in dollars per year, all variables were measured on a four-point scale.

## IMPLICATIONS AND CONCLUSIONS

Several important conclusions can be drawn from this study. First, exporters are motivated mainly by proactive, that is, internal factors. These motivations do not seem to shift dramatically over time but are rather stable. The two types of motivations seem to result in a number of important differences among firms.

Proactive firms seem to have a larger sales volume and be more service oriented than reactive firms. Proactive firms also seem to be more marketing and strategy oriented than reactive firms, whose major concerns rest with operational issues. Proactive firms are also much less willing to seek or use outside assistance for their exporting effort when compared to reactive firms.

These results present a series of interesting issues for export policy makers. The relative stability of motivations over time indicates that export promotion efforts aimed at drastically changing the motivations of firms have little chance of being very successful. A better strategy would be to aim at increasing the impact of motivations on firms by reinforcing the proactive and reactive motivations. Such a reinforcement could be carried out by providing a more conducive environment for proactive motivations through incentives such as tax or accounting measures and by emphasizing in governmental communications the possible and likely future problems for nonexporters. The main thrust should, of course, emphasize proactive motivations.

In terms of direct export assistance, governmental authorities seem best advised to focus mainly on operational issues such as distribution coordination, communication, and financial information. These are the issues that are of main concern to reactively motivated firms, who are also the ones most willing to seek and accept governmental assistance.

REFERENCES

Bilkey, Warren J., and Tesar, George. "The Export Behavior of Smaller Sized Wisconsin Manufacturing Firms." Journal of International Business Studies, Spring/Summer 1977, pp. 93-98.

Cavusgil, Tamer S., Bilkey, Warren J., and Tesar, George. "A Note on the Export Behavior of Firms: Exporter Profiles." Journal of International Business Studies, Spring/Summer 1979, pp. 91-97.

Cavusgil, Tamer, and Nevin, John R. "Internal Determinants of Export Marketing Behavior: An Empirical Investigation." Journal of Marketing Research 18 (February 1981):114-19.

Czinkota, Michael R. "Making Use of the Export Motivation of Smaller Sized U.S. Manufacturers in Export Promotion." Paper presented at the 1980 Annual Meeting of the Academy of International Business, New Orleans.

Hollander, Myles, and Wolfe, Douglas A. Nonparametric Statistical Methods. New York: John Wiley, 1973.

Pavord, William C., and Bogart, Raymond G. "The Dynamics of the Decision to Export." Akron Business and Economic Review 6, no. 1 (Spring 1975):6-11.

Reid, Stanley D. "A Behavioral Approach to Export Decision-Making." In Marketing in the 80's: Changes and Challenges, edited by R. F. Bagozzi et al. Chicago: American Marketing Association, 1980, pp. 265-68.

Stobaugh, Robert B. "The Neotechnology Account of International Trade." In The Product Life Cycle and International Trade, edited by Louis T. Wells, Jr. Cambridge, Mass.: Harvard University Press, 1974.

U.S. Department of Commerce, Industry and Trade Administration. "Seven Surprising Facts about Exporting." Washington, D.C., n.d.

Weil, Frank A. Statement at Hearings before the Subcommittee on International Finance of the Committee on Banking, Housing, and Urban Affairs, Export Policy, Part 3, U.S. Senate, 35th Cong., 2d sess., February 23, 1978, Washington, D.C.

Wiedersheim-Paul, F., Olson, H. C., and Welch, L. S. "Pre-Export Activity: The First Step in Internationalization." Journal of International Business Studies, Spring/Summer 1978, pp. 47-58.

# 2

# THE IMPACT OF SIZE ON EXPORT BEHAVIOR IN SMALL FIRMS

## Stan Reid

Many countries, in efforts to improve exporting performance, are placing more emphasis on providing export assistance and export promotion programs for smaller firms. Such firms are generally regarded as reluctant to enter international markets because they are assumed to suffer from size disadvantages that are felt to be major obstacles in pursuing foreign opportunities.

In spite of this commonly held view of the small firm, little evidence has been produced to suggest the size characteristics that may be critical for international expansion. Indeed, there is not only no commonly held view as to what constitutes a small firm, but there has been no sustained research effort to identify the characteristics of such firms in a way that makes any definition of small behaviorally valid for export policy makers.

This chapter provides an overview of the issues associated with identifying relevant size criteria and presents a conceptual framework for investigating the relationships between different measures of firm size and export behavior in small firms. It describes both the methodology for operationalizing valid size constructs and the empirical results from using these size measures in export behavior research.

---

The author acknowledges the financial support of the American Marketing Association and the Canadian Federation of Independent Business for the study from which these data were drawn.

SIZE AS A CRITICAL ISSUE

It is surprising that the concept of "small-size firm" remains virtually unquestioned in spite of the fact that as presently operationalized it has little practical or theoretical justification. One obvious explanation for this is that statutory definitions impose their own distinctions. A study carried out by the Georgia Institute of Technology (1975) found 75 different national definitions of small business. Even within national boundaries there is little consistency. Not only can state and federal agencies in the United States differ in their definitions of small business, but within the states themselves there is considerable lack of uniformity (Nappi and Vora, 1980). Indeed, as Peterson (1977, p. 60) points out, "no country has a single legal definition of small business. All definitions were linked to special legislation establishing such things as small business development corporations or loan guarantee institutions."

The small-size firm, it would appear, as presently conceived is a legal artifact. This suggests that much of the research results on the relationships between size and export activity in such firms are nongeneralizable. Some researchers acknowledge the severity of the methodological problems and remain doubtful as to whether export studies investigating the effect of size across different types of organizational enterprises can provide substantive results (Hirsch and Adar, 1974a). The issue is further complicated by the use of different size criteria whose validity are assumed but never demonstrated. This has naturally led to a general inconclusiveness as to the impact of size on small-firm export activity.

While firm size is often regarded by export researchers as a critical structural determinant in the exporting activity of an enterprise, the evidence to support the effect of any specific or group size criterion on export behavior is conflicting (Reid, 1981a; Bilkey, 1978). While discrepancies in the findings can be partly adduced to the different dimensions of export behavior under investigation, it is reasonable to expect that they are principally due to both the lack of commonality in the measures employed for size and the absence of a framework that is capable of operationalizing valid measures for size, irrespective of the research context.

For example, some researchers use asset size (Garnier, 1974; Drinkwalter, 1971), others use firm sales (Czinkota, 1980; Abdel-Malek, 1974, 1978; Hirsch and Adar, 1974a &b; Hecht and Siegel, 1973), and yet others use the number of employees (McConnell, 1979; Suntook, 1978; Bilkey and Tesar, 1977). Garnier (1974), Cavusgil (1976), and Cavusgil and Nevin (1979) employed all three measures. These differences in basis of measurement, one may add, are not accidental and seem to be occasioned by both mundane and vulgar research considerations.*

It is clear that there is need for a theoretically meaningful framework that would identify "size" as a valid construct that is neither situational specific nor artifactual and that is directly implicated in export behavior. As Nappi and Vora (1980, p. 26) conclude:

> Because government agencies, commissions, trade
> associations, and academicians have defined small
> business in many different ways, the accuracy of con-
> clusions reached in research studies based on these
> definitions is subject to question. Consequently it is
> very difficult to develop a systematic data base on the
> base of past research findings. . . . it is recommended
> that simplicity and understanding be used as core cri-
> teria in developing a consensus definition or set of defi-
> nitions.

## DEFINING SIZE AND THE SMALL FIRM

In an effort to avoid some of the problems indicated in finding an appropriate definition for the small firm, McGuire (1976, p. 118) rejects structural measures and calls for the use of behavioral criteria that would appear to have more face validity than existing size indicators. He argues that

> a small business enterprise is a profit-oriented or-
> ganization in which there can be rationally only one
> profit center. This definition conforms closely both
> to the traditional economist's concept of the small
> firm and to what the general public conceives to be a
> small company. For analytical purposes, it sets
> small companies apart from large because it focuses
> directly upon an unfractionated entrepreneurial func-
> tion which is the individual identified with success or
> failure, is easily identifiable.

The basic advantage of McGuire's conceptualization for the analyst of export behavior is that it avoids arbitrary definitions,

---

*An overview of some selective findings on the relationships between export behavior and size are shown in Table 2.1.

provides units with a common and significant organizational characteristic, and offers an opportunity to examine impact of size as an
independent variable in a meaningful fashion.

For all the importance ascribed to the impact of size on export behavior, few researchers have provided justification as to why
it should be of importance in export behavior. Among these are
Hirsch (1971), Hirsch and Adar (1974a), and McFetridge and Weatherly (1977) who have concluded that large size is likely to confer
advantages only in situations where there exists physical indivisi-
bility of some firm inputs such as research and development activity, critical level of fixed costs associated with marketing tasks
such as advertising promotions, and economies of scale in foreign
marketing. In these instances size can provide opportunities for
achieving either internal economies of scale through specialization
or for possibly lowering transaction costs associated with purchasing specialized services on the open market.

However, a pervasive feature of most major exporting countries is the presence of numerous types and forms of government
and private institutions, facilities, programs, fiscal incentives,
and aids aimed at encouraging export activity among smaller enterprises (Mayer and Flynn, 1973; Vernon and Ryans, 1975; Pointon,
1978a; Linden, 1980; Reid, 1981b). This suggests that many of the
advantages a large firm is expected to automatically have over the
smaller firm in exporting may be mitigated by the presence and use
of specialist export management services. Both Hirsch and Adar
(1974a) and McFetridge and Weatherly (1977) have of course cau-
tioned against overgeneralizations about the relationships between
firm size and export behavior. These writers suggest that evidence
of a continuous relationship between size and export intensity may
not only be obscuring what is in reality a series of step functions
(McFetridge and Weatherly, 1977) but that other factors such as
type of product and structure of local and foreign demands may be
implicated in export performance.


OPERATIONALIZING THE SIZE CONSTRUCT

It would seem then that researchers investigating the impact
of size on export behavior among small firms have a twofold task.
They should insure first that the export activity of similar type
units (that is, the small firm) are under examination, and second
that the size criteria that are employed should be appropriate measures for the export behavior concerned. A survey of some of the
major studies of exporting activity shows little consistency in the
type of export behavior researched, the level of measurement of

TABLE 2.1

Selected Export Studies, Measures of Firm Size, and Their Relationships with Export Behavior

| Authors | | Country | Actual Number of Firms Investigated | Level of Measurement | Export Behavior Investigated | Measures of Size Employed | | |
|---|---|---|---|---|---|---|---|---|
| | | | | | | Number of Employees | Size of Sales | Size of Assets |
| Tookey | 1964 | United Kingdom | 54 | interval | exports/total sales | a | | |
| Cooper, Hartley | 1970 | United Kingdom | 41 | interval | exports/total sales | a, c* | | |
| Drinkwalter | 1971 | Canada | 155 | interval | export performance (exports/total sales) | | | a |
| Hecht and Siegel | 1973 | Canada | 309 | nominal | exporting versus nonexporting | a | | |
| Hirsch and Adar | 1974a | Denmark, Holland, and Israel | 485 | interval | export performance export/total sales | | a | |
| Hirsch and Adar | 1974b | Denmark, Holland, and Israel | 270 | nominal | market preference | | a | |
| Hirsch and Lev | 1974 | Denmark, Holland, and Israel | 378 | interval | export concentration | | a | |
| Garnier | 1974 | Canada | 171 | nominal | exporting versus nonexporting | a | a | a |
| Vernon and Ryans | 1975 | United States | 142 | nominal | election and use of DISC incentive | | a | |
| McFetridge and Weatherly | 1977 | Canada | 324 | interval | exports/total sales | | c | |

| Author | Year | Country | N | Scale | Dependent variable | | |
|---|---|---|---|---|---|---|---|
| Bilkey and Tesar | 1974 | United States | 423 | ordinal | stages of export development | c | c |
| Abdul-Malek | 1978 | Canada | 166 | interval | export involvement export/total sales | a | c |
| Knoop and Sanders | 1978 | Canada | 170 | ordinal | export attitudes | a | |
| Suntook | 1978 | United Kingdom | 280 | interval | export/total sales | a | |
| Pointon | 1978b | United Kingdom | 122 | interval | export information usage | a | |
| Crookell and Graham | 1979 | Canada | 134 | interval | export/total sales | | b |
| Cavusgil and Nevin | 1979 | United States | 473 | nominal | exporting versus nonexporting | N.R. | N.R. |
| McConnell | 1979 | United States | 148 | nominal | exporters versus nonexporters | a | |
| Czinkota | 1980 | United States | 219 | ordinal | stages of export | | |
| Johnston and Czinkota | 1980 | United States | — | — | exporting practices and attitudes between small- and medium-sized firms | | c |
| Rabino | 1980 | United States | 195 | interval | attitude toward DISC | a | a |

a = positive relationship with export behavior investigated.
b = negative relationship with export behavior investigated.
c = no significant relationship found.
N.R. = no relationship reported.
* = dependent on industry.

23

the dependent variable, or the size indicator employed (Table 2.1).
Both number of employers and size of sales seem to be the most
favored measure for size.

There is prima facie evidence that such commonly used
variables for size may not only be highly intercorrelated but that
they may be strongly correlated with other variables that are not
often identified but that may offer conceptually valid explanations
for the observed impact of firm size on export behavior. Such
variables represent firm contextual characteristics that are likely
to affect demand for the firm's offerings or its ability to supply its
products competitively (Reid, 1981a).

The literature in organizational behavior supports the existence of a causal relationship between size as measured by the number of employees and increasing functional specialization (Child,
1973); size as measured by annual sales and orientation toward
mass production technology and functional specialization (Khandwalla,
1974); and product development with product competition, technological change, and the perceived importance of the marketing area
(Khandwalla, 1976). While these results may be restricted to the
firm operating in the domestic environment, since no evidence is
given as to whether the enterprise is engaged in foreign market activity, they do give some additional perspectives to the debate on
firm size.

It would seem that the greater the functional specialization
and differentiation in the enterprise, the more likely it would have
"extra resources" to pursue foreign opportunities and the greater
possibility of reducing its costs of collection and interpretation of
the continuous flow of information from foreign markets to which it
is exposed.

This view is supported by Tookey (1964, p. 55), who concludes:

> This lack of trained staff was an obvious handicap to
> some firms, for example in the lack of knowledge of
> sources of information about overseas markets, in
> lack of ability to interpret the information when ob-
> tained, and in a tendency to avoid exporting because
> of the complex problems involved.

While the aggregate number of employees is of significance,
their distribution in the enterprise is also of importance. For example both the absolute number of technical and academic employees
and extent of specialization would appear critical for both the production and marketing capabilities of the firm. In this respect product-
line diversity, a likely derivative of scale of technology, may have
its own impact on the firm's ability to be export competitive both in

giving an array of products to the prospective foreign market or in providing a stimulus for achieving economies of scale through longer production runs.

The firm's age and its perceived relative competitive strength are two other variables, not as obviously related to size, that deserve investigation as contributors to the export activity of the enterprise. Analysts such as Bilkey and Tesar (1977) who support a developmental model of the export process implicitly assume some relationship between firm age and exporting activity. The empirical evidence is contradictory; some findings (Snavely et al., 1964; Daniels, 1971; Welch and Wiedersheim-Paul, 1978) offer limited support for this view while others (Litvak and Maule, 1971; Garnier, 1974; Lee and Brasch, 1977) point out that younger firms tend to be more interested in foreign markets at an earlier stage of their development. It would seem that managerial dynamism and the firm's relative competitive ability can obviously play a role in explaining these discrepancies. An empirical investigation was conducted to test the validity of the size measures.

METHODOLOGY

Forming the basis of this analysis are 89 Canadian firms meeting the following criteria: the firm was Canadian-owned and had a nondivisionalized status with the corporate decision locus situated in the province of Ontario, the firm had between 100 and 500 employees, and the firm was grouped in one of the following three industry classifications: furniture, metal fabrication, and machinery industries (not electrical). The data used in this research were part of a larger study (Reid, 1981b) investigating exporting behavior in Canadian manufacturers and were collected by administering structured mail and personal interviews to managers responsible for export decisions.

The specific behavior under investigation is intended export activity. Multiple measures were employed for the dependent variable in order to capture the major underlying dimension of export performance.* These were specifically the intention or likelihood of exporting to new foreign markets in the next 12 months ($X_1$), the intention or likelihood of increasing present proportion of export

---

*See Reid (1981b, pp. 76-104) for extensive discussion of survey methodology and reliability issues associated with measurement of the dependent variable.

sales to current markets ($X_2$), the intention to introduce new products ($X_3$), the proportionate change in firm export sales expected in the next 12 months ($X_4$), and the number of new countries intending entry into within the next 12 months ($X_5$). These measures tap the extent of multimarket expansion, the extent of commitment to existing foreign markets, and the firm commitment to export sales (Reid and Mayer, 1980).

Five additional measures for size were included along with such traditional indicators as number of employees, size in sales, and size in assets. These were age of firm in years; number of employees with academic degrees; number of technical employees such as engineers, scientists, designers, and technicians; extent of functional specialization indicated by the presence of specialist functions such as marketing, sales, production or manufacturing, accounts or finance, research and development managers; and perceived company profile measured by an additive scale.

## RESULTS

Respondents included in this study were predominantly owners of the enterprises (63 percent), with general managers (12 percent) and vice-presidents (12 percent) forming the remaining dominant occupational categories. The majority of the firms were engaged in metal fabrication (49 percent), with furniture and metal manufacturing comprising 27 and 21 percent, respectively. Of the 89 firms, 71 were presently exporting and the remainder were non-exporters. Reliability measures for the dependent variable, exporting behavior, and the independent variable, perceived company profile, are shown in Tables 2.2 and 2.3, respectively.

Many of the size measures showed little intercorrelation and consistently significant bivariate associations with export behavior were shown only by the variable "number of employees." Both number of academic employees and technical employees showed a negative relationship with the age of the firm, suggesting that younger firms tend to have more highly trained personnel. However, the older the firm was, the higher it was evaluated among firms in the same industry. The extent of functional specialization, size of firm's sales and assets, and number of employees were found to be highly correlated as expected (see Table 2.4).

The uncontrolled effect of "firm size" variables on export activity is revealing (see Table 2.5). While the absolute number of employees shows significant association with all aspects of export activity, its effect is more dominant when multimarket expansion is considered. The numbers of academic and technical employees

TABLE 2.2

Characteristics of Dependent Variable

| Dependent Variable | Measure | Reliability Measure and Coefficient |
|---|---|---|
| Intention to export to new markets ($X_1$) within the next 12 months | 6-point intention scale | concurrent .52 (89)[a] |
| Intention to introduce new products ($X_2$) into foreign markets within the next 12 months | 6-point intention scale | concurrent .30 (71)[b] |
| Intention to increase present ($X_3$) proportion of export/total sales within the next 12 months | 6-point intention scale | test-retest .88 (71)[a] |
| Expected absolute percent change ($X_4$) in export sales within the next 12 months | 9-point change scale | test-retest .55 (71)[a] |
| Expected number of new countries ($X_5$) exporting to in next 12 months | number of new countries | test-retest .62 (89)[a] |

[a]significant at p $\leq$ 0.001
[b]significant at p $\leq$ .002

TABLE 2.3

Characteristics of Profile Scale

| Scale | Operational Definition | Measure | Number and Type of Items | Items Chosen by | Reliability Coefficient |
|---|---|---|---|---|---|
| Perceived company profile | Firms' evaluation relative to industry | 5-point rating scale using substantially above average to substantially below average | 8 items Profitability, sales growth, marketing and selling capability, distribution and price | Item-scale analysis | .72* |

*Cronbach's reliability coefficient.

TABLE 2.4

Intercorrelations of Firm Size Variables

| Variable | Age | Size Employees | Size Technical | Size Academic | Functional Specialization | Number of Products | Size Sales | Size Assets | Company Profile |
|---|---|---|---|---|---|---|---|---|---|
| Age | | | | | | | | | |
| Size (employees) | .05 | | | | | | | | |
| Size (technical) | -.39 | .07 | | | | | | | |
| Size (academic) | -.14 | .18 | -.006 | | | | | | |
| Functional specialization | .11 | .46 | .02 | .05 | | | | | |
| Number of products | .16 | .17 | .15 | .13 | .01 | | | | |
| Size (sales) | .18 | .69 | -.002 | .04 | .36 | .02 | | | |
| Size (assets) | .04 | .58 | -.007 | .10 | .42 | .09 | .006 | | |
| Company profile | .54 | .14 | .11 | .12 | .09 | .18 | .04 | .02 | |

Note: Zero order gamma is measure of association used.

29

TABLE 2.5

Bivariate Relationships between Firm Size Variables and Export Activity

| Variable | Export Activity | | | | |
|---|---|---|---|---|---|
| | $X_1$ | $X_2$ | $X_3$ | $X_4$ | $X_5$ |
| | N = 89 | N = 71 | N = 71 | N = 71 | N = 89 |
| Age[a] | -.03 | -.14[e] | .01 | .16[d] | .03 |
| Number of employees[a] | .27[c] | .16[d] | .24[c] | .22[d] | .31[c] |
| Number of academic employees[a] | .19[d] | .23[c] | .09 | .27[c] | -.06 |
| Number of technical employees[a] | .30[c] | .29[c] | .10 | .03 | .18[d] |
| Number of products[a] | .15[d] | .06 | .17[d] | .17[d] | .11 |
| Functional specialization[b] | .10 | .23 | .15 | .19 | .11 |
| Size of sales[b] | .21 | -.01 | .05 | .08 | .37 |
| Size in assets[b] | .26 | -.01 | .05 | .08 | .37 |
| Company profile[a] | .15 | .10 | .28 | .09 | .25 |

[a]Pearson $\tau$
[b]Gamma $(\delta)$
[c]$p \leq .01$
[d]$p \leq .05$
[e]$p \leq .10$

show strong correlations with "introducing new product" kind of activity. However, the numbers of academic employees and technical personnel have a differential impact on export behavior. For example, absolute increases in the magnitude of export sales is more strongly associated with the presence of academic trained personnel. On the other hand, the presence of technical employees is directly related to multimarket expansion type of behavior.

Size as indicated through sales and assets has a specific impact on new market export activity but appears unrelated to either type or extent of export commitment as indicated by export sales performance measures, a finding contrary to much of the existing evidence. In some instances both product-line assortment and functional specialization behaved contrary to expectations.

The number of products manufactured had little relationship to new product introduction activity and showed weak but significant associations primarily with export-commitment type behavior. The level of functional specialization showed its most significant variation with new product and absolute export sales activity.

Two further proxies for firm size, age, and perceived company profile had mixed correlations with export activity. Older firms were less likely to engage in new product introduction behavior and more likely to increase the absolute level of export sales. Firms that saw themselves as above average in their respective industries were more likely to enter a greater number of new foreign markets and increase their existing proportion of export sales.


## DEFINING THE SIZE CONSTRUCT

The results of the bivariate analyses suggest that groups of these size measures employed in the research are interdependent and interrelated. Furthermore, there is indicative evidence of some underlying size constructs that seem to behave similarly to the traditional single measures. In order to determine the degree to which alternative size constructs could be operationalized, the size variables were subjected to principal components factor analysis. The initial factors were then orthogonally rotated using the varimax criterion (Kim and Mueller, 1978). The resultant factor analysis yielded three interpretable and logical dimensions (see Table 2.6).

The first factor (Size A), for example, loaded on traditional size factors, number of employees, firm sales, assets and functional specialization, while the other major factor (Size B) loaded principally on number of academic and technical employees. These factors accounted for a greater part of the explained variance

TABLE 2.6

Factor Analysis of Firm Size Variables
(Varimax Rotation)

| Variable | Factor I | Factor II | Factor III |
|---|---|---|---|
| Age | .04 | -.16 | .73 |
| Number of employees | .84 | .10 | .04 |
| Number of academic employees | .04 | .76 | -.36 |
| Number of technical employees | .08 | .90 | -.01 |
| Functional specialization | .40 | .03 | .08 |
| Number of products | .08 | .21 | .53 |
| Size in sales | .78 | -.03 | .13 |
| Size in assets | .62 | .04 | |
| Company profile | .26 | -.07 | .66 |
| Eigen value | 2.1 | 1.7 | .66 |
| Percent of variance explained | 47.2 | 38.1 | 14.7 |
| | Size A | Size B | Size C |

TABLE 2.7

Bivariate Relationship between Firm Size Factors
and Export Behaviors
(Pearson r)

| Size Construct | $X_1$ N = 89 | $X_2$ N = 71 | $X_3$ N = 71 | $X_4$ N = 71 | $X_5$ N = 89 |
|---|---|---|---|---|---|
| Size A | .27[b] | .15 | .17[c] | .17 | .31[a] |
| Size B | .29[a] | .20[c] | -.06 | .19[b] | .11 |

[a]$p < .01$
[b]$p < .05$
[c]$p < .10$

(85.3 percent). The third factor (Size C), which explained the remaining variance (14.7 percent), represented a "reputational visi-
bility" construct arising from age, number of products, and firm's
relative profile. The validity of these inferred size constructs was
further tested by analyzing their relationship with the dependent
variable export behavior.

Size as indicated by assets, employees, functional specialization, and sales—in other words the traditional notion of size—was
significantly associated with both exporting to new markets and number of new markets intending to export to. The larger a firm was,
by these criteria, the more likely it was to increase its proportion
of export sales. Although the greater number of technical and academic employees a firm had the more likely it was to enter a new
foreign market, this size feature was not found to be associated
with multiple market entry activity. This size factor was of far
more significance in new product activity and change in absolute
level of export sales (see Table 2.7).

The variations in behavior of the two size factors offer com-
pelling evidence for the validity of measures (Heeler and Ray, 1972)
and support the position taken that firm size has multidimensional
properties and is a construct having components that are associated
with different types of export behavior.

CONCLUSION

This investigation not only supports the view that multiple
measures for firm size is a theoretical valid concept that can be
operationalized, but, more importantly, shows that such measures
are likely to be differentially involved in export activity. The results indicate that absolute size using traditional indicators predominantly affects the export entry into new foreign markets. This
suggests that in small firms export market expansion is strongly
influenced by the presence of financial and human resources best
represented by sales, assets, number of employees, and, to a
lesser extent, availability of a stock of managerial personnel. In
contrast such export behavior as introduction of new products and
export sales performance is directly related to the skill intensity
of the small firm.

These findings suggest that export policies aimed at improving the export activity of small firms should recognize that export
market expansion and export performance are distinguishable export activities that are not influenced by the same small-firm characteristics. It seems likely that the provision of facilitating institutions that remove the financial and managerial burden of entering

new markets would stimulate new export entry among small firms
while these incentives that encourage technological sophistication
and upgrading of managerial skills are likely to encourage export
performance as it is currently regarded.

Given that this study is based on a new operationalization of
both export behavior and the "size" construct and is restricted to a
specific category of firms, the findings can be said to be exploratory. However, a research methodology is presented that allows
for generalization of research findings, unrestricted by geography,
national origin, or other type of domain considerations that have
affected previous investigations of the export behavior of small
firms.

## REFERENCES

Abdel-Malek, T. Managerial Export Orientation: A Canadian Study.
London, Ontario: School of Business Administration, University
of Western Ontario, 1974.

Abdel-Malek, T. "Export Marketing Orientation in Small Firms."
American Journal of Small Business 3 (July 1978) : 25-34.

Bilkey, W. "An Attempted Integration of the Literature on the Export Behavior of Firms." Journal of International Business
Studies 9 (Spring/Summer 1978):33-46.

Bilkey, W., and G. Tesar. "The Export Behavior of Smaller-
Sized Wisconsin Manufacturing Firms." Journal of International
Business Studies 8 (Spring/Summer 1977):93-98.

Cavusgil, S. T. "Organizational Determinants of Firms' Export
Behavior: An Empirical Analysis." Ph.D. dissertation, The
University of Wisconsin, Madison, 1976.

Cavusgil, S. T., and J. Nevin. "Determinants of Exporting Marketing Behavior: An Empirical Investigation." Working paper,
University of Wisconsin, 1979.

Child, J. "Predicting and Understanding Organization Structure."
Administrative Science Quarterly 18 (June 1973):168-95.

Cooper, R., K. Hartley, and C. Harvey. Export Performance and
the Pressure of Demand: A Study of Firms. London: George
Allen and Unwin, 1970.

Crookell, H., and I. Graham. "International Marketing and Canadian Industrial Strategy." The Business Quarterly 44 (Spring
1979):28-34.

Czinkota, M. R. "Making Use of the Export Motivation of Smaller
Sized U.S. Manufacturers in Export Promotion." Paper pre-
sented to the 1980 Annual Meeting of the Academy of International
Business, New Orleans, October 1980.

Daniels, J. D. Recent Foreign Direct Manufacturing Investment in
the United States: An Interview Study of the Decision Process.
New York: Praeger Publishers, 1971.

Drinkwalter, D. A. "Some Economic Characteristics of Canadian
Exporting Firms." Ph.D. dissertation, University of Western
Ontario, 1971.

Garnier, G. Characteristics and Problems of Small and Medium
Exporting Firms in the Quebec Manufacturing Sector with Special
Emphasis on Those Using Advanced Production Techniques.
Ottawa: Technological Innovation Studies Program, Department
of Industry, Trade, and Commerce, August 1974.

Georgia Institute of Technology. An International Compilation of
Small Scale Industry Definitions. Industrial Development Division, Engineering Experiment Station, Georgia Institute of Technology, Atlanta, January 1975.

Hecht, M. R., and J. P. Siegel. A Study of Manufacturing Firms
in Canada with Special Emphasis on Small and Medium Sized
Firms. Ottawa: Technological Innovation Studies Program, Department of Industry, Trade, and Commerce, 1973.

Heeler, R. M., and M. Ray. "Measure Validation in Marketing."
Journal of Marketing Research 9 (November 1972):361-70.

Hirsch, S. The Export Performance of Six Manufacturing Industries.
New York: Praeger Publishers, 1971.

Hirsch, S., and A. Adar (a). "Firm Size and Export Performance."
World Development 2 (July 1974):41-46.

Hirsch, S., and A. Adar (b). "Protected Markets and Firms' Export Distribution." World Development 2 (August 1974):29-36.

Hirsch, S., and B. Lev. "The Firm's Export Concentration: Determinants and Applications." World Development 2 (June 1974).

Johnston, W. J., and M. R. Czinkota. "Exporting: Does Sales Volume Make a Difference?" Paper presented to the 1980 Annual Meeting of the Academy of International Business, New Orleans, October 1980.

Khandwalla, P. N. "Mass Output Orientation of Operations Technology and Organization Structure." Administrative Science Quarterly 19 (March 1974):25-31.

Khandwalla, P. N. "The Techno-economic Ecology of Corporate Strategy." Journal of Management Studies 12 (February 1976): 62-75.

Kim, J. O., and C. W. Mueller. Factor Analysis: Statistical Methods and Practical Issues. New York: Sage Publications, 1978.

Knoop, R., and A. Sanders. Furniture Industry: Attitudes Towards Exporting. Montreal: Concordia University, May 1978.

Lee, W., and J. Brasch. "The Adoption of Export as an Innovation Strategy." Journal of International Business Studies 8 (Fall 1977):85-93.

Linden, S. Developing a Mode of Exporter Identification: An Attempt to Integrate U.S. Government Export Promotion Initiatives with Company Development. Office of Export Planning and Evaluation, U.S. Department of Commerce, March 1980.

Litvak, I. A., and C. Maule. Canadian Entrepreneurship: A Study of Small Newly Established Firms. Ottawa: Technological Innovation Studies Program, Department of Industry, Trade, and Commerce, 1971, pp. 43-44.

Mayer, C., and J. Flynn. "Canadian Small Business Abroad: Opportunities, Aids and Experiences." The Business Quarterly 38 (Winter 1973):33-45.

McConnell, J. "The Export Decision: An Empirical Study of Firm Behavior." Economic Geography 55 (July 1979):171-83.

McFetridge, D., and L. Weatherly. Notes on the Economies of Large Firm Size, No. 20. Ottawa: Ministry of Supply and Services, Royal Commission on Corporate Concentration, 1977.

McGuire, J. W. "The Small Enterprise in Economics and Organization Theory." Journal of Contemporary Business 5 (Spring 1976):118.

Nappi, A. T., and J. Vora. "Small Business Eligibility: A Definitional Issue." Journal of Small Business Management 18 (October 1980):22-27.

Peterson, R. Small Business: Building a Balanced Economy. Erin, Ontario: Porcepic Press, 1977.

Pointon, T. (a). "Measuring the Gains from Government Export Promotion." European Journal of Marketing 12, no. 6 (1978): 451-61.

Pointon, T. (b). "The Information Needs of Exporters." Marketing (UK), July 1978, pp. 53-58.

Rabino, S. "An Attitudinal Evaluation of an Export Incentive Program: The Case of DISC." Columbia Journal of World Business 15 (Spring 1980):61-65.

Reid, S. D. (a). "Methodological and Theoretical Issues in Export Behavior Research." In Proceedings of Administrative Sciences Association of Canada, edited by K. Dhawan. Dalhousie University, Nova Scotia, May 1981, pp. 99-106.

Reid, S. D. (b). "Export Behavior in the Small Canadian-Owned Manufacturing Enterprise—An Empirical Investigation." Ph.D. thesis 1981, York University, pp. 114-20, 138.

Reid, S. D. "A Behavioral Approach to Export Decision-Making." In Marketing in the 1980's: Changes and Challenges, edited by R. Bagozzi et al. Chicago: American Marketing Association, July 1980, pp. 265-69.

Reid, S. D., and C. Mayer. "Exporting Behavior and Decision-Maker Characteristics." In Marketing 1980: Towards Excellence in the Eighties, Vol. I, edited by V. Jones. ASAC Proceedings, University of Calgary, 1980, pp. 298-307.

Snavely, W. P., P. Weiner, H. Ulbrich, and E. Enright. Export Survey of the Greater Hartford Area. Storrs: University of Connecticut, 1964.

Suntook, F. "How British Industry Exports." Marketing (UK), June 1978, pp. 29-34.

Tookey, D. A. "Factors Associated with Success in Exporting." Journal of Management Studies 1 (March 1964):48-66.

Vernon, I., and J. Ryans. "The Awareness and Election of an Export Incentive: The DISC Case." Baylor Business Studies 6, no. 4 (1975):19-26.

Welch, L., and F. Wiedersheim-Paul. Domestic Expansion and the Internationalization Process, Working Paper No. 2. Uppsala, Sweden: Centre for International Business Studies, University of Uppsala, 1978.

# 3

# A STUDY OF EXPORT BEHAVIOR OF SMALL- AND MEDIUM-SIZED MANUFACTURING FIRMS IN THREE CANADIAN PROVINCES

Mary R. Brooks
Philip J. Rosson

Exporting plays an important role in the Canadian economy. Merchandise exports in 1979 were in the order of $65 billion Canadian, or 23 percent of GNP (Export Canada, 1980). In recent years a devalued dollar has meant an increased demand for Canadian goods in foreign markets. Yet, despite the dependence of Canadians on exporting, few studies of the export behavior of Canadian firms have been undertaken. Various researchers have examined the reasons for export success, but few have investigated the motivation for exporting or the perceptions exporters and nonexporters have of doing business on an international scale. Much stands to be gained from an understanding of these motivations and perceptions as well as identifying the major sources of information on exporting used in the decision-making process.

Only two Canadian studies, Garnier (1974) and Reid (1980b), have focused on small- and medium-sized firms. Yet this size of firm is of central concern to government policy makers seeking to expand Canadian export involvement. For this reasons, it is felt that a study of current Canadian export behavior is in order. As well as providing data of a distinctly Canadian nature, it may well be that the findings of this study can be compared to those studies of export behavior in other countries.

In this light, the broad objective of this study was to develop comprehensive exporter and nonexporter profiles of small- and medium-sized Canadian firms.

BACKGROUND

The literature review begins by considering published Canadian exporting studies and then progresses to those from other countries. Abdel-Malek's (1974) study is noteworthy. It is an extensive one, involving 166 firms and including a wide range of Canadian exporting and nonexporting firms, from all but the Atlantic Provinces. Abdel-Malek investigates the characteristics of export-oriented firms, concentrating largely on firms' perceptions of market opportunities, government programs, foreign intermediaries, and customers. The study also encompasses decision-maker characteristics and firms' assessments of domestic versus foreign sales. A second Canadian study is that of Crookell and Graham (1979). This study aimed at identifying exporting companies' perceptions of the skills most important to be successful in exporting. The study reveals that exporters view product performance as providing the most important competitive edge, with marketing skills ranked second. A third study by Garnier (1974) examined the relationship of firm size and technological character to exporting. Recent empirical export research has also been conducted by Reid (1980b) into the information-seeking activities of firms as these relate to exporting. While these studies provide insight, those of Abdel-Malek and Garnier are now somewhat dated and a need exists for an up-to-date review of Canadian exporting behavior.

Non-Canadian studies reviewed generally fell into one or more of the following categories:

● Those looking at the stimuli, both internal and external, leading to a firm's export decision
● Those evaluating different perceptual factors affecting the export decision
● Those discussing both firm and decision-maker characteristics that affect the export decision.

Internal and External Stimuli

A variety of potential internal and external stimuli have been suggested in a number of studies. For example, internal stimuli mentioned range from a firm's unique competence that leads to the exploitation of the particular asset in world markets, to the existence of excess capacity in management resources, marketing, finance, or production requiring broader market utilization (Wiedersheim-Paul, Olson, and Welch, 1978). Stimuli such as the existence of adverse home market conditions (Bilkey, 1978; Pavord

and Bogart, 1975) and the possession of patents and distribution ef-
ficiencies (Pavord and Bogart, 1975) are also seen as initiators.
Company or management strengths are perceived to be competitive
assets to be exploited in foreign markets (Tookey, 1964; Cunningham and Spigel, 1971; Bilkey and Tesar, 1977).

Simmonds and Smith (1968), Simpson and Kujawa (1974), and
Pavord and Bogart (1975) have all shown that it is the receipt of an
unsolicited export order that is a most important factor in inducing
a decision to enter export markets. Reid (1980c) argues that this
view is too simplistic; a complex decision such as this would be the
result of a set of factors and the "unsolicited order" cannot stand
alone. Other factors such as adverse market conditions and fluc-
tuating exchange rates must also be considered simultaneously.


Perceptual Factors

In the Simpson and Kujawa (1974) study, factors identified as
being significant in the export decision included the firm's perceptions of the risk, profit, and costs in foreign operations compared
to domestic operations. Exporting decision makers felt that the
risks involved in exporting were higher but offset by higher profits.
In addition, nonexporters clearly felt that the various cost factors
(executive time, packaging and insurance costs, clerical time, and
shipping costs) were higher than did exporters.


Firm and Decision-Maker Characteristics

Various studies find support for the premise that the decision
to export is more likely to be made in firms where top management
has an international orientation (Wiedersheim-Paul, Olson, and
Welch, 1978; Cunningham and Spigel, 1971; Bilkey, 1978).

Decision-maker characteristics have also been cited as an
important internal influence on a firm's export behavior. While in
many firms this type of major policy decision would be a group one,
Mintzberg's (1973) study concluded that in medium-sized firms,
single decision makers tended to be encountered. Therefore the
characteristics of individual decision makers must be considered
as having a decided impact on the export decision. Wiedersheim-
Paul, Olson, and Welch affirm Mintzberg's view in an exporting
context. Simpson and Kujawa found a significant difference in the
level of education between decision makers in exporting and nonexporting firms: the former tended to be college graduates whereas
the latter had "some college" education. Pinney (1970) found support

for the premise that export decision makers also tend to be younger. Contrary findings are suggested; Garnier's (1974) study of Quebec firms found that the characteristics of the entrepreneurs, for example, education, had no statistically significant influence. Part of the international orientation of top management previously mentioned is, of course, the international orientation of a single decision maker. Several studies have demonstrated that where decision makers have foreign experience, having lived abroad or studied a foreign language, active exporting is more likely to be found (Simmonds and Smith, 1968; Langston and Teas, 1976).

Also of interest is the usage of information sources in both preexport and postexport stages. Reid's (1980b) study of small- to medium-sized Canadian firms in selected industries finds a low awareness and usage of export information sources. It is important to determine which sources of exporting information are used by exporters and nonexporters in order to evaluate their decision making.

In view of the research findings, the following hypotheses are worth studying in the Canadian context:

$H_1$: Exporters perceive the risks of exporting to be less than nonexporters.

$H_2$: Exporters perceive the profits from exporting to be greater than nonexporters.

$H_3$: Exporters perceive the costs and management time required for exporting to be less than nonexporters.

$H_4$: The major stimulus for a firm's initial decision to export is the receipt of an unsolicited order from abroad.

$H_5$: Exporters are more active in seeking information on export market opportunities than nonexporters.

$H_6$: Exporters perceive their firms as having greater company and management strengths than nonexporters.

$H_7$: Exporting firms have decision makers that are younger, better educated, have a better knowledge of foreign languages, and more of an international orientation.

METHODOLOGY

A mail survey of 575 Ontario, Nova Scotia, and New Brunswick firms was carried out. A random sample of 350 Ontario firms was selected from Scott's Industrial Directory of Ontario (12th ed.), excluding large firms (500 employees or more) and also very small firms (less than 50 employees). The sample also included 116 Nova Scotia and 109 New Brunswick firms. In order to obtain an adequate data base and meet the above size criteria, a census of Nova Scotia and New Brunswick exporting firms was required. These, as well as the randomly selected nonexporting firms, were obtained from the Nova Scotia Directory of Manufacturers, 1977-78 and New Brunswick Manufacturers and Products, 1978.

The questionnaire used in this study was one being used in studies of export behavior in Maine and New Mexico in the United States, as well as in Norway. Appropriate changes were made to "Canadianize" the original U.S. instrument.

Each company in the sample was sent an individually typed letter addressed to the president or general manager of the company as named in the directory. A prepaid reply envelope was included for the return of the questionnaire. A follow-up letter with questionnaire and prepaid reply envelope was later mailed to nonrespondents.

The response breakdown was as shown in Table 3.1. The highest response rate occurred among exporters, in spite of the fact that it was stressed in both the initial and follow-up accompanying letters that nonexporter responses were also important to the study. Budget limitations precluded further contacts with nonexporter nonrespondents.

TABLE 3.1

Response Rate

|  | Province | | |
| --- | --- | --- | --- |
|  | Ontario | Nova Scotia | New Brunswick |
| Total responses | 177 | 55 | 46 |
| Number deleted* | 14 | 5 | 6 |
| Usable responses | 163 | 50 | 40 |
| Overall usable response rate (percent) | 47 | 43 | 37 |
| Current exporter | 135 | 41 | 28 |
| Nonexporter | 27 | 9 | 12 |
| No response | 1 | — | — |

*Deletion due to not meeting firm size criterion.

Table 3.2 shows a fairly even representation of size categories in the sample of companies. Table 3.3 shows the distribution of respondents by 1979 dollar sales. Using this measure, the majority of firms fall in the over $5 million sales category.

The respondents were also spread through many different sectors of the manufacturing industry, so that the sample was truly cross-sectional. More than 10 respondents were found in 12 of the 20 categories. The largest response category was for food manufacturing, followed by machinery and lumber.

For 59 percent of the exporters, the United States was the largest export market. The United Kingdom, Australia, and Japan were the next most important markets for Canadian goods. In all, 29 countries were cited by the 224 exporters as being their most important export market in 1979.

## FINDINGS

This chapter presents the initial findings of the study. The seven hypotheses are tested utilizing t-tests, chi-square tests, and frequency counts; significance, where relevant, being established at the .05 level.

### Hypotheses 1-3

The exporter and nonexporter mean responses presented in Table 3.4 show that Canadian exporters do perceive the risks and the majority of costs of exporting to be significantly lower than do nonexporters. The costs that are not perceived to be significantly different are production costs, which could reasonably be considered as similar given that the difference is in the end-market destination; and clerical costs—perhaps the additional paper work for managing export business is seen as minimal. These findings for hypotheses 1 and 3 support those of Simpson and Kujawa (1974). However, contrary to Simpson and Kujawa, the findings do not support the second hypothesis, that profit perception is significantly different. Both exporters and nonexporters perceive little difference between the profit obtainable from export sales versus domestic sales.

### Hypothesis 4

This hypothesis concerned the major stimulus for a firm's initial export decision. Although many studies have found that the

TABLE 3.2

Size of Firm
(number of employees)

| | Number of Respondents | | | | | | | | |
| | Ontario | | | Nova Scotia | | | New Brunswick | | |
| Firm Size | E* | NE* | Total | E | NE | Total | E | NE | Total |
|---|---|---|---|---|---|---|---|---|---|
| 50-99 employees | 38 | 19 | 57 | 13 | 3 | 16 | 7 | 3 | 10 |
| 100-249 employees | 54 | 6 | 60 | 15 | 1 | 16 | 11 | 6 | 17 |
| 250-500 employees | 38 | 3 | 41 | 10 | 4 | 14 | 10 | 3 | 13 |
| No response | | | 5 | | | 4 | | | — |
| Total | | | 163 | | | 50 | | | 40 |

*E = exporter, NE = nonexporter.

TABLE 3.3

Size of Firm
(1979 dollar sales)

| | Number of Respondents | | | | | | | | |
| | Ontario | | | Nova Scotia | | | New Brunswick | | |
| Sales | E* | NE* | Total | E | NE | Total | E | NE | Total |
|---|---|---|---|---|---|---|---|---|---|
| Less than $999,999 | 4 | — | 4 | 1 | — | 1 | — | 1 | 1 |
| $1 million-$4,999,999 | 28 | 13 | 41 | 12 | 4 | 16 | 5 | 2 | 7 |
| $5 million or more | 98 | 13 | 111 | 27 | 4 | 31 | 23 | 9 | 32 |
| No response | | | 7 | | | 2 | | | — |
| Total | | | 163 | | | 50 | | | 40 |

*E = exporter, NE = nonexporter.

45

TABLE 3.4

Perceptions of Risk, Profit, and Cost in Exporting

| Variable[a] | Mean Response | | Significance |
|---|---|---|---|
| | Exporter | Nonexporter | |
| Risks | 3.57 | 4.04 | .00 |
| Profits | 2.92 | 2.88 | N.S.[b] |
| Costs | | | |
| Production | 3.07 | 3.19 | N.S. |
| Assembly | 3.14 | 3.37 | .04 |
| Packaging and handling | 3.76 | 4.15 | .00 |
| Shipping | 4.18 | 4.58 | .00 |
| Insurance | 3.93 | 4.28 | .02 |
| In-transit damage | 3.52 | 4.00 | .00 |
| Clerical | 3.93 | 3.90 | N.S. |
| Management time required | | | |
| To locate customers | 4.08 | 4.41 | .01 |
| To negotiate sales | 4.00 | 4.24 | .05 |
| For after-sale customer contacts | 3.52 | 3.90 | .03 |

[a]5-point ordinal scale: 1 = much less than domestic to 5 = much more than domestic.
[b]Not significant at the .05 level.

46

receipt of an unsolicited order from abroad is the most important initial stimulus, this is not borne out in this study. Table 3.5 shows that the internal factor—excess production capacity—is the single most important stimulus for this sample of firms. Unsolicited orders were second most important, and it is interesting to note that, for 18 firms, more than one stimulus was reported. This lends credibility to Reid's (1980c) argument concerning the complexity of the initial export decision.

TABLE 3.5

Initial Export Stimulus for Exporting Firm

| Stimulus | Number of Responses |
|---|---|
| Availability of unutilized production capacity | 57 |
| Receipt of unsolicited order from abroad | 22 |
| Others | 19 |
| More than one above checked | 18 |
| Increased competition in your domestic market | 16 |
| Information on exports you received from a source outside your firm | 13 |
| Identified a market for our product(s) | 13 |
| Accumulation of unsold inventories | 8 |
| Unknown—long exporting history | 8 |
| Profit potential obtainable from additional business | 7 |
| Long-run market growth | 7 |
| Saturation/decline of Canadian market | 5 |
| Subsidiary orders | 4 |
| Original intent | 4 |
| Value of Canadian dollar | 4 |
| A competitor beginning to export | 2 |

Hypothesis 5

Of the various sources providing export information considered, exporters used three information sources significantly more than nonexporters: industrial associations, personal contacts with other executives, and export agents. Overall, the data presented in Table 3.6 show that both federal and provincial government agencies are used substantially by both exporters and nonexporters and that exporters tend to be more active in seeking export market opportunities. Clearly government agencies are seen as valuable information sources as are executives in other firms.

TABLE 3.6

Information Sources on Exporting

| Sources Used | Exporter (percent) | Nonexporter (percent) | $X^2$ Significance |
|---|---|---|---|
| Federal government agency | 77.5[a] | 66.0 | N.S.[b] |
| Provincial government agency | 62.3 | 61.7 | N.S. |
| Chamber of Commerce | 8.8 | 8.5 | N.S. |
| Industrial association | 34.3 | 14.9 | .02 |
| Banks | 12.7 | 6.4 | N.S. |
| Personal contacts with executives outside your firm | 63.7 | 42.6 | .01 |
| Export agent | 41.2 | 17.0 | .03 |
| Other | 26.6 | 10.6 | N.S. |
| None of the above | 2.5 | 8.5 | N.S. |

[a]Read as follows: 77.5 percent of exporters reported using federal government agencies as a source of export information.
[b]Not significant at the .05 level.

Hypothesis 6

Much of the literature reviewed supports the view that exporting firms perceive themselves to have greater company and/or management strengths than do nonexporters. As can be seen in Table 3.7, the findings in this study do not support this view. In eight of nine company factors and four of seven management strengths, the exporter mean response suggests greater strengths but mean differences are small and not statistically significant. Only in one instance is there a significant difference between exporter and nonexporter responses; nonexporters feel that their national network of

TABLE 3.7

Perceived Company and Management Strengths

| Perceptions of | Mean Response[a] | | Significance |
|---|---|---|---|
| | Exporters | Nonexporters | |
| Company strengths | | | |
| Quality of products | 1.64 | 1.70 | N.S.[b] |
| Prices of products | 2.61 | 2.43 | N.S. |
| Capability to develop new products | 2.46 | 2.49 | N.S. |
| Servicing products | 2.24 | 2.28 | N.S. |
| Patents you held | 3.05 | 3.34 | N.S. |
| Overall quality of management | 2.09 | 2.23 | N.S. |
| Network of middlemen in home province | 2.91 | 3.00 | N.S. |
| National network of middlemen | 2.88 | 3.34 | .02 |
| Understanding of customer needs and requirements | 1.90 | 2.09 | N.S. |
| Management strengths | | | |
| Marketing | 2.16 | 2.48 | N.S. |
| Production | 2.01 | 2.09 | N.S. |
| Finance | 2.31 | 2.13 | N.S. |
| Engineering | 2.51 | 2.60 | N.S. |
| Purchasing | 2.63 | 2.47 | N.S. |
| Short-term planning (up to one year) | 2.29 | 2.26 | N.S. |
| Long-range planning (beyond one year) | 2.68 | 2.70 | N.S. |

[a]On a 5-point ordinal scale, 1 = great strength to 5 = great weakness.
[b]Not significant at the .05 level.

49

middlemen is weaker. In all, the findings do not support the notion that exporting companies perceive themselves to be stronger organizations.

Hypothesis 7

Table 3.8 highlights no significant age or educational differences between the decision maker in exporting companies and the one in nonexporting companies. As far as international orientation is concerned, it appears that decision makers in exporting companies have slightly better, although still poor, foreign language skills (primarily French and Spanish). Exporters are also more likely to have visited Latin America than nonexporters, but travel incidence remains low. For other international travel destinations, no significant difference is seen between exporters and nonexporters. Generally, then, the findings do not lend support to the view that decision makers in exporting companies are younger, better-educated, have better foreign language skills, and a more international orientation (as measured by international travel behavior).

CONCLUSIONS

It is apparent that few of the hypotheses tested in this study were supported by the study data. This is interesting insofar as the findings here run contrary to a good number of other studies.

Like other research, the Canadian data show that the nonexporters perceive the costs and risks of exporting to be greater than do exporters. It is clear that these perceptions may well act as an obstacle to exporting for some nonexporting firms considering market expansion, and that room exists for the modification of these concerns about engaging in overseas business. Of interest is the finding that both Canadian exporters and nonexporters view profits from exporting as being somewhat less than the profitability of domestic business. If profit is not the main motivator of expansion overseas, other factors are obviously important, for example, spreading of market risk, and again there is an opportunity for nonexporters to be "sold" on this type of idea. Indeed some of these factors are suggested in Table 3.5, for example, unutilized production capacity, long-run market growth. As has been found in other studies, unsolicited orders are an important export stimulus for many Canadian companies, although other stimuli are also shown to be salient.

TABLE 3.8

Decision-Maker Characteristics

| Characteristic | Mean Response | | Significance |
|---|---|---|---|
| | Exporter | Nonexporter | |
| Age[a] | 3.66 | 3.65 | N.S.[e] |
| Education[b] | 3.84 | 3.63 | N.S. |
| Foreign languages[c] | | | |
| French | 3.84 | 4.30 | .01 |
| Spanish | 4.75 | 4.98 | N.S. |
| Other (4 languages) | | | N.S. |
| International travel[d] | | | |
| United States | 3.00 | 3.00 | N.S. |
| Latin America | 1.62 | 1.35 | .02 |
| Europe | 2.47 | 2.38 | N.S. |
| Africa | 1.29 | 1.19 | N.S. |
| Asia | 1.39 | 1.33 | N.S. |
| India | 1.09 | 1.05 | N.S. |
| Australia | 1.30 | 1.16 | N.S. |

[a] 1 = 18-24, 2 = 25-34, 3 = 35-44, 4 = 45-54, 5 = 55-64, 6 = 65+.

[b] 1 = less than high school    4 = college graduate
2 = high school    5 = school beyond four-year
3 = some college      college
     6 = noncollege postsecondary

[c] Degree of knowledge on a 5-point ordinal scale: 1 = excellent to 5 = not at all.

[d] Extent of travel: 1 = never, 2 = one trip, 3 = two or more trips.

[e] Not significant at the .05 level.

On the question of information activities, the study results show that exporting companies are generally more active in seeking information on exporting than nonexporting firms. This finding is in harmony with other research. Fairly sharp differences are presented for industrial associations, other company executives, and export agents—in each case exporters making significantly more use of these sources. It may well be that government should encourage nonexporter usage of these sources, as well as continued usage of their own resources. In addition, industrial associations might do more to stimulate international trade by their Canadian members, through wider dissemination of export-related information. It would appear that banks and chambers of commerce are viewed as less important sources of export information, given the relatively low level of usage of these institutions by exporter and nonexporter alike. Perhaps these institutions could be encouraged to take a more active role, particularly since the major banks in Canada have international centers.

Two other sets of results present contrasting evidence to those of other researchers. First, the Canadian data indicate that export firms are little different from nonexporting firms, in terms of perceived company and management strengths. Second, little evidence is seen for the view that decision makers in exporting companies are different from those in nonexporting firms. These findings present contrary but Canadian evidence. Perhaps the similarity in firm and decision-maker characteristics between exporters and nonexporters is related to the extraregional expansion strategies of the latter, necessitated by the geographic dispersion and small size of the Canadian market. In this way, although a firm may be a nonexporter it may have a broad market scope. This, in turn, could well have led to the development of similar perceptions of company/ management strengths and an outward market orientation.

Overall, the study reported here provides information on the export behavior of small- and medium-sized Canadian manufacturing firms in 1980. The results are similar in some respects to other research in this field, but contrasts are also provided.

Finally, certain initiatives are suggested by the results for those concerned with stimulating Canadian exports. Further analysis of the study data is planned using multivariate procedures.

REFERENCES

Abdel-Malek, T. (1974). Managerial Export-Orientation: A Canadian Study. London, Ontario: University of Western Ontario.

Bilkey, W. J. (1978). "An Attempted Integration of the Literature on the Export Behavior of Firms." Journal of International Business Studies 9 (Spring):33-46.

Bilkey, W. J., and G. Tesar (1977). "The Export Behavior of Smaller Sized Wisconsin Manufacturing Firms." Journal of International Business Studies 8 (Spring):93-98.

Cavusgil, S. T. (1976). "Organizational Determinants of Firms' Export Behavior: An Empirical Analysis." Ph.D. dissertation, The University of Wisconsin, Madison.

Crookell, H., and I. Graham (1979). "International Marketing and Canadian Industrial Strategy." The Business Quarterly, Spring, pp. 29-34.

Cunningham, M. T., and R. I. Spigel (1971). "A Study in Successful Exporting." British Journal of Marketing, Spring, pp. 2-12.

Doyle, R. W., and N. A. Schommer (1976). "The Decision to Export: Some Implications." Minnesota District Export Council, St. Paul.

Export Canada, 1980-81 (1980). Vancouver, B.C.: Evergreen Press Ltd.

Garnier, Gérard (1974). Characteristics and Problems of Small and Medium Exporting Firms in the Quebec Manufacturing Sector with Special Emphasis on Those Using Advanced Production Techniques. Ottawa: Technological Innovation Studies Program, Department of Industry, Trade, and Commerce.

Langston, C. M., and R. K. Teas (1976). Export Commitment and the Characteristics of Management. Presented at the Annual Meeting of the Midwest Business Association, St. Louis, Missouri.

Mintzberg, H. (1973). The Nature of Managerial Work. New York: Harper & Row.

Pavord, W. C., and R. G. Bogart (1975). "The Dynamics of the Decision to Export." Akron Business and Economic Review, Spring, pp. 6-11.

Perlmutter, H. V. (1969). "The Tortuous Evolution of the Multinational Corporation." Columbia Journal of World Business, January-February, pp. 9-18.

Pinney, J. K. (1970). "Process of Commitment to Foreign Trade." Bulletin published by the Indiana Department of Commerce, Indianapolis.

Reid, Stan (1980a). "A Behavioral Approach to Export Decision-Making." Proceedings, Educator's Conference, edited by R. Bagozzi et al. Chicago: American Marketing Association.

Reid, Stan (1980b). "Information Usage and Export Expansion Strategies in Canadian Manufacturing Enterprises." Presented at Academy of International Business Annual Meeting, New Orleans.

Reid, Stan (1980c). "The Contextual Environment of Foreign Entry: Theoretical and Methodological Issues." Proceedings of South-Western Marketing Association, Annual Meeting, San Antonio, Texas.

Simmonds, K., and H. Smith (1968). "The First Export Order: A Marketing Innovation." British Journal of Marketing, Summer, pp. 93-100.

Simpson, C. L., Jr. (1973). "The Export Decision: An Interview Study of the Decision Process in Tennessee Manufacturing Firms." Ph.D. dissertation, Georgia State University, Atlanta.

Simpson, C. L., Jr., and D. Kujawa (1974). "The Export Decision Process: An Empirical Enquiry." Journal of International Business Studies, Spring, pp. 107-17.

Snavely, W. P., P. Weiner, H. H. Ulbrich, and E. J. Enright (1964). Export Survey of the Greater Hartford Area. Storrs: University of Connecticut.

Tookey, D. A. (1964). "Factors Associated with Success in Exporting." Journal of Management Studies, March, pp. 48-64.

Wiedersheim-Paul, F., H. C. Olson, and L. S. Welch (1978). "Pre-Export Activity: The First Step in Internationalization." Journal of International Business Studies 9 (Spring/Summer):47-57.

Welch, L. S., and F. Wiedersheim-Paul (1977). "Extra Regional Expansion—Internationalization Within the Domestic Market?" First draft of a working paper prepared at the Centre of International Business Studies, Department of Business Administration, University of Uppsala, Sweden.

# 4

# AN EMPIRICAL STUDY OF NORWEGIAN EXPORT BEHAVIOR

## Pat Joynt

Export behavior is an important factor in evaluating the economic well-being of a nation. Any national unit on this globe must generate enough export to compensate for imports. Norway, until recently, has experienced a chronic balance of payments deficit and presently has one of the smallest productivity increases in Europe. While the resource oil may compensate for the lack of gains in productivity in the short run, and thus a balanced budget, the long-term effects of this new natural resource can be damaging to the productivity of the nation in other sectors. The study reported here looks at a small segment of this phenomenon, namely export behavior. Eighty-five Norwegian organizations were surveyed and classified as small- and medium-sized firms as defined by having less than 500 employees.

The research is designed to further understand export motivating and inhibiting factors. It is expected that further analysis of the data will permit the development of useful preexport and postexport stages that firms typically go through in moving toward internationalization of operations.

In addition, a comparative analysis of export behavior in the United States and Norway will aid in further extending export stimulation theory, as well as in providing guidelines for strategies to increase exports. The study is envisaged as the first in a continuing series of studies focusing on export behavior (Bilkey, 1970;

I wish to thank Erik Ranheim, who assisted me in the collection of data.

de la Torre, 1972; Johanson and Wiedersheim-Paul, 1975; Langston, 1976; Naor, 1980; Czinkota and Johnston, 1981; Czinkota and La Londe, 1980; Prent, 1980; and Astrup, 1980).

The eventual objectives of this research endeavor are to:

● Develop comprehensive profiles of small- and medium-sized exporting firms
● Determine the major motivating and inhibiting factors with regard to the export behavior of these firms
● Develop a classification of such firms by useful preexport and postexport stages
● Determine theoretical and strategy implications regarding small- and medium-sized firms
● Compare export behavior in Norway and the United States

Bilkey and Tesar (1977) identified the following six stages of international development on the part of small- and medium-sized firms with respect to export decision making:

● Management is not interested in exporting.
● Management would fill an unsolicited export order, but would make no efforts to explore the feasibility of exporting.
● Management actively explores the feasibility of exporting.
● The firm exports on an experimental (trial test) basis.
● The firm is an experienced exporter to one country and adjusts exports optimally to changing exchange rates, tariffs, and so on.
● Management explores the feasibility of exporting to many countries.

The preliminary findings reported here show that the Norwegian firms surveyed tended to emphasize the final three stages, while the U.S. firms surveyed by Bilkey and Tesar (1977) and Naor (1980) showed that U.S. firms emphasized all the stages. Since close to half of Norway's gross national product involves exports and imports and the U.S. percentage is under 10 percent, the above general findings seem obvious. Perceptual factors relating to management and objective factors relating to other categories have been found instrumental in influencing the export propensity of firms. This study focuses mainly on the management factors involved.

PREVIOUS THEORETICAL WORK IN THE
EXPORT BEHAVIOR OF FIRMS

The export behavior of firms has been a topic of major interest in international business research since the early 1960s. According to Naor (1980) most of the empirical research has attempted to develop internal and external factors that explain a firm's export behavior. The majority of the research has used the large firm as the unit of analysis. Thorelli (1966) and Perlmutter (1969) studied the foreign attitude of top management related to export decisions; Pinney (1970) studied the significance of internal change agents; and Langston and Teas (1976) the foreign orientation of decision makers.

The quality of management has received much attention (Tookey, 1964; Simpson, 1973; Tesar, 1975; and Naor, 1980). The firm's environment is also an important factor as Pinney (1970), Tesar (1975), Joynt (1979), and Naor (1980) point out. Tesar found that the role of other firms was most important in moving firms to export behavior, while Pavord and Bogart (1975) found adverse home market conditions as most important. Other factors such as size, competitive advantages, the firm's goals, history, product lines, and information have been studied.

Czinkota and La Londe (1980) surveyed over 300 small- and medium-sized U.S. firms and found the following general implications for the firms involved. In the initial stage, which was defined as "completely uninterested firm," sales volume was usually less than $5 million and the firm had less than 100 employees. In stage two, which is defined as the "partially interested firm," export volume was found to be below $200,000 and sales abroad usually involved less than ten customers. The size profiles of stage one were much the same. Stage three, which is the "exploring firm," exported about $500,000 worth of merchandise to less than 20 customers and had the same size profiles as stage one. Stage four, which was defined as the "experimental exporter," had $750,000 worth of goods shipped to less than ten customers and had the same size profiles as in stage one. In stage five the annual sales volume is below $10 million and most of the firms employed 100 or less employees. Export volume is slightly below $1.5 million shipped to an average of 40 customers. The president is the major decision maker with strong input from marketing. Profit advantage, unique products, and technological advantage are the main factors motivating exports.

The final stage can be defined as the experienced large exporter and most firms have an average annual sales volume of below $50 million and employ between 100 and 250 persons. Average annual export volume is about $6 million shipped to about 140 customers. The president and the marketing manager are the main export decision makers in the firm. The main motivating factors are profit advantage, competitive pressures, and a unique product.

One important implication of the Czinkota and La Londe research was in the area of international business education.

Identifying the needs of business has shown that firms
are attempting to improve in the area of selling, communication and customer service in the international
context. These needs seem to indicate the necessity
for increasing foreign language training and a stronger
emphasis on marketing and logistic in the education
of international business majors (p. 23).

Czinkota and Johnston (1981, p. 7) used the following variables
in their attempt to classify firms with respect to export decisions:

Background of firms: Demographic characteristics of firms,
such as size and age, the export distribution, the beginning of export activities, and the motivation for exporting. Also the event-
oriented background of the firm such as receipt of an unsolicited
order, and threshold points for the change of behavior.

Importance and problems: Variables relevant to the export
effort of firms such as advertising, sales effort, information gathering, and their impact on the firm.

Perceived customer value: How the exporting firm perceives
that the customer will benefit from the variables that are of relevance to the exporter.

Internal improvement: The improvement in export performance the firm believes it could obtain if the firm were to place
more emphasis on the issues relevant to exporting.

Governmental assistance: The improvement in export performance the firm believes it could obtain if the U.S. Department of
Commerce were to perform exporting tasks for the firm.

Export perceptions: The attitudes management displays toward exporting and its impact on the firm.

Product orientation: The extent to which the export offering
of the firm consists of the physical product. The opposite of software orientation.

Decision makers: The amount of input various people in the
firm have into the export decision process.

Prent (1980), in sampling 70 Norwegian firms, found the following factors present in the export decision:

Extra production capacity
Reaction to an unexpected export order
Increased competition in the home market
Information on export possibilities from external sources
Increase in inventories
Home market is too small

Increased prices in foreign markets
Risk minimization
Positive response from an export exhibit
Season swings in the home market are different from the international market
Need for a larger market
Products do not sell in the home market
Desire to have larger sales

In the majority of the U.S. studies mentioned above, Canada was the initial and primary country used for export. The Norwegian behavior in the area of export behavior is slightly more complex. Astrup (1980), in a study of internationalization of Norwegian firms in the Common Market (the Common Market accounts for the majority of Norwegian exports and imports), found the following results:

| Country used for establishing a daughter firm | Number of firms |
|---|---|
| England | 13 |
| Denmark | 11 |
| Netherlands | 4 |
| West Germany | 4 |
| Belgium | 3 |
| Italy | 3 |
| Ireland | 2 |
| France | 1 |

(Sweden is not included in this study; however, the Norwegian export behavior here is similar to that of England.)

Samdal (1975) found that Norwegian firms engaging in export had the following technologies:

| Main technology | Number |
|---|---|
| Factory production | 97 |
| Chemical production | 53 |
| Lumber production | 21 |
| Metals | 20 |
| Food and drink products | 19 |
| Clothing and textiles | 12 |
| Mineral products | 10 |
| Wood fabrication | 7 |

In addition Samdal found that 32 percent of these firms were vertically integrated, that is, there was a direct connection between production abroad and at home. Of the firms, 60 percent were horizontally integrated, that is, production was done in Norway. Finally, 8 percent could be classified as conglomerate, that is, different things were made at home and abroad.

METHODOLOGY

Mintzberg (1970) and Joynt (1979) found that in medium-sized firms single decision makers are a usual encounter. The research design used here involves a questionnaire survey sent to single decision makers in 85 Norwegian firms. The data were collected in the spring of 1980. The questionnaire includes items developed from exploratory interviews by Naor (1980), as well as items pertaining in particular to perceptual motivators and inhibitors developed in previous research (Tookey, 1964; Simpson and Kujawa, 1974; Sinai, 1970; Bilkey and Tesar, 1977; and Naor, 1980). Naor reported that motivators for exporting included perceptual factors such as long-term and short-term profit expectations, production of domestically seasonal products, or entry of a domestic competitor into export markets. Inhibitors to export behavior included risk, high cost perceptions, and infrastructural and institutional obstacles.

Nominal and ordinal types of data will be generated by question responses to compare with the previous work of Naor (1980). The results presented here will be a raw summary of the questions and data obtained. Further analysis will include nonparametric tests to determine significant stimuli-type and environmental factors as well as comparing mean responses of decision makers of exporting firms in Norway and the United States.

ANALYSIS

Researchers tend to be cautious about accepting a new theory or information concerning a new theory (evidence) as valid. When confronted with a great deal of uncertainty or new information, they avoid drawing conclusions and instead call for additional information and research. This strategy is consistent with generations of scientific traditions, in that hypotheses must be carefully developed, tested, and proven, and cause and effect must be demonstrated. Unfortunately, practical managers often don't have the luxury of putting off decisions until certainty arrives, thus the managers' action or inaction is a decision. In an effort to compromise both schools of thought, the next section of the study will present the results of the survey of 85 Norwegian firms in the spring of 1980 in complete detail. Further analysis and refinement of these data will be done in future work as was reported in the methodology section.

## NORWEGIAN EXPORT STUDY

First we are interested in your opinions as to the advantages of exporting in general.

1. In your opinion how great are the risks of exporting as compared to the risks involved in sales to the domestic (U.S.) market? (Check the response that corresponds to your opinion.)

| Much Less Than Domestic | Somewhat Less Than Domestic | About the Same as Domestic | Somewhat More Than Domestic | Much More Than Domestic |
|---|---|---|---|---|
| 1 | 3 | 21 | 47 | 13 |

2. In your opinion how do _profits_ to be gained from exporting generally compare to profits from domestic sales? (Check one response.)

| Much Less Than Domestic | Somewhat Less Than Domestic | About the Same as Domestic | Somewhat More Than Domestic | Much More Than Domestic |
|---|---|---|---|---|
| 5 | 36 | 24 | 18 | 2 |

3. Now please rate how each of the following _costs_ of exporting compares to costs of domestic sales. (Check one response for each cost item.)

| | Much Less Than Domestic | Somewhat Less Than Domestic | About the Same as Domestic | Somewhat More Than Domestic | Much More Than Domestic |
|---|---|---|---|---|---|
| Production costs | 1 | 3 | 52 | 21 | 8 |
| Packaging and handling costs | 1 | 0 | 36 | 38 | 10 |
| Shipping costs | 1 | 1 | 7 | 37 | 37 |
| Insurance costs | 1 | 28 | 36 | 19 | 0 |
| In-transit damage costs | 2 | 28 | 37 | 16 | 0 |
| Management time required: | | | | | |
| to locate potential customers | 3 | 9 | 35 | 38 | 0 |
| to negotiate sales | 2 | 12 | 40 | 31 | 0 |
| after-sale contacts with customers | 2 | 6 | 23 | 38 | 16 |

4. Which of the following was the major reason behind your firm's original decision to engage in export activities. (Please check one response.)

| | |
|---|---|
| 19 | Receipt of unsolicited order from abroad |
| 2 | A competitor beginning to export |
| 7 | Accumulation of unsold inventories |
| 17 | Availability of unutilized production capacity |
| 13 | Increased competition in your domestic market |
| 4 | Information on exports you received from a source outside your firm |
| 9 | Desire for more production, more rational production, larger market |
| 1 | Filling of season swings in the domestic market |
| 3 | Production of fish products is dependent on exports |
| 6 | No special reason |
| 4 | Do not export |

5. From which of the following sources have you received information on exporting in the last five years? (Please check all that apply.)

| | |
|---|---|
| 18 | Department of Commerce |
| 12 | Department of State |
| 60 | Department of Industry |
| 60 | Export Council |
| 11 | Export finance |
| 24 | Banks |
| 61 | Personal contact with an external businessperson |
| 33 | Magazines, newspapers, and so on |
| 17 | Export/import agent |
| 2 | None of the above |
| 30 | Other sources |

6. Which of the sources of information listed above were most helpful to you:

| | |
|---|---|
| 2 | Department of State |
| 21 | Export Council |
| 20 | Personal contact |
| 1 | Magazines |
| 9 | Export/import agent |
| 11 | Other sources |

7. We are interested in your perceptions of your company's strengths and weaknesses. Please rate each of the following items as it applies to your company.

| | Great Strength | Strength | Neither Strength nor Weakness | Weakness | Great Weakness |
|---|---|---|---|---|---|
| Quality of your products | 48 | 31 | 6 | 0 | 0 |
| Prices of your products | 5 | 20 | 25 | 30 | 3 |
| Capability to develop new products | 12 | 26 | 29 | 13 | 3 |
| Servicing your products | 13 | 23 | 42 | 5 | 3 |
| Patents you hold | 9 | 11 | 38 | 4 | 5 |
| Overall quality of your management | 8 | 34 | 35 | 7 | 0 |
| Network of middlemen in Norway | 14 | 32 | 32 | 4 | 0 |
| National network of middle-men external to Norway | 12 | 23 | 33 | 11 | 1 |
| Understanding of customer needs and requirements | 16 | 47 | 16 | 5 | 0 |

8. Now specifically in the area of management, what are your company's strengths and weaknesses:

| | Great Strength | Strength | Neither Strength nor Weakness | Weakness | Great Weakness |
|---|---|---|---|---|---|
| Marketing | 9 | 35 | 23 | 17 | 1 |
| Production | 13 | 48 | 18 | 6 | 0 |
| Finance | 9 | 31 | 31 | 12 | 1 |
| Engineering (product development) | 10 | 27 | 32 | 14 | 2 |
| Purchasing | 6 | 28 | 44 | 5 | 1 |
| Short-term planning (up to one year) | 11 | 32 | 32 | 8 | 1 |
| Long-range planning (beyond one year) | 10 | 16 | 28 | 26 | 4 |

9. Using the lists from Questions 11 and 12 please list in order the three areas in which your company is strongest (1 being strongest).

| | |
|---|---|
| 44 | Quality of the product |
| 8 | Marketing |
| 8 | Product development |
| 4 | Price |
| 4 | Quality of management |
| 4 | Production |

10. Please list in order the three areas in which your company is weakest (1 being weakest).

| | |
|---|---|
| 19 | Price |
| 12 | Long-range planning |
| 11 | Marketing |
| 11 | Product development |
| 9 | Finance |
| 5 | Patents |

Further analyses of the first ten questions tend to reveal several behavioral patterns that are contrary to much of the existing theory. The first two questions tend to illustrate that the typical Norwegian firm is interested in exporting in spite of the fact that profits are lower and risks are higher. In addition, question 3 shows that most of the costs associated with export are higher when compared to the domestic market. The lack of a positive motivation factor for doing business abroad—such as higher profits, lower risks, or lower costs—did not emerge in this study and one is left with this basic factor unanswered. In follow-up interviews with some of the participants the writer found that many felt exporting was a natural part of Norwegian business life. Few companies in the United States limit their operation to a single state, and Norway with its population of 4 million might be considered as having business behavior similar to a state rather than a large country. This development deserves further attention in future research of this type.

Further analysis of the companies' strengths and weaknesses showed that the quality of the product emerged as the most important strength. Norwegian machinery, chemicals, candy, boats, furniture, and electronics (question 12) have a worldwide reputation of good quality. Unfortunately, the recent failures of Tandberg and many companies in the textile area raise serious doubts as to how long this image of good quality can continue to exist. The German rise and fall in this area is possibly a similar phenomenon worth consideration in a Norwegian context.

Question 11 found that the average size of the firms sampled was close to 150 employees. Joynt (1979) also found that the industrial revolution came to Norway during this century with the result that most Norwegian companies are relatively young and small compared with other nations. Because of this the strategy of finding small niches in the international market is often typical here. There are many cases of this strategy, where a small Norwegian company will take on the large internationals. A good example of this is Norsk Data, a small company less than 20 years old that has been highly successful in the computer hardware market.

The following questions represent certain traits of the firms' export behavior:

13. Approximately what percent of your firm's gross sales were to customers outside of Norway in each of these years? (Please check one response for each year.)

|  | 1978 | 1979 | 1980 |
| --- | --- | --- | --- |
| None | 6 | 5 | 4 |
| Less than 5 percent | 8 | 10 | 10 |
| 5-9 percent | 13 | 9 | 8 |
| 10-19 percent | 9 | 11 | 12 |
| 20-29 percent | 15 | 17 | 16 |
| 30-50 percent | 18 | 18 | 22 |
| 50 percent or more | 16 | 15 | 13 |

14. For how many years has your firm engaged in exporting:

| | |
| --- | --- |
| 3 | 0 years |
| 23 | 1-10 years |
| 31 | 10-20 years |
| 14 | 20-50 years |
| 9 | over 50 years |

15. What country was your firm's largest customer for exporting in 1977 and 1978, and what country do you expect to be your largest customer in 1979?

|  | 1978 | 1979 | Expected 1980 |
| --- | --- | --- | --- |
| Sweden | 29 | 28 | 29 |
| England | 10 | 10 | 10 |
| Denmark | 11 | 8 | 8 |
| Germany | 6 | 6 | 6 |
| United States | 5 | 4 | 6 |
| Yugoslavia | 1 | 2 | 2 |
| USSR | 2 | 2 | 1 |
| Nigeria | 2 | 4 | 2 |
| Austria | 2 | 3 | 2 |

Finally, we would like some information about you:

16. What positions do you hold in your company: (Check all that apply.)

| | |
|---|---|
| 8 | President or assistant |
| 8 | Vice-president, sales |
| 6 | Vice-president, marketing |
| 0 | Vice-president, production |
| 10 | Vice-president, finance |
| 1 | General manager |
| 2 | Plant supervisor |
| 3 | Export manager |
| 8 | Other (please specify) |

17. What was the last grade you completed in school?

| | |
|---|---|
| 2 | Less than high school |
| 21 | High school |
| 10 | Some college |
| 45 | College graduate |
| 7 | School beyond four-year college degree |

18. Where did you receive your education? (Check all that apply.)

| | |
|---|---|
| 62 | Norway |
| 23 | Another country |

19. Please indicate any foreign languages you speak and how good your knowledge is of each.

| | Excellent | Good | Fair | Poor | Not at All |
|---|---|---|---|---|---|
| English | 37 | 30 | 16 | 2 | 0 |
| German | 13 | 24 | 32 | 15 | 1 |
| French | 6 | 3 | 12 | 37 | 27 |
| Spanish | 2 | 2 | 2 | 8 | 71 |

Further analysis of Norwegian export behavior shows that certain trends have been common. In the late 1960s export to the United States, Canada, and Japan declined considerably, followed by a period of decline in European markets. At this point the United States, Canada, and Japan trends reversed themselves; however, trade to underdeveloped countries fell sharply. Presently, Norway sends 75 percent of its exports to Western Europe and about 10 percent to the United States, Canada, and Japan. Less than 5 percent is to underdeveloped nations, yet the government has a policy of giving 1 percent of the GNP as aid to underdeveloped nations.

The results found here tend to illustrate that the average small Norwegian firm has over 30 percent of gross sales as export, and this result tends to contradict much of the prior theory, which suggests that only large firms have well-established export behavior. The fact that Sweden, Denmark, and England are major trade partners is not surprising from a theoretical point of view. However, Finland, which borders on Norway, is not found on the list given with question 15. Follow-up interviews showed that the factors of language, culture, and political ideology often emerged as prohibiting factors. In addition, this country borders Norway from the north, which is an area that has little industry.

CONCLUSIONS

Since this research is both exploratory and preliminary, it is prudent to point out several factors related to interpreting the results. Although additional information is needed to clarify the reasons underlying the above results, one may hypothesize that export behavior in a firm goes through several stages. This is consistent with the results found in earlier studies (Bilkey and Tesar, 1977), although this study tends to support multiple reasons for starting the export process. The most likely reasons are receipt of an unsolicited order from abroad, availability of unutilized production capacity, and increased competition in domestic markets.

Norwegian firms tended to evaluate themselves as strong in production, engineering, and finance and relatively weaker in marketing, purchasing, and planning. The strongest competitive factor appears to be the quality of the product and one of the weakest factors is the price.

Machinery, tree transport, and chemicals are the most important product lines or main technologies, and Sweden, England, and Denmark are the major export countries for Norway.

The exploration into the export behavior of Norwegian firms yielded new insights into this relatively new field of study. Perhaps future research can integrate additional factors as well as different countries with the concepts and factors surveyed here. The reports reported here are part of a large research plan that will include data from the United States, France, and Canada as well as statistical analysis of the present data.

SELECTED REFERENCES

Astrup, B. "Norske industrietableringer i EF-landene" (Norwegian Industrial Statistics in EEC Companies). Norges Industri 4 (1980).

Bilkey, W. J. Industrial Stimulation. Lexington, Mass.: Heath Lexington Books, 1970.

Bilkey, W. J., and Tesar, G. "The Export Behavior of Smaller Sized Wisconsin Manufacturing Firms." Journal of International Business Studies, Spring/Summer 1977.

Czinkota, M. R., and Johnston, W. J. "Segmenting U.S. Firms for Export Development." Journal of Business Research 9, no. 4 (1981).

Czinkota, M. R., and La Londe, B. J. "An Analysis of Export Development Strategies in Selected U.S. Industries." WPS 80-17 Ohio State University, 1980.

de la Torre, J., Jr. "Marketing Factors in Manufactured Exports from Developing Countries." In The Product Life Cycle and International Trade, edited by L. T. Wells. Cambridge, Mass.: Harvard University Press, 1972.

Johanson, J., and Wiedersheim-Paul, F. "The Internationalization of the Firm—Four Swedish Case Studies." The Journal of Management Studies, October 1975.

Joynt, P. D. "Contingency Theories of Administration." Doctoral thesis, Brunel University, 1979.

Langston, C. M. "A Reappraisal of Export Marketing Theory." International Business Seminar, New York, 1976.

Langston, C. M., and Teas, R. K. "Export Commitment and Characteristics of Management." MBA seminar, St. Louis, 1976.

Mintzberg, H. "Managerial Work Analysis from Observation." Working Paper, McGill University, 1970.

Naor, J. "An Empirical Investigation of the Export Behavior of Small and Medium Sized Firms." Unpublished work from 1979, 1980, University of Maine, 1980.

Pavord, W. C., and Bogart, R. G. "The Dynamics of the Decision to Export." Akron Business and Economic Review 6, no. 1 (1975).

Perlmutter, H. V. "The Tortuous Evolution of the Multinational Corporation." Columbia Journal of World Business, January-February 1969.

Pinney, J. K. "Process of Commitment to Foreign Trade." Indiana Department of Commerce, 1970.

Prent, T. "Ofte tilfeldige arsaker til at bedrifter gar ut pa export" (Main Reasons Why Companies Export). Norges Utenrikshandel 7, no. 8 (1980). (The article has drawn information gathered from an early stage of this study.)

Samdal, I. "Teorier om direkte investeringer belyst ved en under-søkelse av norske produksjonsselskaper i utlandet" (Theories of Direct Investment: A Study of Norwegian Manufacturing Abroad). University of Oslo, 1975.

Simpson, C. L. "The Export Decision: An Interview Study of the Decision Process in Tennessee Manufacturing Firms." Doctoral thesis, Georgia State University, 1973.

Simpson, C. L., and Kujawa, D. "The Export Decision Process: An Empirical Enquiry." Journal of International Business Studies, Spring 1974.

Sinai, C. C. "An Investigation of Selected Characteristics of Export Participating Manufacturing Firms." Doctoral thesis, University of Washington, 1970.

Tesar, G. "Empirical Study of Export Operations among Small and Medium Sized Firms." Doctoral thesis, University of Wisconsin, 1975.

Thorelli, H. B. "The Multinational Corporation as a Change Agent." Southern Journal of Business, July 1966.

Tookey, D. A. "Factors Associated with Success in Exporting." The Journal of Management Studies, March 1964.

# 5

## EXPORTERS AND NONEXPORTERS:
## A PROFILE OF SMALL
## MANUFACTURING FIRMS IN GEORGIA

Ernest W. Ogram, Jr.

Significant increases in exports are needed to reduce the recorded U.S. balance of trade deficit of $24.7 billion (f.a.s.) for 1979 (compared to the 1976 deficit of $5.6 billion). A substantial portion of the trade balance deficit resulted from an estimated $56.7 billion deficit for oil imports in 1980, which is likely to continue for the foreseeable future. U.S. trade balance deficits result in job losses at home. Each additional $15,000 increase in exports creates one new job. This is particularly significant in view of the U.S. economy's unemployment rate of 7.4 percent for 1980. Additional jobs are also created by the so-called multiplier effect as wages and profits earned through additional exports are expended on consumer goods, which in turn may induce increased expenditures on capital goods, thus creating additional employment. In a recent interview, C. Fred Bergsten, the former assistant secretary of the Treasury for international affairs, commented that "one out of every five jobs in the United States depends on exports."[1] It is anticipated that the study will be able to identify high-potential exporters in Georgia who currently are not exporting.

To this writer's knowledge, four somewhat related U.S. studies have appeared in the last decade: two in Tennessee, one in Minnesota, and one in Connecticut. Such a study has never been undertaken for Georgia firms. In addition, this study on Georgia differs in two respects from those previously undertaken in other states. First, the present study focuses exclusively on smaller manufacturing companies. Second, companies are matched (one exporter and one nonexporter) by product and size by either employment or sales volume. Although not a distinguishing characteristic of the study, insofar as possible, companies included came from product categories that represent significant or potential export sales volume for the state. These included carpets, computers and peripherals, agricultural machinery, food and packaging machinery, health care equipment, and apparel.

The basic justification for concentrating only on small manufacturing firms is that according to U.S. Department of Commerce data, small businesses are big in export. About 60 percent of all U.S. exporters have fewer than 100 employees. In addition, "a comprehensive survey of manufacturing firms in Hartford, Connecticut indicated that 69 out of 145 firms in exporting each employed fewer than 50 employees."[2] Small companies therefore are and can be competitive in the overseas market.

The primary reason for matching companies was to establish basic congruity in as many areas as possible and thus eliminate factors such as product category, employment, and annual sales volume as relevant variables for purposes of comparison between exporters and nonexporters. Common reasons given in the other states' studies for not exporting are: "I don't have a product that is exportable" or "I'm too small to export."

## OBJECTIVE

The primary objective of this study is to develop a profile of exporters and nonexporters for small manufacturing firms within the state of Georgia. Seventeen pairs of firms are to be used in the study. One company in each pair is an exporter and one a nonexporter. Each company is matched as to type of product; size is based on annual sales volume or employment when sales volume is not available. A subsidiary objective of the research is to identify nonexporting firms that have a high export potential.

## METHODOLOGY

The interview process was utilized in attempting to learn from chief executive officers (CEOs) or other senior officers of single-product companies in the majority of cases the relative importance of internal and external stimuli and environmental variables involved in the decision-making process in deciding whether or not to export.

The following stimuli were examined:

Internal:      Profit
               Excess domestic capacity
               Competition

Productive efficiency
Seasonal products
Management philosophy

External:    Insurance against domestic recession
             Orders from foreign buyers
             Trade mission activities—federal, state, local
             Foreign and domestic trade fairs
             U.S. Department of Commerce export activity
             General state of domestic economy
             DISC

Environmental
Variables:   A. Perception of risk
                Foreign country expropriations
                Cost involving product adaptation, price,
                   packaging, communication, insurance,
                   clerical, shipping, and management
                   time
                Foreign exchange controls
                Devaluation
             B. Other: level of education

The interviewer, in addition to acquiring hard data on sales, employment profits, and so on, from each company, was interested in how the person being interviewed perceived the risks, opportunities, and costs in deciding whether or not to export. The interview guide involved ordinal responses along with some open-ended questions.

DEFINITIONS

For purposes of the study, the term "exporter" is defined as a small Georgia company in manufacturing, employing under 250 workers, exporting one or more of its products on a regular basis. The figure of 250 employees was used as a reference point for inclusion in the study inasmuch as it is the figure used by the Small Business Administration (SBA) in defining a manufacturing company eligible for SBA loans.

The time period of three years is used as a general guide for involvement in exporting since it was felt that companies with only one to two years' experience in exporting in many instances should be considered new to exporting. Thus, their perceptions of the relative importance of external and internal stimuli along with the environmental variables may differ to a considerable degree compared to firms that have been established in exporting over a longer period of time.

The term "exporting on a regular basis" indicates a firm whose exports over the last three years have averaged 1 percent of its annual sales.

A "nonexporter" would be defined as a small Georgia manufacturer not currently engaged in exporting. This could therefore include a company that has never exported or one that has exported in the previous period but for one reason or another has decided to phase out its export activity.

Other parameters for including a company in the study are the following:

It must be a manufacturing firm incorporated within the state of Georgia.

A high priority is given to including firms that either currently represent significant export product categories within Georgia or those that may have considerable export potential such as apparel, carpets, food and packaging, machinery, agricultural machinery and equipment, health care equipment, computers and software.

Total sales of sample firms ranged between $250,000 and $4 million, although exceptions below $250,000 and above $4 million were considered.

As mentioned previously, for the firm to be included in the study employment will range to 250 with the possibility of one or two exceptions above 250.

In order to minimize transportation costs involved in the interview process, wherever possible, firms were drawn from an area with a radius of 50 miles from downtown Atlanta.

Matching firms were identified by four-digit Standard Industrial Classification (SIC) categories.

The general rule was that a match took place between an exporter and a nonexporter as long as there was no more than 10 percent difference in sales volume or employment.

Company interviews with the CEO or a senior official have been completed in the following product categories:

| Product Category | Number of Company Interviews |
| --- | --- |
| Agricultural machinery | 8 |
| Food machinery | 6 |
| Carpets | 12 |

| | |
|---|---|
| Computers and peripherals | 2 |
| Apparel | 4 |
| Health care equipment | 2 |
| Total | 34 |

## FINDINGS

The general findings of the study are the following:

Exporters consider themselves as a group to be more aggressive than conservative in their management philosophy in terms of looking for new markets.

Profit is a major factor in nearly all cases for getting into exporting—superseding travel, competition, available assistance, and everything else.

Generally, exporters had a lower risk and a higher profit perception.

R&D as a percentage of sales ran somewhat higher for exporters than for nonexporters.

Level and type (technical or general) of education was not important in determining whether or not the firm exported.

The number of years in business does not appear to have been a contributing factor in determining whether or not a company exported.

Exporters in general operated at a slightly higher percentage of operating capacity and in a number of instances it was mentioned that this was because of exporting.

There appear to be no significant differences in wage rates between those companies exporting and those not exporting.

Exporters generally took a broader view of their potential market, that is, local, state, regional, and overseas as market potential; whereas nonexporters took a much narrower view of their potential market.

More exporters than nonexporters had utilized support services offered by the Department of Commerce and other service organizations such as banks and freight forwarders. All exporters had some awareness of these services. Also, most of the nonexporters who were unaware of the Department of Commerce programs or other types of assistance did express interest in knowing about them.

Travel to a foreign market did not appear to be an important consideration in deciding whether or not to export by either exporters or nonexporters; so having a first-hand look at the market and potential buyers did not seem to be very important.

DISC was considered as significant for exports of smaller manufacturers.

Government regulations and unnecessary paperwork was perceived as a significant barrier to exporting by both exporters and nonexporters.

There was a consensus among exporters that a greater amount of top management's time was necessary in an exporting compared to a company that was not exporting.

## COMPANY CHARACTERISTICS

Tables 5.1 and 5.2 represent the broad areas of differences in responses given by executives interviewed in two of the major product areas included in the study, agricultural machinery and carpets. All company names have been changed for both product categories and all companies are family owned, a characteristic common to over 70 percent of the firms in the study.

In addition, the comments quoted by those interviewed in these two product categories represent a somewhat common pattern of perceptions for risk, profit, and cost in exporting as well as general attitudes in management philosophy in all six product categories.

## OTHER FINDINGS: COST PERCEPTIONS

Concerning the pattern of responses in this category, Tables 5.1 and 5.2 indicate there were differences between exporters and nonexporters regarding clerical, packaging, transportation, and communication costs.

Generally, nonexporters perceived that all clerical, packaging, transportation, and communication costs were higher. For exporters the general pattern of responses indicated that although packaging costs were higher, clerical, transportation, and communication costs were either the same or moderately higher compared to the domestic market.

There was a general absence of comments from both exporters and nonexporters concerning perceptions of product adaptation in exporting. When pressed on the point a number of exporters and nonexporters in these two product categories stated that there was no reason to adapt their product for foreign markets since the end use was the same no matter whether it was used in the domestic or the overseas market.

TABLE 5.1

Company Characteristics: Agricultural Machinery, 1977

| Company Description | Risk and Profit Perception in Export | Percent of Capacity | Reason for Exporting | Reason for Not Exporting | Cost Perceptions in Exporting | Exports as Percent of Total Sales | General Management Philosophy |
|---|---|---|---|---|---|---|---|
| LARCHMONT MFG. (E)* Family owned, in bus. 46 yrs.; emp.: 52; manufacturing multi-purpose spraying equip.; avg. hourly rate $7.00 (incl. fringes). Sales avg. $2 mil. but signif. increase last 2 yrs. | We never lost money on overseas accounts but we have on domestic accounts where they have not paid. | 90 | Customer wrote for a quote and we sold on that basis, we did not answer these at first but we do now; no adaptation needed. | Restrictions by foreign governments are important. | Packaging costs considerably greater; same is true with shipping costs because locally we just sell in Georgia; clerical cost also higher because of increased paperwork. | $\frac{3}{R+D}$ Close to 3 percent this year and next | Overaggressive on sales but conservative on financial matters; we only sell on irrevocable letter of credit. |
| KINGSBRIDGE CULTIVATORS (NE)* Family corp.; emp: 45; in bus. 39 yrs.; build diff. types spreaders; avg. hourly rate $4.50 + $1.00 for fringes. Sales increase last 3 yrs. moderate, now $2.3 mil. | No need to export; we sell all we make; risks are greater in exporting. | 95 | | There is no need to concern ourselves with all the extra headaches. | All costs are higher except clerical. | $\frac{0}{R+D}$ Less than 1 percent | My father makes all the decisions and he is a little on the conservative side. |

| Company | Risk | | | Costs | | |
|---|---|---|---|---|---|---|
| ACHUGA PRODUCTS (E) Family owned; manufactures grain handling equip.; emp.: 42; avg. hourly rate $4.50. Sales $1.9 mil. up 2.5 times in 5 yrs. | Risks are somewhat greater but so are the profits. | 90 | My son went to a workshop where they talked about it; then I got someone from the Department of Commerce to talk to us. | Insurance, packaging, and clerical costs are somewhat higher. | $\frac{1}{R+D}$ Nothing this year. Probably close to 1 percent next year. | Centralized completely but we are always on the lookout for new markets overseas. |
| J. H. BICK CO. (NE) Family bus.; makes tillers; emp.: 35. Growth rate and sales 25 percent in last 2 yrs., now $1.4 mil. Avg. hourly rate $3.75 | Have always thought it was risky and the returns did not justify the higher risks. | 90 | Tried it once and it did not work; no follow-up orders— was less than 1 percent of our sales for that year. | All the costs are higher than domestic; I'd be spread too thin since I'd have to do it myself. | $\frac{0}{R+D}$ A little more than 1 percent | I am my own boss. It could not be any other way. We might take another look at export in another year or so. |

*E = exporter; NE = nonexporter.

TABLE 5.2

Company Characteristics: Tufted Carpet Industry

| Company Description | Risk and Profit Perception in Export | 1977 Percent of Capacity | Reasons for Exporting | Reasons for Not Exporting | Cost Perceptions in Exporting | 1977 Export Percent of Sales | General Management Philosophy |
|---|---|---|---|---|---|---|---|
| DELMON INTL (E)* Family owned; in bus. 44 yrs.; custom carpets; total emp. 70; avg. hr. rate $4; sales past 5 yrs. $2.6 mil. avg. | Initial and present risk greater (not getting paid and exchange controls). Stopped exports to S. Africa because couldn't compete pricewise with European competitor. | 60 | High profit potential, foreign market more impt.; increase in productive efficiency; competition began exporting. No adaptation needed. | | Clerical costs higher; other costs the same; paid by buyer; seller quoted f.a.s. price in dollars. | 1 percent constant R & D 2 percent constant | Always looking for new markets, incl. overseas; somewhat conservative in budgeting. |
| MARGO PRODUCTS (NE)* Family owned; in bus. 6 yrs.; comm. carpets; emp. 63; wage $5.05; sales $3.5 mil. in 1977 (signif. increase in last 2 yrs.) | Risks appear to be . . . greater in exporting . . . got burned twice . . . doesn't seem to be more money in exporting. | 100 | | Based on lack of contacts, unfamiliarity with exporting procedures. Not actively seeking new markets; can sell everything now. | Clerical, packaging, and communication costs greater in exporting. | 0 R & D 1 percent but increasing to 2 percent in next 2 yrs. | Somewhat conservative in fiscal matters. |

| | | | | | | |
|---|---|---|---|---|---|---|
| ROBINSON TUFTING (E) Family owned; in bus. 4 yrs.; comm. and res. carpets; emp. 104; wage N/A; sales est. at $2-4 mil, in 1977. | Risks are greater but so are profits . . . profits down because of added costs for extra paperwork are enormous. | 90 | We're always on the lookout for new markets . . . got order from Canada . . . got (us) started. No product adaptation needed. Possibilities in Mid-East seem excellent. | Packaging costs greater; double wrap for exports. Clerical, transportation, and communication costs somewhat higher. | 1 percent (74) 3 percent (77) R & D 1 percent but increasing | Very aggressive in looking for new markets everywhere. Management structure very centralized. In spite of fast changes in technology, will stay competitive. |
| AJAX CARPETS (NE) Family owned; in bus. 20 yrs.; emp. 95; wages $4.50; sales past 5 yrs. $3 mil. | Risks are so great but profit is same as domestic. | 85 | In 77 received two export orders (Canada and United Kingdom.) Until the past year felt it not worth the effort because all attention has been domestic. | Clerical, packaging, transportation, and communication costs are much greater. Paperwork is increasingly burdensome. | 1 percent R & D 0 percent and no plans for change | Management considers itself very aggressive in all areas. |

*E = exporter; NE = nonexporter.

On the matter of pricing perception for the overseas market, although this did not appear explicitly in any of the quoted comments, there was a general recognition, especially among exporters in the open-ended part of the interview guide, that higher costs (of the type mentioned above) would result in higher export prices compared to the domestic market.

EXPORT PROBLEMS

There was a consensus among exporters in all six product categories that their major export problems appeared to be the following: competing with foreign suppliers, acquiring the necessary funds to finance export sales, finding good foreign markets, and knowing and keeping up with export procedures and import requirements in potential market areas overseas.

COMPARISON WITH OTHER STUDIES

Table 5.3 compares the similarities and differences of a representative sample of other state studies to this study. (Those studies not included involved Wisconsin, New Mexico, Maine, Oregon, and Kansas.) The format and thrust of the Georgia study evolved from these previous studies spanning almost two decades.

One of the findings of the Connecticut study (1962) by Jack Enright in differentiating between exporters and nonexporters stated that nonexporters considered themselves too small to be involved in exporting. As mentioned previously, the current study eliminates the size variable in the decision-making process because matched pairs of firms were used, an exporter and a nonexporter within 10 percent of the sales volume. Since sales volume data were not available or available only within broad ranges (because in many cases family firms were reluctant to give this type of information), employment data were used.

The Minnesota study commissioned by the Minnesota District Export Council in 1976 was the first attempt to the writer's knowledge to match importers and exporters by SIC code. A two-digit SIC code was used for matching firms by product category. The present study utilizes four-digit SIC codes. An example of the advantages of the latter would involve using the two-digit code for apparel, SIC 23, which includes all types of apparel for which there is very little export potential for the generalized category. When two additional digits are added, over 30 additional subcategories are available for study. In the case of SIC 2327 (men's and boys' trousers and jeans) and 2328 (men's and boys' work clothing) there is export potential and as a result four firms bearing these numbers were utilized in the study.

## OVERALL COMPARISON

In the first three studies (Connecticut, both Tennessee studies) a recurring theme that came out again and again was the way most firms got into exporting was as a result of an unsolicited order. In the Minnesota study and in the present study the unsolicited order was of a second order of importance. Perhaps time would have some explanatory value here because of the greater awareness companies have of the opportunities in exporting. This could be the result of better educational efforts on the part of the U.S. Department of Commerce, university, and other state and local educational programs.

In four of the five studies cited in Table 5.3 profit is mentioned as either an important factor or the most important reason for getting involved in exporting. In the first Tennessee study profit was listed as important by only 20 percent of the sample firms studied.

Aggressive management philosophy became a critical variable in explaining how companies get started in exporting. This was mentioned in both the Minnesota and Georgia studies but not in the earlier studies.

## ANTICIPATED CONTRIBUTION OF RESEARCH

A profile of small manufacturing firms in Georgia differentiating exporters and nonexporters should be helpful to those in government at the federal and state levels and those outside—the trade associations and other private groups involved in promoting exports. The data tabulated revealed that certain characteristics were evident for all or most exporting firms, such as operating at a higher percentage of operating capacity, a broader view of their potential market, aggressive management style, low-risk perception for exporting or a higher percentage of R & D to sales, and, should many of the same characteristics be present in the nonexporting group, the companies should be thought of as prime candidates for becoming involved in exporting. In other words, once these high-potential export companies are identified in the nonexport group they could be given special consideration by both government and industry groups to make them aware of the short- and long-term

TABLE 5.3

Comparison of State Studies

| Name of State and Year | Purpose | Methodology | Findings |
|---|---|---|---|
| Connecticut (1962) | Establish profile of Es and NEs. 61 percent are small manufacturers and 39 percent are nonmanufacturing. | Mail questionnaire to 145 Es, 142 NEs, and 12 former Es. No attempt made to include specific product categories. | Similarities between Es and NEs in age, number of employees, and gross sales. Differences: many NEs (1) operate from one plant, (2) price and patent disadvantages, (3) too small for exporting. Most Es got started with unsolicited order and sell in national market. NEs sell in regional market. |
| Tennessee (1) (1972) | To develop profile of state Es and to examine variables that kept Es from increasing exports to help develop market for state products abroad. | 4,000 small, medium, and large mfg. firms mailed questionnaires in east, middle, and west part of state. No specific product categories used. | Larger firms export smaller percent of total sales. No significant differences in profit margins between heavy and light exports (heavy exports more than 5 percent). Heavy E had higher growth rate in export sales and more active in search for export market. Firms in this category had higher export profits compared to domestic sales. |

| | | | |
|---|---|---|---|
| Tennessee (2) (1973) | To profile decision maker in E and NE firms and to determine perceptions of risks and cost, benefits in exporting. | Interviews with 120 mfg. firms: 50 Es, 70 NEs. Nonparametric statistical sampling used to determine significance of internal/external stimuli in E. No specific product categories used. | Unsolicited orders (external stimuli) most frequent reason to become E. External and internal stimuli not sufficient to initiate foreign sales. Perception of good profit, low cost, and risk also needed. E not generally interested in DISC. Profits significant for 20 percent of Es. |
| Minnesota (1976) | To survey Es and NEs to determine effective ways to influence Es to become better Es. | Interviews with CEOs of 15 pairs of firms of various sizes. Rough match (two-digit SIC in some cases) between Es and NEs for product and service firms. | Es more aggressive philosophy. Competition and travel play minor role in decision-making process but good profit critical factor and awareness of export assistance; significant problem areas: lack of understanding procedure, culture, communications, and language. |
| Georgia (1981) | To develop profile of Es and NEs for small manufacturing firms and identify NEs that have high export potential. | Interviews top mgmt.: 17 matched pairs of firms (four-digit SIC). One E matched with one NE by product category and size (sales or employment). | Profits and aggressive management philosophy most important for firms getting into exporting. For E also higher percent R & D, higher percent of capacity, broader view of market, utilized support services. Level and type of education, travel, and number of years in business not important for E. |

Note: E = exporter; NE = nonexporter.

83

advantages of exporting and provide such high-potential exporters with innovative educational programs calculated to bring a number of these nonexporters into exporting.

In addition, the feedback from both groups of firms (exporters and nonexporters) would be of assistance in helping federal, state, and local government agencies involved in export promotion to evaluate more fully their existing efforts in this area.

Finally, by focusing on small manufacturing firms whose product categories are or could be significant in the state's export trade, a base is established for more intensive research. A further study of a comparative nature could be directed toward determining if any significant differences occur in the decision variables when large numbers of firms are examined in each of the six product categories included in the study.

NOTES

1. Agency for International Development's weekly nationwide public affairs television program, "Overseas Mission," Front Lines, June 23, 1977.

2. Export Marketing for Smaller Firms, 3rd ed. (Washington, D.C.: Small Business Administration, 1971), p. 2.

# 6

## COMPARISON OF WISCONSIN AND VIRGINIA SMALL- AND MEDIUM-SIZED EXPORTERS: AGGRESSIVE AND PASSIVE EXPORTERS

### George Tesar
### Jesse S. Tarleton

Interest in export operations and export development is rapidly growing worldwide. National governments, individual states, and economic regions are actively interested in stimulating exports among their small- and medium-sized manufacturing firms. Both government and the private sector are interested in drafting comprehensive statements of export policy to provide specific guidelines for export development.[1]

The above effort, however, faces several major problems. First, even though the interest in export operations and export development is growing, very little empirical research is available on which a sound conceptual and theoretical foundation for export stimulation can be built.[2] Second, the empirical research that does exist is frequently overlooked by the public policy decision makers, primarily because they do not understand the applicability of the results of this type of research to their specific situations. Third, many of the public policy decision makers, as well as the representatives of the U.S. Department of Commerce, are convinced that all one has to do is to present the small- and medium-sized firms with export opportunities or actual orders and these firms will export automatically. This is not the case.

Small- and medium-sized firms differ greatly. Small- and medium-sized exporters also differ greatly. Before small- or medium-sized manufacturing firms will become actively involved in export operations as a result of public policy action or direct intervention by the U.S. Department of Commerce, a great deal of additional empirical research is needed. We need to learn more about their internal operations, their market behavior, and their style of management.

Based on an examination of past research in the area of export operations, export development, and export stimulation, it is possible to classify individual studies into three categories.[3] The first category of research includes relatively unsophisticated convenient sample studies designed to evaluate normatively apparent export behavior. These studies were conducted approximately between 1964 and 1970. The second category of research lasted approximately from 1970 to 1973. In this relatively short period small sample studies were conducted using simple statistical techniques of analysis. These studies generally examined the exporters only and attempted to identify their outstanding characteristics.

The third category of research, and perhaps the most important, began approximately in 1973 and is continuing into the present. This category includes a broad international effort to study export operations, export development, and export stimulation. It includes large-scale empirical studies using univariate and multivariate statistical techniques to analyze large sample sizes. A number of these studies have focused not only on the identification of the critical differences between exporters and nonexporters, but also on the differences among exporters. Several studies have attempted to develop profiles of exporters based on several managerial and operational factors of the firms.

One of the significant shortcomings of the empirical research currently available is the fact that these studies are one-time studies. Replication of individual studies in the same socioeconomic or business environment or in another socioeconomic or business environment has not been done. Yet replication of even the smaller-scale studies is critically needed. Replication of empirical studies in exports is needed for three fundamental reasons: to verify the internal consistency of the studies themselves, to verify the findings of the studies, and to build a sound conceptual and theoretical foundation for export operations, export development, and export stimulation.

The purpose of this chapter is to report on the first attempt to systematically replicate one large-scale empirical study. The chapter discusses a comparison of empirical results from the 1974 Wisconsin study and the 1981 Virginia study of small- and medium-sized manufacturing firms.[4]

The Virginia study was conducted within the same research framework as the Wisconsin study. The same assumptions were made regarding the firms, the same questionnaire was used, and the same techniques of analysis were used. Theoretically, the Virginia study recognized the same objectives and limitations. The Wisconsin study includes 474 Wisconsin-based and -owned small- and medium-sized manufacturing firms and the Virginia study includes 190 Virginia-based and -owned small- and medium-sized manufacturing firms.

For the purpose of this presentation, only one portion of the study has been analyzed; that is, this chapter focuses only on the differences between aggressive and passive exporters. The aggressive exporters were defined as those that sought the first export order, the passive exporters as those that did not seek the first export order.

## PRESENTATION OF FINDINGS

The presentation of findings from the comparison is organized into four major parts. The first part presents the comparison between the aggressive and passive exporters in terms of their planning processes, their perceived differential advantage, and their growth objectives. Figure 6.1 is the pictorial presentation of the comparative framework.

FIGURE 6.1

Comparative Framework for 1974 Wisconsin Study and
1981 Virginia Study Regarding Planning, Perceived
Advantage, and Corporate Growth

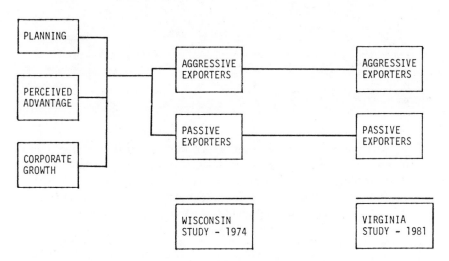

Source: The four figures in this chapter were compiled by the authors.

The second part of the comparison focuses on the differences between the aggressive and passive exporters in terms of sales volume, employment, and capital investment of the firms in each study. These three factors are considered to be the standard indicators of a firm's size. The pictorial presentation of the comparative framework is in Figure 6.2.

FIGURE 6.2

Comparative Framework for 1974 Wisconsin Study and
1981 Virginia Study Regarding Sales Volume,
Employment, and Capital Investment

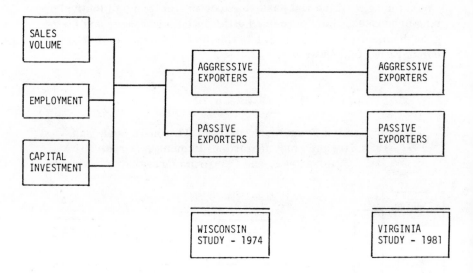

The third part of the comparison focuses on the perceptions of these firms regarding how much export operations would potentially contribute to a set of specific corporate objectives. In addition, this part also examines the existence of corporate policy toward exports and the existence of corporate structure to evaluate exports. Future export markets are also examined along with whether or not the firm in the study systematically explored the possibility to export. The pictorial presentation of the comparative framework is in Figure 6.3.

FIGURE 6.3

Comparative Framework for 1974 Wisconsin Study
and 1981 Virginia Study Regarding a Set
of Export-Related Factors

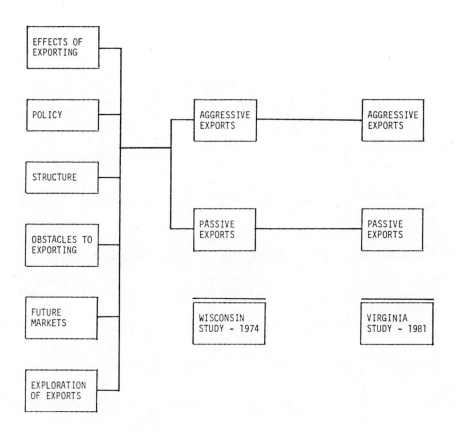

Finally, the fourth part of this comparison examines the
actual export performance of both aggressive and passive exporters. Factors dealing with export motivation, perceived risk in
exporting, years of export experience, percentage of sales volume
derived from exports, number of visits to foreign markets, and
informational needs of exporters are presented in this part. The
pictorial presentation of the comparative framework is made in
Figure 6.4.

FIGURE 6.4

Comparative Framework for 1974 Wisconsin Study and
1981 Virginia Study Regarding Export Performance

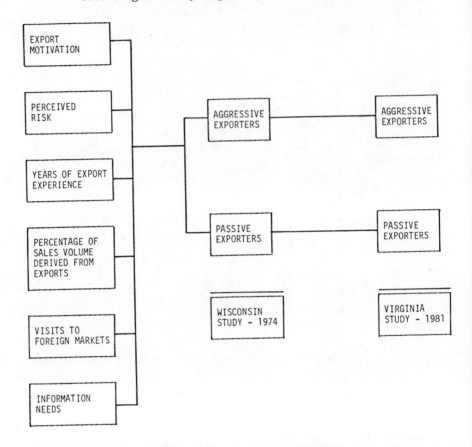

## THE OVERALL FINDINGS AND CONSIDERATIONS

The replication of the Wisconsin study in Virginia was a relatively simple process that did not produce any unexpected negative
results. The study was conducted in approximately the same time
of the year, it was produced and implemented in the same manner,
and the same care was taken in data collection. The only difference
was that a follow-up mailing was not used in the Virginia study.
Therefore, the sample size is somewhat smaller but still statistically representative of the number of small- and medium-sized
manufacturing firms in Virginia.

Because of the time differential, it was expected that there
would be some differences regarding awareness of the importance of

exports. This expectation was based on changes in the external business environment stressing the importance of exports nation-wide. That is, awareness of the importance of exports is greater in 1981 than it was in 1974. Indeed, these differences are apparent in the fourth part of the comparison.

In summary, no unexpected major differences were found with respect to the execution, evaluation, and internal configuration of the studies. The Virginia study provides a sound and robust data base.


## PART 1: PLANNING PROCESS, PERCEIVED ADVANTAGES, AND GROWTH OBJECTIVES

The rank order of the planning alternatives differ between the two sample groups; they are presented in Table 6.1. The Wisconsin exporters ranked "expansion of market share" as the first planning alternative while the Virginia exporters ranked "new market develop-ment" as the first planning alternative. The major difference be-tween the two sample groups was accounted for by the "development of foreign markets" alternative. The Wisconsin exporters ranked it as their last alternative while the Virginia exporters ranked it fourth.

Within the sample groups, statistically significant differences were found among three planning alternatives: new market develop-ment, new product development, and development of foreign mar-kets. The only statistically significant differences in the Virginia sample group were found with respect to the planning alternative "development of foreign markets." More of the passive exporters in the Virginia sample group plan to develop foreign markets.

The rank order of perceived advantages (presented in Table 6.2) differs substantially. The Wisconsin sample group perceived "strong management" as their most important advantage while for the Virginia sample group it was "competitive price." Advantages including "efficient production techniques," "technology," and "unique product" are included in the top four perceived advantages in both sample groups.

Statistically significant differences in both sample groups exist in the case of the "efficient marketing techniques" advantage. In the Virginia sample group "adequate assets" also account for statistically significant differences.

There are virtually no differences between the rank order of firms' goals and the average readings on the thermometer scale for each goal. The overall average readings for both sample groups are within two percentage points. There are larger differences between the two sample groups for specific goals such as "high growth rate." The results are presented in Table 6.3.

TABLE 6.1

Types of Exporters versus Planning Alternatives
(percentages)

| Planning Alternatives (ranked) | Wisconsin Study | | Planning Alternatives (ranked) | Virginia Study | |
|---|---|---|---|---|---|
| | Aggressive 40 percent (66) | Passive 60 percent (101) | | Aggressive 49 percent (28) | Passive 51 percent (29) |
| Expansion of your market share | 42 | 58 | New market development | 46 | 54 |
| New market development | 46 | 54* | New product development | 47 | 53 |
| Greater national distribution | 43 | 57 | Expansion of your market share | 46 | 54 |
| Diversification into other businesses | 38 | 62 | Development of foreign markets | 43 | 57* |
| New product development | 7 | 93* | Greater national distribution | 49 | 51 |
| Development of foreign markets | 54 | 46* | Diversification into other businesses | 44 | 56 |

*Statistically significant differences on 0.05 level.

## TABLE 6.2

### Types of Exporters versus Perceived Advantages
(percentages)

| Perceived Advantages (ranked) | Wisconsin Study | | Perceived Advantages (ranked) | Virginia Study | |
|---|---|---|---|---|---|
| | Aggressive 40 percent (66) | Passive 60 percent (101) | | Aggressive 49 percent (28) | Passive 51 percent (29) |
| Strong management | 39 | 61 | Competitive price | 53 | 47 |
| Efficient production methods | 38 | 62 | Technology | 50 | 50 |
| Technology | 42 | 58 | Efficient production methods | 56 | 44 |
| Unique product | 41 | 59 | Unique product | 44 | 56 |
| Competitive price | 35 | 65 | Efficient distribution | 60 | 40 |
| Adequate assets | 31 | 69 | Strong management | 58 | 42 |
| Efficient marketing techniques | 52 | 48* | Proximity to markets | 35 | 65 |
| Efficient distribution | 48 | 52 | Efficient marketing techniques | 74 | 26* |
| Dynamic sales force | 50 | 50 | Adequate assets | 72 | 28* |
| Proximity to markets | 28 | 72 | Dynamic sales force | 64 | 36 |

*Statistically significant differences on 0.05 level.

93

TABLE 6.3

Types of Exporters versus Average Reading on the Thermometer Scale for Each Goal
(0–100)

| Goal | Wisconsin Study | | Virginia Study | |
|---|---|---|---|---|
| | Aggressive | Passive | Aggressive | Passive |
| High profit rate on investment | 73 | 69 | 66 | 67 |
| High growth rate | 63 | 53 | 56 | 54 |
| Security of investment | 60 | 64 | 52 | 59 |
| Development and/or security of your markets | 73 | 68 | 78 | 78 |
| Contribution to the development of the U.S. economy | 39 | 34 | 30 | 47 |
| Average | 58 | 62 | 56 | 61 |

## PART 2: SALES VOLUME, EMPLOYMENT, AND CAPITAL EQUIPMENT

Tables 6.4, 6.5, and 6.6 present the comparison between the two sample groups. It was found in the Wisconsin sample group that there are no statistically significant differences between the two types of exporters with respect to the three factors. However, the Virginia sample group produced statistically significant differences between the two types of exporters for all three factors. The aggressive exporters in Virginia tend to have higher sales volume, higher levels of employment, and also higher levels of capital investment.

The above findings are important. The reasons for these differences might be accounted for by the time differential; in any case they need further verification, primarily because of their importance for the development of public policy. These findings might be used as motivation factors for firms that want to grow; that is, those firms that seek export orders are more likely to grow.


## PART 3: EXPORT OPERATIONS AND CORPORATE OBJECTIVES

The perceived effect of exports on various considerations are presented in Table 6.7. The major differences are found with respect to the first three considerations between the two sample groups. The Virginia group has higher expectations from exports regarding firm's profits, firm's growth, and security of your firm's investment. The average readings measured on a scale from 1 to 5 also differ between the two sample groups. Again, this difference might be accounted for by the time differential. The Virginia firms might be more aware of the importance of exports.

The Wisconsin sample group produced statistically significant differences with respect to the existence of fixed policy regarding exports; the Virginia sample group did not. That is, the Wisconsin aggressive exporters tend to have a fixed policy regarding exports, while the Virginia aggressive exporters tend not to. The results are presented in Table 6.8.

The same results were produced in the case of the existence of a formal structure for evaluating exports (see Table 6.9).

The perceived obstacles to exporting were divided into two categories. The first category concerns obstacles that appear to be important at the beginning of export operations. No statistically significant differences were found either in the ranking of these obstacles or within the two sample groups.

## TABLE 6.4

Kolmogorov-Smirnov Test: Differences between Types of Exporters—Sales Volume

Let $Sn_1(X)$ = The observed cumulative step function of responses for aggressive exporters.
$Sn_2(X)$ = The observed cumulative step function of responses for passive exporters.

Cumulative Proportions of Responses

| | 0 | Under $100,000 | $100,000–$249,999 | $250,000–$499,999 | $500,000–$999,999 | $1.0–$4.9 Million | $5.0–$9.9 Million | $10.0–$49.9 Million | Over $50.0 Million |
|---|---|---|---|---|---|---|---|---|---|
| **Wisconsin study** | | | | | | | | | |
| | 1 | 3 | 0 | 9 | 9 | 21 | 5 | 9 | 9 |
| | 1 | 4 | 4 | 13 | 22 | 43 | 48 | 57 | 66 |
| $Sn_1(X)$ = | .015 | .060 | .060 | .197 | .333 | .652 | .727 | .863 | 1.000 |
| | 2 | 2 | 9 | 10 | 17 | 45 | 5 | 10 | 1 |
| | 2 | 4 | 13 | 23 | 40 | 85 | 90 | 100 | 101 |
| $Sn_2(X)$ = | .020 | .040 | .129 | .228 | .396 | .842 | .890 | .990 | 1.000 |
| $D_1 = \lvert Sn_1(X) - Sn_2(X) \rvert$ = | .005 | .020 | .069 | .031 | .063 | .190 | .163 | .127 | 0 |

Chi-square = 4.24; $p < .25$ (2 d.f.)

| | 0 | Under $100,000 | $100,000–$249,999 | $250,000–$499,999 | $500,000–$999,999 | $1.0–$4.9 Million | $5.0–$9.9 Million | $10.0–$49.9 Million | Over $50.0 Million |
|---|---|---|---|---|---|---|---|---|---|
| **Virginia study** | | | | | | | | | |
| | 0 | 0 | 3 | 1 | 2 | 6 | 3 | 7 | 8 |
| | 0 | 0 | 3 | 4 | 6 | 12 | 15 | 22 | 27 |
| $Sn_1(X)$ = | .000 | .000 | .111 | .148 | .222 | .444 | .555 | .815 | 1.000 |
| | 0 | 0 | 2 | 3 | 2 | 16 | 2 | 3 | 0 |
| | 0 | 0 | 2 | 5 | 7 | 23 | 25 | 28 | 28 |
| $Sn_2(X)$ = | .000 | .000 | .071 | .179 | .250 | .821 | .893 | 1.000 | 1.000 |
| $D_1 = \lvert Sn_1(X) - Sn_2(X) \rvert$ = | .000 | .000 | .040 | .031 | .028 | .377 | .338 | .185 | 0 |

Chi-square = 7.82; $p < .025$ (2 d.f.)

TABLE 6.5

Kolmogorov-Smirnov Test:  Differences between Types of Exporters-Employment

Let $Sn_1(X)$ = The observed cumulative step function of responses for aggressive exporters.
  $Sn_2(X)$ = The observed cumulative step function of responses for passive exporters.

| | | | | Cumulative Proportions of Responses | | | |
|---|---|---|---|---|---|---|---|
| | 0 | Under 25 | 25-99 | 100-249 | 250-499 | 500-1,000 | Over 1,000 |
| **Wisconsin study** | | | | | | | |
| $Sn_1(X) =$ | 2 | 15 | 21 | 12 | 3 | 7 | 6 |
| | 2 | 17 | 38 | 50 | 53 | 60 | 66 |
| | .030 | .258 | .576 | .758 | .803 | .909 | 1.000 |
| $Sn_2(X) =$ | 1 | 30 | 41 | 18 | 6 | 2 | 3 |
| | 1 | 31 | 72 | 90 | 96 | 98 | 101 |
| | .010 | .307 | .713 | .891 | .950 | .970 | 1.000 |
| $D_1 = \left| Sn_1(X) - Sn_2(X) \right| =$ | .020 | .049 | .137 | .133 | .147 | .061 | 1.000 |
| Chi-square = 3.45; $p < .25$ (2 d.f.) | | | | | | | |
| **Virginia study** | | | | | | | |
| $Sn_1(X) =$ | 0 | 5 | 4 | 10 | 2 | 3 | 3 |
| | 0 | 5 | 9 | 19 | 21 | 24 | 27 |
| | .000 | .185 | .333 | .704 | .778 | .889 | 1.000 |
| $Sn_2(X) =$ | 0 | 11 | 11 | 6 | 0 | 0 | 1 |
| | 0 | 11 | 22 | 28 | 28 | 28 | 29 |
| | .000 | .379 | .759 | .966 | .966 | .966 | 1.000 |
| $D_1 = \left| Sn_1(X) - Sn_2(X) \right| =$ | .000 | .194 | .426 | .262 | .188 | .077 | 1.000 |
| Chi-square = 10.15; $p < .01$ (2 d.f.) | | | | | | | |

## TABLE 6.6

Kolmogorov-Smirnov Test: Differences between Types of Exporters—Capital Investment

Let $Sn_1(X)$ = The observed cumulative step function of responses for aggressive exporters.
$Sn_2(X)$ = The observed cumulative step function of responses for passive exporters.

| | 0 | Under $100,000 | $100,000–$249,999 | $250,000–$499,999 | $500,000–$999,999 | $1.0–$4.9 Million | $5.0–$9.9 Million | $10.0–$49.9 Million | Over $50.0 Million |
|---|---|---|---|---|---|---|---|---|---|
| | | | | | Cumulative Proportions of Responses | | | | |
| **Wisconsin study** | | | | | | | | | |
| | 4 | 8 | 9 | 16 | 4 | 9 | 5 | 6 | 5 |
| | 4 | 12 | 21 | 37 | 41 | 50 | 55 | 61 | 66 |
| $Sn_1(X)$ = | .060 | .182 | .318 | .560 | .621 | .758 | .833 | .924 | 1.000 |
| | 6 | 17 | 15 | 18 | 18 | 18 | 3 | 5 | 1 |
| | 6 | 23 | 38 | 56 | 74 | 92 | 95 | 100 | 101 |
| $Sn_2(X)$ = | .059 | .228 | .376 | .554 | .733 | .910 | .940 | .990 | 1.000 |
| $D_1 = \lvert Sn_1(X) - Sn_2(X)\rvert$ = | .001 | .046 | .058 | .006 | .112 | .152 | .107 | .066 | 0 |
| Chi–square = 3.69; p < .25 (2 d.f.) | | | | | | | | | |
| **Virginia study** | | | | | | | | | |
| | 0 | 0 | 6 | 2 | 2 | 7 | 2 | 5 | 2 |
| | 0 | 0 | 6 | 8 | 10 | 17 | 19 | 24 | 26 |
| $Sn_1(X)$ = | .000 | .000 | .231 | .308 | .385 | .654 | .731 | .923 | 1.000 |
| | 0 | 4 | 5 | 5 | 2 | 10 | 0 | 1 | 0 |
| | 0 | 4 | 9 | 14 | 16 | 26 | 26 | 27 | 27 |
| $Sn_2(X)$ = | .000 | .148 | .333 | .519 | .593 | .963 | .963 | 1.000 | 1.000 |
| $D_1 = \lvert Sn_1(X) - Sn_2(X)\rvert$ = | .000 | .148 | .102 | .211 | .208 | .309 | .232 | .077 | 0 |
| Chi–square = 5.06; p < .10 (2 d.f.) | | | | | | | | | |

TABLE 6.7

Types of Exporters versus the Effect of Exporting on Considerations Listed
(measured on scale 1–5)

| Considerations | Wisconsin Study | | Virginia Study | |
|---|---|---|---|---|
| | Aggressive | Passive | Aggressive | Passive |
| Your firm's profits | 3.85 | 3.15 | 4.19 | 4.19 |
| Your firm's growth | 4.03 | 3.40 | 4.24 | 4.04 |
| Security of your firm's investment | 3.42 | 2.71 | 3.63 | 3.22 |
| Development and/or security of your markets | 3.67 | 2.72 | 3.68 | 3.78 |
| Contribution to the development of the U.S. economy | 3.75 | 2.92 | 3.50 | 3.77 |
| Average | 3.74 | 2.98 | 3.85 | 3.80 |

## TABLE 6.8

### Types of Exporters versus Existence of
### Fixed Policy Regarding Exports
### (percentages)

| Policy | Wisconsin Study[a] | | Virginia Study[b] | |
|---|---|---|---|---|
| | Aggressive 42 percent (63) | Passive 58 percent (88) | Aggressive 49 percent (27) | Passive 51 percent (28) |
| Yes | 52 | 48 | 53 | 47 |
| No | 35 | 65 | 47 | 53 |

[a]Statistically significant differences on 0.05 level.
[b]No significant differences.


## TABLE 6.9

### Types of Exporters versus Existence of Evaluation Structure
### (percentages)

| Structure | Wisconsin Study[a] | | Virginia Study[b] | |
|---|---|---|---|---|
| | Aggressive 38 percent (58) | Passive 62 percent (95) | Aggressive 49 percent (27) | Passive 51 percent (28) |
| Yes | 61 | 39 | 67 | 33 |
| No | 33 | 67 | 43 | 57 |

[a]Statistically significant differences on 0.05 level.
[b]No significant differences.

Table 6.10 also presents the second category of obstacles identified as ongoing obstacles to exporting. These obstacles become operational after the firm begins to export. There are some differences in the ranking of these obstacles between the two sample groups; however, these differences are not statistically significant.

The perceived future export markets are presented in Table 6.11; the three top markets are the same for both sample groups: Canada, Western Europe, and South America in that order. More of the aggressive exporters in the Wisconsin sample group perceived South America as a more important future market. There are statistically significant differences between the aggressive and passive exporters in the Wisconsin sample group regarding this future market for exports. The rest of the differences are in ranking order only and are not substantial.

Table 6.12 indicates that in both sample groups there are statistically significant differences between the two types of exporters regarding exploration of the possibility to export. The aggressive exporters in both sample groups systematically explored possibilities to export their products.

PART 4: ACTUAL EXPORT PERFORMANCE

Factors influencing initiation of export operations among the aggressive exporters for both sample groups are presented in Table 6.13. In both cases "unique qualities of your product" and "technological advantage" are quoted as the leading factors in initiation of exports by the aggressive exporters in both sample groups. The rank order of the subsequent factors differs for the two sample groups, but the differences tend to be minor ones.

Factors influencing initiation of exports operations among the passive exporters is presented in Table 6.14. The two top factors initiating export operations in both sample groups are "general inquiry from abroad" and "manufacturer's agent." The rank order factors in this category differ slightly. The most important finding once again suggests that the U.S. Department of Commerce or the state government's export expansion effort has little, if any, impact on the initiation of exports among both sample groups.

The amount of perceived risk in export operations by both types of exporters in both sample groups is presented in Table 6.15. The differences between the two types of exporters in each sample group are not statistically significant. However, more of the aggressive exporters in the Virginia sample group perceive that the amount of risk encountered in exporting is less than in domestic operation. More passive exporters in both sample groups feel that the amount of risk encountered in exporting is more than in domestic operations.

TABLE 6.10

Types of Exporters versus Perceived Obstacles to Exporting
(percentages)

| | Wisconsin Study | | Virginia Study | |
|---|---|---|---|---|
| Obstacles to Exporting | Aggressive 49 percent (66) | Passive 60 percent (101) | Aggressive 49 percent (28) | Passive 51 percent (29) |
| **Initiating obstacles (ranked)** | | | | |
| Foreign opportunities are difficult to determine. | 40 | 60 | 38 | 62 |
| Shipping documents, export licenses, and other paper work requires too much time. | 31 | 69 | 33 | 67 |
| It costs too much money to get started in exporting. | 24 | 76 | 50 | 50 |
| **Ongoing obstacles (ranked)** | | | | |
| Adequate representation in foreign markets is difficult to obtain. | 39 | 61 | 42 | 58 |
| Service is difficult if not impossible in foreign markets. | 36 | 64 | 37 | 63 |
| Different product standards and consumer habits make U.S. products unsuitable for exports. | 36 | 64 | 14 | 86 |
| It is difficult to collect your money overseas. | 34 | 66 | 31 | 69 |
| High cost of doing business in export markets consumes any possible profits. | 47 | 53 | 55 | 45 |
| Foreign business practices are difficult to understand. | 50 | 50 | 14 | 86 |
| It is difficult to convert some currencies into U.S. dollars. | 50 | 50 | 0 | 100 |

TABLE 6.11

Types of Exporters versus Perceived Future Markets
(percentages)

| | Wisconsin Study | | | Virginia Study | | |
|---|---|---|---|---|---|---|
| Future Markets (ranked) | Aggressive 40 percent (66) | Passive 60 percent (101) | Future Markets (ranked) | Aggressive 49 percent (28) | Passive 51 percent (29) |
| Canada | 43 | 57 | Canada | 41 | 59 |
| Western Europe* | 49 | 51 | Western Europe | 52 | 48 |
| South America | 47 | 53 | South America | 55 | 45 |
| Mexico | 47 | 53 | Central America | 58 | 42 |
| Japan* | 63 | 37 | Middle East (including Egypt) | 57 | 43 |
| Australia and New Zealand | 57 | 43 | Mexico | 60 | 40 |
| Central America | 47 | 53 | Japan | 73 | 27 |
| Middle East (including Egypt) | 41 | 59 | Australia and New Zealand | 60 | 40 |
| Africa (excluding Egypt) | 45 | 55 | Peoples Republic of China | 40 | 60 |
| East Europe | 73 | 27 | Africa (excluding Egypt) | 63 | 37 |
| Soviet Union | 62 | 38 | Other Asia (excluding Japan and PRC) | 63 | 37 |
| Other Asia (excluding Japan and PRC) | 42 | 58 | Eastern Europe | 75 | 25 |
| Peoples Republic of China | 42 | 58 | Soviet Union | 0 | 0 |

*Statistically significant differences on 0.05 level.

103

## TABLE 6.12

Types of Exporters versus Exploration
of the Possibility to Export
(percentages)

| | Wisconsin Study* | | Virginia Study* | |
|---|---|---|---|---|
| Explored | Aggressive 39 percent (65) | Passive 61 percent (100) | Aggressive 49 percent (25) | Passive 51 percent (26) |
| Yes | 54 | 46 | 61 | 39 |
| No | 24 | 76 | 28 | 72 |

*Statistically significant differences in both studies on 0.05 level.

The years of export experience between the two sample groups do not differ, as is shown in Table 6.16. The Virginia sample group produced a somewhat different distribution of years of experience in exporting; it appears that the aggressive exporters in this sample group have been exporting longer than the aggressive exporters in the Wisconsin sample group. The passive exporters in both sample groups appear to be recently exposed to export operations.

Table 6.17 presents a summary of the percentages of sales volume generated from exports. The aggressive exporters in both sample groups tend to generate over 10 percent of their sales volume from export operation, while the passive exporters in both groups tend to generate less than 10 percent of sales volume from exports. These differences are statistically significant.

Export markets for both sample groups are presented in Table 6.18. The rank order of the export markets differ. The Virginia sample group tends to generate a higher level of exports to all of the markets. In both cases Canada and Western Europe constitute the most desirable markets for firms in both sample groups.

There are statistically significant differences between the aggressive and passive exporters in both sample groups with respect to the frequency of visits to foreign markets. The aggressive exporters tend to visit foreign markets more frequently than the passive exporters. This information is presented in Table 6.19.

TABLE 6.13

Factors Influencing Initiation of Export Operations for Aggressive Exporters (percentages)

| Factors | Wisconsin Study 100 percent (66) | Factors | Virginia Study 100 percent (28) |
|---|---|---|---|
| Unique qualities of your product | 58 | Unique qualities of your product | 32 |
| Technological advantage | 39 | Technological advantage | 29 |
| Marketing advantage | 33 | Price advantage | 25 |
| Financial advantage | 32 | Financial advantage | 25 |
| Exclusive information about a foreign market or a customer | 24 | Declining domestic sales | 25 |
| Patented product | 21 | Marketing advantage | 21 |
| Competitive pressure | 20 | Overproduction | 18 |
| Price advantage | 15 | Exclusive information about a foreign market or a customer | 14 |
| Efficient distribution network | 12 | Patented product | 11 |
| Declining domestic sales | 9 | Competitive pressures | 7 |
| Overproduction | 9 | Managerial advantage | 7 |
| Managerial advantage | 6 | Efficient distribution network | 4 |
| Proximity to ports | 6 | Proximity to ports | 4 |

TABLE 6.14

Factors Influencing Initiation of Export Operations for Passive Exporters
(percentages)

| Factors | Wisconsin Study 100 percent (101) | Factors | Virginia Study 100 percent (29) |
|---|---|---|---|
| General inquiry from abroad | 57 | General inquiry from abroad | 38 |
| Manufacturer's agent | 17 | Manufacturer's Agent | 28 |
| Distributor | 16 | Export agent | 17 |
| Foreign distributor | 12 | Distributor | 14 |
| Export agent | 12 | Foreign distributor | 10 |
| U.S. Department of Commerce | 7 | Domestic competitors | 7 |
| Domestic competitors | 4 | Wholesaler | 7 |
| Wholesaler | 2 | U.S. Department of Commerce | 0 |
| State government's export expansion effort | 1 | State government's export expansion effort | 0 |
| Bank | 1 | Bank | 0 |

## TABLE 6.15

### Types of Exporters versus Risk Encountered in Exporting
### (percentages)

| | Wisconsin Study* | | Virginia Study* | |
|---|---|---|---|---|
| Amount of Risk | Aggressive 40 percent (66) | Passive 60 percent (99) | Aggressive 48 percent (27) | Passive 52 percent (29) |
| Less than in domestic operations | 52 | 48 | 75 | 25 |
| Equal to domestic operations | 40 | 60 | 50 | 50 |
| More than in domestic operations | 36 | 64 | 36 | 64 |

*No significant differences in both studies.

## TABLE 6.16

### Types of Exporters versus Years of Export Performance
### (percentages)

| | Wisconsin Study* | | Virginia Study* | |
|---|---|---|---|---|
| Years of Export Experience | Aggressive 40 percent (66) | Passive 60 percent (98) | Aggressive 52 percent (28) | Passive 48 percent (26) |
| Less than 1 year | 44 | 56 | 25 | 75 |
| 1 to 2 years | 19 | 81 | 33 | 67 |
| 3 to 5 years | 36 | 64 | 40 | 60 |
| 6 to 10 years | 50 | 50 | 77 | 23 |
| 11 to 20 years | 42 | 58 | 29 | 71 |
| Over 20 years | 42 | 58 | 64 | 36 |

*No significant differences in both studies.

TABLE 6.17

Types of Exporters versus Percentage of
Sales Generated from Exports
(percentages)

| | Wisconsin Study* | | Virginia Study* | |
|---|---|---|---|---|
| | Aggressive 40 percent (66) | Passive 60 percent (101) | Aggressive 49 percent (27) | Passive 51 percent (28) |
| Percent of Sales | | | | |
| Less than 10 percent | 32 | 68 | 37 | 63 |
| Over 10 percent | 65 | 35 | 70 | 30 |

*Statistically significant differences in both studies on 0.05
level.

The exporters were also asked what type of information would
be useful for their export operations. Table 6.20 presents the findings. The first four types of information in both sample groups
relates to market share potential, pricing, foreign competition, and
economic conditions. There are statistically significant differences
between the aggressive and passive exporters in the Wisconsin sample group regarding these types of information; the aggressive exporters have more uses for these types of information. In the
Virginia sample group only the "foreign competition" factor produced statistically significant differences. The rank order of the
rest of the factors tends to be similar.

CONCLUSION

This study focused on the comparison between two sample
groups: the 1974 Wisconsin study and the 1981 Virginia study. The
objective was to replicate the Wisconsin study to determine the internal consistency of the study, to verify the findings of the study,
and to provide a foundation for development of a conceptual and
theoretical foundation for export operations, export development,
and export stimulation. The comparison provided a number of
similarities and no major differences. Based on this conclusion it
can be assumed that the Wisconsin study can be considered to meet
all three of the considerations listed above.

TABLE 6.18

Types of Exporters versus Average Percentage of Exports Derived from Each Market
(percentages)

| Export Markets | Wisconsin Study | | Export Markets | Virginia Study | |
| | Aggressive | Passive | | Aggressive | Passive |
| --- | --- | --- | --- | --- | --- |
| Canada | 40 | 42 | Western Europe | 38 | 47 |
| Western Europe | 22 | 11 | Canada | 38 | 39 |
| South America | 3 | 6 | Japan | 30 | 51 |
| Central America | 3 | 5 | Eastern Europe | 35 | 26 |
| Japan | 5 | 3 | South America | 23 | 41 |
| Mexico | 2 | 3 | Central America | 34 | 17 |
| Middle East (including Egypt) | 2 | 4 | Middle East (including Egypt) | 22 | 23 |
| Australia and New Zealand | 1 | 3 | Africa (excluding Egypt) | 6 | 38 |
| Eastern Europe | 1 | 1 | Other Asian countries | 18 | 8 |
| Other Asia (excluding Japan and PRC) | 1 | 1 | Mexico | 10 | 11 |
| Africa (excluding Egypt) | 1 | 1 | Australia and New Zealand | 6 | 4 |
| Soviet Union | 1 | 0 | Soviet Union | 0 | 0 |
| Peoples Republic of China | 0 | 0 | Peoples Republic of China | 0 | 0 |

TABLE 6.19

Types of Exporters versus Frequency of
Visits to Foreign Markets
(percentages)

| Frequency of Visits | Wisconsin Study* | | Virginia Study* | |
| --- | --- | --- | --- | --- |
| | Aggressive 38 percent (58) | Passive 62 percent (96) | Aggressive 49 percent (27) | Passive 51 percent (28) |
| About twice a year | 78 | 22 | 50 | 50 |
| About once a year | 56 | 44 | 57 | 43 |
| About once every two years | 30 | 70 | 75 | 25 |
| Seldom | 29 | 61 | 38 | 62 |
| Never | 10 | 90 | 25 | 75 |

*Statistically significant differences in both studies on 0.05 level.

It might be useful to replicate the Wisconsin study again in an international setting, in order to increase the research capability for large-scale empirical studies in exporting. The results from a comparison of the Wisconsin study and an international study might be useful in developing an international profile of exporting firms and would make a substantial contribution to the conceptual and theoretical foundation of exports.

TABLE 6.20

Types of Exporters versus Types of Useful Information
(percentages)

| | Wisconsin Study | | | Virginia Study | |
| Types of Information (ranked) | Aggressive 40 percent (66) | Passive 60 percent (101) | Types of Information (ranked) | Aggressive 49 percent (28) | Passive 51 percent (29) |
|---|---|---|---|---|---|
| Market share potential* | 49 | 51 | Market share potential | 51 | 49 |
| Pricing* | 55 | 45 | Pricing | 50 | 50 |
| Foreign competition* | 60 | 40 | Foreign competition* | 67 | 33 |
| Economic conditions* | 53 | 47 | Economic conditions | 58 | 42 |
| Consumer information | 48 | 52 | Export financing | 61 | 39 |
| Export shipping* | 52 | 48 | Export shipping | 56 | 44 |
| Product performance* | 64 | 36 | Quotas and tariffs | 56 | 44 |
| Domestic competition | 51 | 49 | Domestic competition | 57 | 43 |
| Product design* | 56 | 44 | Export licensing | 57 | 43 |
| Quotas and tariffs* | 65 | 35 | Political conditions | 50 | 50 |
| Export financing | 47 | 53 | Product design | 62 | 38 |
| Export licensing | 47 | 53 | Product performance | 54 | 46 |
| Packaging* | 60 | 40 | Packaging | 55 | 45 |
| Political conditions* | 59 | 41 | Consumer information | 70 | 30 |
| Sociocultural information | 73 | 27 | Sociocultural information | 0 | 0 |

*Statistically significant differences on 0.05 level.

111

NOTES

1. Proposed Wisconsin State Export Policy statement available from George Tesar, College of Business and Economics, University of Wisconsin-Whitewater, April 10, 1981.

2. Tamer Cavusgil and George Tesar, "A Bibliography on the Empirical Studies of Firms' Export Behavior," unpublished paper, College of Business and Economics, University of Wisconsin-Whitewater, August 1978.

3. Warren J. Bilkey, "An Attempted Integration of the Literature on the Export Behavior of Firms," Journal of International Business Studies, Spring/Summer 1978, pp. 33-46.

4. George Tesar, "Empirical Study of Export Operations among Small and Medium-Sized Manufacturing Firms," Ph.D. dissertation, Graduate School of Business Administration, University of Wisconsin-Madison, 1975.

# 7

## COMPARATIVE EXPORT BEHAVIOR OF SMALL CANADIAN FIRMS IN THE PRINTING AND ELECTRICAL INDUSTRIES

### Gérard Garnier

The theory of exports is not new; it makes up the largest part of international trade theory and, as such, is undoubtedly one of the oldest branches of economic theory. It contends that goods are exchanged between nations on the basis of price alone (and therefore of costs of production) and that each country exports those goods in which it has a comparative advantage—those using intensively the factors of production that are abundant and therefore cheap in that country. Although widely accepted before World War II, the theory of international trade and its macroeconomic approach have since been severely attacked.

Many experts admit that this theory should be viewed as a general framework to explain the main currents of exchange between countries but that it cannot be used as a practical guide to help a particular firm to decide whether it should export its products or not and to select the potentially most promising markets for these products. It cannot even help a country select the industries that have the best export potential.

In reaction against this theoretical macroeconomic approach, several specialists have, in the last 20 years, tackled the export problem from a resolutely microeconomic and empirical point of view. Using questionnaires and interviews they have tried to understand the export behavior of individual firms to isolate the factors that trigger the export mechanism. Many empirical studies have been conducted along that line in Great Britain (Simmonds and Smith, 1968; Hunt, Froggart, and Hovell, 1967), in the United States (Simpson and Kujawa, 1974), and in Sweden (Johanson and Wiedersheim-Paul, 1975; Wiedersheim-Paul, Olson, and Welch, 1978) to name only a few countries, all reaching very similar conclusions.

We now have a much better understanding of the export process. However, many studies treat exporting firms as a global, homogeneous group, which they are not. There still is a lack of interindustry comparisons that would stress not only the characteristics that are common to all exporters but also the elements that are specific to each industry, in other words a theory that would combine the micro and the macro approaches.

This chapter has far more modest objectives: It will simply report the main conclusions of two studies that were conducted in 1977 in Canada on the export behavior of predominantly small- and medium-sized firms in two industries: the commercial printing and the electrical and electronics industries. The basic purpose of this report is to stress the similarities but also to insist on the differences in these two industries, differences that can explain their different export performance. The chapter will also present a theoretical scheme of export behavior.

Many factors have an impact on the decision of a specific firm, particularly of a small firm, to export or to refrain from so doing: some are very general, very diffuse; others are very specific. All these factors can be grouped in three broad categories:

The factors that constitute the environment, that is, the characteristics of the country in which the firm is located, and of the industry of which it is a part.

The characteristics of the firm itself: its size, its product line, its amount of research, and so on.

The characteristics of the owner-manager, that is, of the entrepreneur or of the managing team when the firm is larger and assumes a corporate form.

## CHARACTERISTICS OF THE ENVIRONMENT

Canada can be considered as the prototype of an "open economy": between 25 percent and 30 percent of all the goods and services it produces are exported. The general environment is then quite favorable to foreign trade and many government campaigns have been launched to promote and encourage exports.

In addition, the Canadian economy is characterized by an abundance of natural resources, by a small but highly qualified and well-paid labor force, and by a far from negligible stock of capital. Several of its manufacturing sectors are highly research intensive. Therefore Canada has a comparative advantage in natural-resource-intensive goods and to a lesser extent in research-intensive goods. On the other hand it is highly disadvantaged in the production of cheap labor-intensive goods.

More than the general environment, the specific characteristics of the industry have an influence on the export propensity of a firm. Many elements make up these characteristics, but three groups of factors seem to be particularly important: the size distribution of firms, that is, the relative importance of small and large firms; the relative factor intensity of the industry (whether labor, capital, natural resource, or research intensive); and the stability or variability of the sales.

The commercial printing and the electrical and electronics industries were selected because at first they seemed to represent the two extreme points among manufacturing industries on the export spectrum: The electrical and electronics industries being highly research intensive seemed to be destined to a brilliant export performance. In actuality, their performance is far from brilliant and explanations had to be found for this surprising behavior. On the other hand the commercial printing industry is mainly a capital-intensive industry (therefore not enjoying a comparative advantage) with seemingly unexportable products: It therefore represented a challenge and the ideal instrument to study the export process.

The study on the electrical industry was in fact limited to two major industrial groups: SIC group 335: producers of telecommunication equipment, and SIC group 336: producers of industrial electrical equipment. At the end of 1976 the two groups included a total of 461 firms. Together they represented 1.5 percent of all manufacturing firms in Canada, employed 3.5 percent of all production workers, accounted for 3.7 percent of the total value added by manufacturing and for 2.4 percent of sales.

To a large extent the industry is made up of small- and medium-sized firms: 60 percent of the firms included in the two groups had fewer than 50 employees, 94 percent had less than 500 employees. In 1975, 44 percent had sales of under $1 million. In short, 85 percent of all firms accounted for 29 percent of sales; whereas at the other extreme, 2 percent of the firms accounted for 25 percent of sales.

Another characteristic of the industry is its cyclical nature with wide swings in the level of sales. A third one is its highly research-intensive character: With R & D expenses representing about 3.5 percent of sales in 1976, it is one of the most technologically advanced industries in Canada.

As to the exports of the two groups, in 1976 they represented 1.0 percent of all Canadian exports (1.4 percent of exports of manufactured products). Foreign sales represented 16.4 percent of their Canadian sales (19.4 percent for telecommunications equipment and 12.3 percent for industrial equipment), far below the average of 26 percent of sales for all Canadian exporters.

The commercial printing industry is very different: with 2,078 printing firms (in 1975) it represented 7 percent of all manufacturing establishments, employed 2.6 percent of all manufacturing workers, accounted for 2.1 percent of the total value added, but for only 1.5 percent of sales. To a larger extent than the electric industry it is made up of small firms: 92 percent of all printing firms employ less than 50 people. Only 3 percent of all firms have more than 100 employees, but these 65 largest firms account for 42 percent of the sales of the industry.

The industry itself makes very little research, the bulk of R & D expenses being made by manufacturers of printing equipment. It is characterized by the fact that most of its products are bulky and extremely heavy in relation to their intrinsic value, therefore expensive to ship. Consequently, 81 percent of all firms make the largest part of their sales within a 50-mile radius around their shop; only 2 percent sell beyond a 500-mile radius.

As to exports, in 1975 they represented 0.23 percent of total Canadian exports. They amounted to 5.6 percent of the industry's Canadian sales, which is very little. The industry's sales are also cyclical, though to a lesser extent than those of the electric industry.

In summary, the two industries have these points in common: First, they are made up of a majority of small firms with a few large firms accounting for the bulk of sales. Second they are rather cyclical. On the other hand the electrical industry is research and technology intensive, whereas the other uses a very widespread technology.

To some extent these characteristics can explain the general export performance of each industry. The influence of size will be dealt with more fully in the characteristics of the firm, but many surveys have indicated that export performance is related to size: An industry dominated by small firms is less likely to export as much as another one in which large firms are abundant. This can explain the rather disappointing export performance of both industries. On the other hand, the instability of domestic demand may be an incentive to diversify the sources of revenue and therefore a factor favoring export.

Finally, the research-intensive character of the electrical industry is a factor in favor of export and can explain its performance relative to that of the printing industry: The former exports about three or four times as much per dollar of domestic sales as the latter.


CHARACTERISTICS OF THE FIRMS

The surveys took place in 1977, mainly through a mail questionnaire; a limited number of direct interviews were also conducted to check and complement the data. In the electrical industry, 450 firms (practically the whole population) were contacted: 66 returned their questionnaire in a usable form (14 percent of the population). Of the 66 responding firms, 60 (91 percent of the sample) were classified as exporters.

In the printing industry, a sample of 500 firms was drawn at random, but only 39 returned the questionnaire in a usable form (8 percent of the sample and less than 2 percent of the population). Of the 39 respondents, 17 (43 percent) were classified as exporters. Under these conditions, the respondents cannot be claimed to be really representative of the population, particularly because both samples include a much higher proportion of exporters than the population. No statistical inference can therefore be made and comparisons between exporters and nonexporters, particularly in the electrical industry, will be presented only for illustrative purposes.

Nevertheless, as the main objective of the study is simply to analyze the export process, the following data, backed with results obtained by other researchers, keep all their validity.

Except for the high percentage of exporters, both samples present about the same general characteristics as the population from which they were drawn. The following analysis will concentrate on the main factors that have a direct impact on export performance: size, underutilization of productive capacity, characteristics of products, and factor (research) intensity.


Size: The Importance of Small-Sized
Firms in Both Samples

In the printing sample, 73 percent of the respondents have 50 employees or less; at the other end, 22 percent of them have more than 100 employees. In other words, the sample contains a higher percentage of relatively large firms than the population. In the same sample, exporters seem to be larger than nonexporters, size being measured either as number of employees or amount of sales. Several studies have confirmed this relationship between size and export status and performance: As a general rule there is a larger percentage of exporters among large firms than among small firms.

The same phenomenon appears in the electrical sample but because of the limited number of nonexporters the difference is not statistically significant. This sample is also dominated by small firms: 49 percent of the respondents have 50 employees or less; at the other extreme, 40 percent have more than 100 employees (5 percent have 1,000 or more employees). The better export performance of the electrical compared to the printing industry is probably due in part to the higher proportion of larger firms.

The relationship between size and export performance is related to two factors: an organization and a risk factor. Large firms have more specialized functions: They can afford to have some people specializing in the foreign sector of their operations. In short, they can devote more time and resources to looking for foreign customers than the smaller-sized firms. In addition, selling in a foreign and less-well-known market entails a higher risk than selling to domestic customers. The smaller firm with its limited resources cannot take as much risk as the larger one, since the consequences of an unfavorable operation will have far more serious consequences on its results and perhaps even endanger its survival.

## Cyclical Nature of Sales and Underutilization of Productive Capacity

Data furnished by the responding firms on a five-year basis show that sales can vary substantially from year to year, causing considerable uncertainty. One consequence of the cyclical behavior of sales is the widespread underutilization of productive capacity in both industries: For instance, in the printing industry, only 23 percent of the respondents indicated that they were working at full capacity in 1977 (full capacity being defined as 95 percent or more of technical capacity), 74 percent were functioning between 50 and 95 percent of capacity, whereas 3 percent were using less than 50 percent of capacity. In the electrical industry, the situation is as follows: 28 percent of respondents were using their full capacity, 62 percent were between 50 and 95 percent of capacity, and 10 percent were under 50 percent of capacity. The data did not allow identification of significant differences between exporters and nonexporters.

In short, there is no doubt that the sometimes considerable variations of revenues caused by abrupt changes in domestic demand constitute a powerful inducement for management to try to stabilize these revenues by diversifying the sources of revenue; they can then be considered as an inducement to export.

## Characteristics of Products

The most immediate cause for export success is the nature of the product or service offered by the exporting firm. However, it sometimes is very difficult to pinpoint the exact characteristics that are responsible for the export success or failure of a product.

The printing industry is characterized by a wide variety of products ranging from books, newspapers, advertising pamphlets and brochures, to banknotes, wrapping material, art bindings, and so on. Most firms offer a large number of products, but generally one or two products make up the largest part of sales: For 32 percent of the respondents, the main product accounted for between 50 percent and 75 percent of sales; for 24 percent it represented over 75 percent of revenues. This concentration is an additional factor of cyclical instability of revenues.

There are two kinds of printing firms: those that sell a very specialized product like banknotes, theater tickets, artistic book bindings; then there are the general printing firms that offer advertising material, envelopes, even newspapers and magazines—all products that do not require any special skill or machinery. The second category has fewer chances of exporting than the first because few customers will apply to a printing firm in another country for their day-to-day needs when printing services are so easily available close to their office. In addition, printing products are generally bulky and heavy in relation to their low intrinsic value and therefore are very sensitive, pricewise, to transportation costs. Another factor that reinforces the above elements is the importance of service in getting new customers and in keeping old ones. However, service means different things to different firms: For some, it is the ability to fill an order in a very short time (theater tickets), to respect agreed-upon deadlines; for others, it means confidentiality and security (banknotes, financial reports, catalogs); for others, technical help (photographic, artistic). In many cases, service requires personal contact and trust between customer and printer. Most respondents have stressed the importance of personal contact by the president himself in getting new clients and keeping old ones. On the other hand, price was rarely mentioned as the determining factor. Price is important for some standardized products like newspapers and advertising material, but even then a customer will seldom change printers only for a question of price.

All this points to the difficulty of exporting for the general printer: It explains why the respondents in general made 62 percent of their sales within 25 miles around their factory and 85 percent of their sales within a 100-mile radius. Another consequence is that volume of export is a function of the amount of time the chief executive spends abroad trying to get foreign business, and therefore it depends on his attitude toward foreign sales.

The case of the electrical industry is slightly different: Most firms produce only a limited number of products (or product lines). Most of these are finished products sold to the final consumer; however, an important group of firms makes complete systems to be integrated without any change into larger systems like whole telephone systems or airport communication systems. Finally, a minority makes parts and components that will be used by other firms to make their own products. So the characteristics of the products are fundamental: On the whole, they are technically very sophisticated and highly specialized. In addition, most products are either custom-made to the specifications of the client or built in small series with possibility of adaptation to specific needs. Only 15 percent of all respondents made only standardized, mass-produced electrical products.

Therefore, the customer and his specific requirements are all-important. This is reflected in the client-supplier relationships. Although most electrical firms have a large number of clients, many are dependent on a few customers for the largest part of their business: about half the respondents depend on their five largest customers for over half of their revenues; about 25 percent have three-quarters of their total sales coming from their five main clients. Most clients are large firms: government departments and agencies (Canadian and foreign: NASA), large aeronautical firms, electricity generating firms, radio and TV stations.

Because of the importance of fairly frequent service to customers, physical proximity is definitely an asset; on this account the products exported by Canadian firms are disadvantaged, since the largest potential customers are abroad, most of them in the United States. On the other hand, the whole of North America can be considered as one integrated market with regard to electrical products: U.S. firms in advanced technological fields will not hesitate to buy from Canadian firms if the latter have the best products, give the best service, and have a good reputation for reliability. This unity of the market is reinforced by the identity of electrical standards and norms in Canada and the United States and by the cultural similarity between engineers in both countries. However, this advantage is lost when other foreign (European) markets are considered.

The electrical industry is a very competitive field, but few respondents (16 percent) in the sample mentioned price as the main competitive element, precisely because few make mass-produced items. The most important competitive factors are the quality of the product, the technology it embodies, delivery times, and service to the clients.

Characteristics of the Production Process
and the Importance of Factor Intensity

These characteristics make a bridge between the macroeconomic and microeconomic approaches to export. According to

international trade theory, trade is based on price and cost considerations alone, these prices reflecting both the intensity of utilization and the cost of the diverse factors of production. As the printing industry is mainly capital intensive and the electrical industry
is mainly labor intensive, and as these factors of production are not
particularly abundant and therefore cheap in Canada, neither industry should export much.

However, in many cases price is not the determining consideration in export. The printing industry does not export much, as
predicted by theory but not for the reasons proposed by that theory.
As to the electrical industry, it is mainly research intensive and as
such it can be expected to be a large exporter. In that line of reasoning all respondents have confirmed the importance of research:
To them it is vital to find new products and improve old ones in order to keep ahead of competition and consequently to retain their
foreign customers.

## CHARACTERISTICS OF THE OWNER-
## MANAGER OR THE DECISION MAKER

The characteristics of the environment and the firm play an
important role in the export decision but they are not decisive. They
can have a negative influence by showing that, due to price considerations or to the characteristics of the product, the chances to suc-
ceed on foreign markets are slim. Inversely they can provide inducement to export, but in all cases the final decision will be made
by one person (or by a team) whose attitudes toward export will be
decisive. In small firms, where power, particularly decision-
making power, is generally concentrated in the hands of one or very
few persons, the characteristics of the decision maker are of primary importance. Four elements are important:

The decision maker's psychological characteristics, particularly his attitude toward things that are new or strange to him and
also his attitude toward risk and uncertainty, are the first element.
Entrepreneurs are supposed to be ready to accept higher levels of
risk and uncertainty than ordinary persons. However, there are
many forms of risk, some more acceptable than others. For instance, an entrepreneur may be ready to accept putting all his money
in the creation of an enterprise in order to launch a new product but
might refuse to gamble the same amount by betting on a horse. In
addition, some persons have a natural distrust for everything that
is foreign or different—inversely, some people are attracted by this
very same foreign character. This attitude toward foreign things

is to some degree connected to the basic psychological traits of the personality, but it is mainly determined by education and life experience. Few studies have been conducted in this field, but it will be assumed here that the higher the level of uncertainty the entrepreneur is ready to accept and the more interested he is in foreign affairs and foreign ways of life, the higher the probability that his firm will be willing to export.

The decision maker's level of education is an element that may play a part in the export decision. It is hypothesized that entrepreneurs with a higher level of education (university graduates) will have a more open mind, will be more interested by foreign things and markets, and therefore will be more willing to evaluate objectively the benefits and costs of exporting.

Life and professional experience are also important elements in that respect. People who have lived in an international atmosphere, who have worked for multinational corporations or international institutions, or who have spent some time in the foreign service will be expected to be more favorable to exporting. Owing to practical difficulties, it was not possible to check directly these three hypotheses in the surveys. Regarding the level of education, it was found that many entrepreneurs had university or technical-school degrees but it was not possible to ascertain whether there was a statistically significant difference between managers of exporting and nonexporting firms with respect to level of education.

The ethnic origin of owners-managers is a fourth important element. Several authors (Simmonds and Smith, 1968; Wiedersheim-Paul, Olson, and Welch, 1978; Garnier, 1974) have shown that among the heads of exporting firms there often was a high percentage of foreign-born persons. These persons lived in another country for part of their lives so that to them selling to their country of origin is not really exporting: They are already familiar with that market and with its customs and so do not feel the uncertainty connected to foreign business. In the commercial printing sample, these foreign-born entrepreneurs represent 21 percent of all entrepreneurs in exporting firms against only 5 percent in nonexporting firms. In the electrical firms, the percentages are 38 percent in exporting firms and 17 percent in nonexporting enterprises.

## EXPORT ACTIVITY IN THE PRINTING AND ELECTRICAL INDUSTRIES

A general problem with small firms is that many are irregular exporters. This makes difficult the definition of an exporter: In the present study every firm that had sold abroad at least once during the years 1972-76 was considered an exporter, irrespective of the year, of the frequency, of foreign sales, of the dollar volume. Using this definition, there were 17 exporters out of 39 respondents (43 percent) in the printing sample and 60 out of 66 respondents (91 percent) in the electrical sample. About two-thirds of the firms (63 percent of printing firms and 64 percent of electrical firms) had exported during each of those five years and therefore could be considered as regular exporters.

It is often claimed that foreign business is only of secondary importance to small firms. If importance is measured by the part of total revenues represented by foreign sales, this was true of the printing firms but not of the electrical enterprises: 47 percent of the exporters in the printing business made 1 percent of their sales or less outside Canada, the rest made between 1 and 25 percent. By opposition, 42 percent of the exporters in the electrical sector realized over 25 percent of their sales outside Canada, of which 23 percent derived over 50 percent of their total revenues from foreign sales. It is obvious that electrical firms are far more involved in foreign business than printing firms.

It is interesting to analyze where the exports of both sectors are going, that is, to what countries. It will be argued that when a small firm starts exporting it will tend to sell first to the geographically or culturally closest foreign country; then gradually it will sell to countries located farther and farther away and to countries with increasingly different cultures and environments. There are two reasons for that behavior; first, an economic reason: by tackling first a neighboring country, the junior exporter can minimize the costs of its first foreign experience. The second reason is related to uncertainty reduction as the geographically or culturally closest countries (for instance France for Quebec-based firms) are generally the markets with which the firm is most familiar. The hypothesis was confirmed in both samples but particularly in the printing sample. In it, 94 percent of all responding exporters sold to the United States and most of them sold only to that country: As an average, the U.S. market absorbed 75 percent of their export sales; 17 percent to the West Indies (part of the British Commonwealth), these islands representing an average of 7 percent of their export sales; then came France (17 percent of firms with 3 percent of total exports); and finally Great Britain.

Among electrical firms, 80 percent of the exporters sold to the United States (33 percent of total exports); 49 percent sold to Latin America (9 percent of exports), 36 percent to European countries other than Great Britain and France, and 31 percent to Great Britain (6 percent of exports). In summary, the larger and more export-oriented electrical firms had more diversified markets than the printing firms, which sold almost exclusively to the United States.

Probably the most critical point in the export process is the decision to export for the first time and the reasons behind that decision. Simpson and Kujawa (1974) pointed out that for small firms that decision was seldom the result of careful strategic planning including a systematic evaluation of the development possibilities open to the firm and a scrutinizing of potentially interesting foreign markets. According to their survey, export would rather come as the result of chance circumstances acting as an "external stimulus" to the firm. Many events can act as the external stimulus but the most frequent is the reception of an inquiry by a foreign firm on the terms and conditions of sales, if not an outright order for the firm's products. This proposition was tested in our two surveys.

In the printing sample, 24 percent of the exporters connected their first foreign sales directly to an unexpected inquiry from a foreign firm, 24 percent to their own marketing efforts abroad, and 52 percent to other causes. Further investigation brought information on these "other causes": In one case the first export sale came as the result of a recommendation by a Canadian consulting firm that was working in Africa under a contract with the Canadian International Development Agency; in two cases the order came from foreign subsidiaries of Canadian firms. One was from a U.S. firm that had bought a Canadian firm; the latter was patronizing a Canadian printer and persuaded the parent company to place an order with it. In all cases the foreign customer was not completely unknown to the Canadian printer or to one of its clients: The order was not a result of the Canadian firm's efforts but it was not completely unexpected and was not a result of the foreign client's either. In all these cases, third parties played a fundamental role by bringing together a foreign potential client and a Canadian supplier; this role is particularly important in view of the fact that printers sell a service as much as a product and that the main selling point is trust and personal contact.

In addition, whereas 94 percent of the exporters have at some time received an inquiry about their products from a foreign firm, only 33 percent of the nonexporters have received one. Whereas all exporters were favorable to accepting the order, only 19 percent of all nonexporters were in favor of it, 14 percent of them turning it down deliberately.

In the electrical sample, the percentages are as follows: 15 percent of the exporters connected their first foreign sale directly to a foreign inquiry, 55 percent to their own marketing efforts, and 30 percent to "other causes." The electrical firms seem to be more dynamic exportwise than the printers.

Practically all electrical firms in the sample had received a foreign request for information at one time or another (95 percent of exporters and 83 percent of nonexporters). However, whereas 81 percent of all exporters were favorable to accepting it, only 40 percent of nonexporters were. In other words, practically everybody had the same possibility of exporting but some accepted it while others refused.

In both samples, some firms exported within the year in which they were created, whereas some waited for more than 30 years before starting to export. In addition, the amount of time elapsed between creation of the firm and reception of the first inquiry by a foreign firm follows about the same distribution as the time between creation and first export: It ranges from 0 to over 20 years. On the other hand, practically all exporters started selling abroad within a very short time after receipt of that first inquiry, the majority exporting within the same year in which they received it (about all printing exporters and 79 percent of electrical exporters).

Two conclusions emerge from these data: first, reception of an inquiry or an order from a foreign firm certainly plays an important role in the export decision process; second, the mere reception of that inquiry is not sufficient by itself to decide the firm to export; it also takes a favorable climate within the firm.

In other words, the proposition presented by Simpson and Kujawa (1974) that small firms are generally passive with regard to export, that they will not move by themselves to look for foreign clients, is generally supported by our data but to different degrees according to the industry. In the most dynamic industries (perhaps the most research intensive) there is a larger percentage of firms that will initiate the search. However, the first foreign inquiry seems to play mainly the part of "attention evoker," of bringing the export problem to the attention of the decision maker. The final decision will depend on internal factors including profitability prospects but also attitude of the decision maker toward export.

## A THEORETICAL MODEL OF THE EXPORT PROCESS IN SMALL FIRMS

The following model applies essentially to small firms, that is, to firms in which limited human and financial resources will limit the rate of expansion, in particular of expansion in foreign markets. It is based on six elements, some of which have been verified by diverse authors, while others still are hypotheses:

It is supposed that the decision-making mechanism is essentially in the hands of one person, the entrepreneur or owner-manager.

The smaller the firm, the closer this hypothesis will approximate reality. This does not mean that the decision maker can decide in complete independence; like everybody he is submitted to outside influences, but in a small enterprise the owner-manager is the official center of authority.

The entrepreneur is supposed to be averse to risk: He may be ready to accept risk and sometimes high levels of risk, but when confronted with two projects promising the same rate of return, will systematically select the one with the lower probable risk.

Exporting will be considered as a phase in the development of a firm, one of the growth strategies open to it. This implies that a firm will first tackle the domestic market in which it will try to acquire a satisfactory share before thinking about foreign business.

When a firm starts exporting it will sell the same products (or services) abroad as it sells on the domestic market. Only after some time, after having acquired some experience of a few foreign markets, will it bring changes to its standard products to adapt them to the specific conditions of these foreign markets.

As a result of limited human and financial resources, a firm will not analyze all possible foreign markets and then decide which are the most promising. Instead it will look at one specific market and decide whether to export to it or not. Actually, most of the time the analysis will start after receipt of an inquiry or of an outright order by a specific foreign firm located in a given country and will be limited to the question: Should we accept it or turn it down? In the best cases, analysis will be sequential and not simultaneous.

In order to keep uncertainty as low as possible, the firm, when it takes the initiative to look for foreign clients, will start with the geographically closest country or with a country that has the same culture, the same language. Only once exports to this country have reached a satisfactory level and most problems have been solved will the firm tackle another neighboring country, and so on.

Given these points, the export (decision-making) process can be viewed as taking place in six successive steps represented schematically in Figure 7.1.

Preexport Activities and Subconscious
Orientation of Decision Maker

Recent theories on export claim that this activity does not represent an abrupt change in the operations of a firm but is the ultimate stage in a gradual increase in the size of the domestic territory covered by the firm (Wiedersheim-Paul, Olson, and Welch,

FIGURE 7.1

The Export Process in a Small Firm

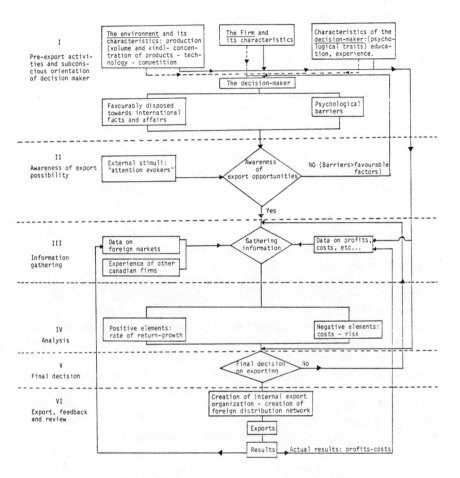

1978). Most firms start by selling to a limited local market, then gradually enlarge their territory until it covers the whole country. This involves a considerable variation in the scale of their operations requiring a concomitant change in production processes and in the whole organizational structure.

The problems it encounters when it sells to distant parts of the national territory are not very different from those it will have to face when entering foreign markets. This is particularly true in a widespread country like Canada with several different regional populations. Therefore it can be claimed that domestic expansion represents the first step toward export. Probably the most difficult adaptation required by the growth process, either at home or abroad, concerns the decision maker, who has to change his mental attitude. In the case of exports, Simmonds and Smith (1968, p. 93) noted that "The survey showed that within [small firms] . . . there was a marked lack of interest in exporting, coupled with a considerable preoccupation with day to day affairs on the home front." Our surveys confirmed that view: The main explanation offered by nonexporters for their behavior was that they never thought about exporting because they were totally absorbed by local business.

Given the importance granted by general newspapers as well as by specialized business magazines and in view of the considerable efforts displayed by the Canadian government to promote exports, it is hardly believable that some businessmen had never heard of export. It is more probable that they did not relate the concept with the concrete fact that their enterprise might sell outside the country. They unconsciously shut off their minds to that idea. The reason is that exporting means selling in foreign markets, which they often visualize as strange, unknown, and dangerous. Simmonds and Smith (1968) as well as Wiedersheim-Paul, Olson, and Welch (1978) have indicated that there are marked differences between individuals in their international dimension that would be reflected in differences in their behavior and more precisely in their attitude toward export. In some people the elements favorable to international affairs (curiosity, general interest)—what can be called the positive elements—prevail over the negative elements (fear of the unknown, of the different). These persons will unconsciously be favorable to exports. In others psychological barriers are stronger and these persons will push everything connected to foreign things to the back of their minds into their subconscious. It was indicated earlier that the ethnic origin, the level of education, as well as life and professional experience are elements that have an influence on this psychological attitude toward foreign elements.

In addition to these psychological traits of the decision maker, which at this stage are of fundamental importance, it was shown that other elements such as the characteristics of the environment and of the firm itself might influence the entrepreneur's predisposition toward exports. However, the last two elements will be particularly important during the fourth and fifth stages.

From Psychological Predisposition to Concrete
Awareness of Export Possibilities

From the conflict between the positive and negative elements will result a certain attitude toward foreign things and affairs at

large. If the negative elements prevail, the decision maker will get
an unconscious bias against anything foreign so that if the opportunity of exporting arises he will automatically reject it. He will keep
his negative attitude until some variations in the environment induce
a change in the balance between the positive and negative forces in
his mind.

On the other hand, if the positive elements prevail, it does
not necessarily follow that the entrepreneur will immediately take
steps to find foreign customers. It simply indicates that he is favorably disposed toward the idea of exporting. However, in general,
he will not move unless some outside event (attention evoker) brings
the export problem to his immediate attention. If such an event does
happen (a foreign order), he is ready to study seriously the possibility of exporting.

## Gathering Information on Foreign
## Markets and Export Formalities

The decision maker (or the person he appoints to that task)
must now get as much information as possible on the foreign customer who has sent the order and more generally on the country in
which that customer resides (importance of market, distribution
channels, prices, and so on). He must also learn about export procedures and difficulties. Finally, he must get information on costs
and risks and gather data that will allow him to determine the price
he will quote.

## Analysis of the Data

Once the data are gathered, they must be analyzed, that is,
divided into two groups: the positive elements, essentially the profit
aspect but also the ensuing possibility of growth and development for
the firm; and the negative elements, that is, the costs and the risks
associated with the operation.

## The Final Decision

The decision maker is now in a position to make a final decision, but this decision will seldom be totally rational. Many subjective, emotional elements will color his appreciation of the positive
and negative elements. It is at this stage that all the elements previously mentioned have their full impact.

If the decision is negative, the export process will be held off until a new offer comes from another foreign customer at a later time and the whole evaluation process will start all over again. If it is positive the firm will have to create a specific internal structure (generally a few people) to deal with foreign clients, and to organize some sort of distribution network in the foreign country.

### Export, Feedback, and Revision of Export Decision

After some time, when export results are available, the data will have to be analyzed and compared to anticipated results and a decision will have to be made to continue exporting, to branch out to new foreign markets, or to stop altogether. The larger the firm, the more formalized and probably the less subjective the whole process will be.

## CONCLUSION

In conclusion, most tests performed on the objective characteristics of firms in the printing and electrical industries failed to reveal any significant difference between exporters and nonexporters, with the exception of size. Likewise, analysis of financial data (including performance ratios), not reported in the present study, did not discriminate between the two groups. It is then concluded that the major determining factor is the personality of the entrepreneur (or of the leading team) and in particular his attitude toward things foreign. This conclusion generally agrees with most of the recent theories on export behavior. However, several parts of the proposed model are still speculative and additional research, particularly in the psychology of exporting entrepreneurs, is still urgently needed. In addition, stricto sensu, the above conclusions are limited to the two specific industries: More industry analyses are needed before a valid generalization can be reached.

## REFERENCES

Garnier, G. "Caractéristiques et problèmes des petites et moyennes entreprises exportatrices du secteur manufacturier au Québec." Report for the Canadian Department of Industry, Trade, and Commerce, August 1974.

Gruber, W., D. Mehta, and R. Vernon. "The R & D Factor in International Trade and International Investment of United States Industries." Journal of Political Economy, February 1967, pp. 20-38.

Hunt, H. G., J. D. Froggart, and P. J. Hovell. "The Management of Export Marketing in Engineering Industries." British Journal of Marketing, Spring 1967, pp. 10-24.

Johanson, J., and F. Wiedersheim-Paul. "The Internationalization of the Firm—Four Swedish Case Studies." Journal of Management Studies, October 1975, pp. 305-22.

Simmonds, K., and H. Smith. "The First Export Order: A Marketing Innovation." British Journal of Marketing, Summer 1968, pp. 93-100.

Simpson, C. L., and D. Kujawa. "The Export Decision Process: An Empirical Enquiry." Journal of International Business Studies, Spring 1974, pp. 107-17.

Wiedersheim-Paul, F., H. Olson, and L. Welch. "Pre-export Activity: The First Step in Internationalization." Journal of International Business Studies, Spring-Summer 1978, pp. 47-58.

# 8

# EXPORT ORIENTATION OF NOVA SCOTIA MANUFACTURERS

Erdener Kaynak
Lois Stevenson

The value of Nova Scotia export products is approaching $1 billion dollars annually and is located, uniquely, near the cross-roads of the major trade routes of the world; the province is in a position to consider exporting as a major business activity. According to the <u>Nova Scotia Directory of Manufacturers 1979/80</u>, Nova Scotia exports have increased from a value of $663 million in 1976 to $943 million in 1979, and it is expected to increase at a faster rate in the future. Further investigation shows that foreign trade accounts for about 20 percent of Canada's gross national product (GNP) and, as such, is an important factor contributing to future maintenance of economic growth, prosperity, production, and employment in this country. Yet little is known about the breakdown of Canadian exports and the actual export behavior of small- and medium-sized firms. A review of academic research literature on the topic of export activity and behavior of firms is limited at best, [1] and relevant material on the Canadian scene is virtually nonexistent.

By understanding the process that firms use in reaching a decision to implement an export strategy, one can identify those factors that encourage or hinder the export process. Such an understanding will enable more firms to consider exporting as an

---

The authors acknowledge with thanks the financial assistance provided by Mount Saint Vincent University and the Center for International Business Studies of Dalhousie University for the completion of this research.

alternative element of their strategy to survive, grow, and prosper in today's highly competitive environment. Canadian companies, like their developed counterparts in the United States and Western Europe, are encountering formidable competition among themselves and from highly efficient foreign companies.[2] Businesses in Nova Scotia need ways of analyzing export markets, the potential exportability of their products, and, equally important, tools for predicting which products are likely to be threatened by import competition, as well as the appropriate marketing strategies to use in exporting.[3]

In order to compete and become successful in this competitive environment and develop or expand foreign markets, it is of utmost importance for Nova Scotia firms to have a profound understanding of the environment and business practices and procedures in export markets and to adopt an international outlook. In this process, the export manager should become an effective liaison between the foreign marketing operations and the domestic marketing and production divisions.

CHANGING NATURE OF EXPORT MARKETING

The lowering of barriers to international trade has resulted in many opportunities for Canadian as well as Nova Scotia companies to profit from export marketing. However, a large number of Canadian companies have entered the export business more by chance than a conscious realization of the advantages to be gained. The obvious advantages are those of utilizing the company's resources to the optimum in both economics of scale of production and use of managerial time and also in diversifying risk during periods of depression or bad economic downturns in the home country. Here the exporting firm aims to dispose of surplus capacity that cannot be sold in the domestic market because of an unexpected economic climate.[4] Simpson discussed factors such as the above as internal stimuli to the export marketing decision and defined these as being excess capacity, seasonal product, entry of domestic competitors into export markets, and profit motivation.[5] These elements were seen as rational or objective-oriented factors affecting the firm's behavior. In his study, Simpson also described external stimuli (less objective-oriented behavior) to the export marketing decision defined as being trade mission activities, trade fairs, sales agent activity, and fortuitous orders from foreign customers. These can act as positive forces to offer incentives to firms to pursue export marketing of their products. Pavord and Bogart found that a saturated domestic market, a desire to reduce

dependence on the domestic market, and declining domestic sales
were the major incentives for the U.S. industrial firms, similar to
the practices in Europe. [6]

For Canadian companies, there are additional advantages to
exporting offered by the declining value of the Canadian dollar, the
increased technological capabilities of Canadian companies, and
the opening of trade with socialist countries that have also offered
attractive trade potential. Generally, exporters who are actually
involved with exporting tend to be stimulated by the need for new
markets to attain a set goal for increase in sales and profits, a way
to use excess capacity and the personal excitement or satisfaction
that accrues to the company's management. Nonexporters, however, are not generally inclined to see these factors as major incentives and thus have not entered export markets. For instance,
a study conducted by Mayer and Flynn of eight Toronto-based small
business firms already involved in export marketing found that the
majority of the firms did so because of fortuitous circumstances,
namely receipt of an unsolicited order. [7] Other companies cited
the following additional reasons for exploring export markets:
small size of Canadian market, highly competitive market, local
"slump" periods, and greater demand in foreign markets.

While there are a number of reasons why firms should include
exporting as one of their marketing functions, there is evidence in
the literature that generally this decision is not approached on a
rational basis. [8] The Simpson study found that excess capacity was
not a significant factor in the decision to export; neither were expansion of profits and reduction of business risks given as prime
motivators. The study further found that unsolicited orders from
foreign customers were the most important individual stimuli influencing the initiation of export activity. Simpson also attempted
to ascertain why firms exposed to the same stimuli responded differently to the export decision. While some firms exposed to, for
example, an unsolicited order from a foreign customer responded
positively by filling the order and thus becoming engaged in the exporting process, other firms reacted negatively and did not fill the
order. The exporters and nonexporters personified by the decision
maker in the firm were found to differ on such decision variables
as education level, profit perception (export in relation to domestic
activity), risk perception, and cost perception (significant difference). Simpson concluded from his study that before nonexporting
firms can be triggered to adopt a positive decision, these perception difficulties must be addressed.

Bilkey and Tesar indicated that the most important factors
in whether the firm actually started exporting were receipt of an
unsolicited order and quality and dynamism of the firm's manage-

ment. [9] In other words, the decision was based more on management's general images of exporting and of foreign lands than economic considerations.

Wiedersheim-Paul, Olson, and Welch found the international orientation of the decision maker to be significant in the firm's decision to export, [10] hence the past history and experience of the decision maker is important too. Competence in managing the elements of the marketing mix is a major determinant of the firm's long-run performance and commitment in international marketing. [11] Because of the risk and uncertainty involved in export marketing, careful manipulation of each aspect of the marketing mix is essential. Empirical research of Cavusgil suggests that the following elements are especially critical: quality and design of the products and packaging for foreign markets, development of distribution channels, competitive pricing, and extension of credit. [12] Firms have been identified as progressing through various steps or stages in the level of export activity. [13] The first stage is that of domestic marketing where the firm has not explored the possibilities of export marketing and is satisfied to supply domestic demand. Some firms, due to fortuitous circumstances, as described above, will enter the second stage, which is identified as initial involvement in exporting, that is, fulfilling an unsolicited order. Usually there is no product adaptation or marketing policy changes and dealings are with psychologically close countries. Realizing the potential profitability of expanded markets, firms then enter a stage where they conduct feasibility studies. With continued successes firms will enter a stage where they are actively involved in exporting, are willing to make changes in the marketing mix to meet export market requirements and also to begin exporting to countries regardless of their psychic or geographic distance. At this stage, some firms, usually larger in size, will enter into international marketing, which involves setting up manufacturing facilities in the export markets to satisfy those local demands.


BARRIERS TO EXPORTING

In general, most small- and medium-sized manufacturers tend to be domestic market oriented and they do not explore export market opportunities. Groke and Kreidle, in their study of smaller-sized Illinois business firms, revealed myopic thinking on the part of the managers who expressed belief that their entire production was being taken by the domestic market and that only local demand existed for their products. [14] Other managers feared they were unable to go through product adaptation or afford higher selling costs involved in export marketing.

In Tookey's survey of the British hosiery and knitwear manu-facturing firms, while most firms agreed on the importance of being willing to adapt products (and packaging to meet local export needs), they foresaw many practical difficulties in the way of adaptation.[15] Variations in style and color increase costs at every stage of handling of an order and act as a hindering factor in the export decision. Tookey also concluded that the principal factors associated with success in exporting are size of the firm, its policy toward exports, the marketing channels it principally uses at home, its willingness to adapt its products to export require-ments, its use of various different export services, and finally the type of quality of product it normally makes. In addition, Tookey felt that firms have taken an unsolicited approach to export market-ing methods because of little consumer research.

Barriers to exporting appear to be divided into two areas: problems encountered by firms in the process of exporting and problems perceived by firms that prevent them from exporting at all.[16] In the first category, barriers or problems were seen as paper work, selecting a reliable distributor, competitive disadvan-tage due to nontariff barriers, honoring letters of credit, and communications with foreign customers. In the second category, perceived barriers to export were lack of exposure to other cultures, large domestic market, lack of staff time, paper work, and manage-ment of export operations and different safety and quality standards. Distribution was seen by Rabino's study as the major problem area in exporting. The other elements of the marketing mix required only slight modification, but distribution was seen as more difficult.

Bilkey found that as firms advance through the export stages their perception of barriers to exporting concentrates on the follow-ing considerations: difficulty in understanding foreign business practices, different product standards and consumer standards in foreign countries that make U.S. products unsuitable for export, difficulty in collecting money from foreign markets, difficulty in obtaining adequate representations in foreign markets, difficulty in obtaining funds necessary to get started (inverse relationship).[17] Other barriers cited were: foreign import quotas, lack of foreign markets information, difficulty with service in foreign markets, shipping documents, export licenses, and other paper work required too much time, and difficulty in converting currencies to Canadian dollars.

Alexandrides outlined the results of this study of Georgia firms where he attempted to discover how firms viewed problems in the export decision.[18] Firms already involved in exporting cited the major obstacle as foreign competition, followed by difficulties in locating foreign markets for their products. Firms not involved

in exporting saw major barriers in development of export sales to
be foreign competition, lack of knowledge about exporting, and location of foreign markets. This study also found thatindustry groups
perceived barriers differently. Overall, these Georgia firms indicated that the greatest help was needed in the location of foreign
markets. The second most significant area was in the payment
procedures, with export procedures (knowledge of techniques involved in making foreign sales) third.

Cavusgil, Moose, and Tesar identified two categories of barriers to exporting: attitudinal constraints (too risky, too complicated, not profitable) and financial, operational constraints (limited resources).[19] Depending on the level of export marketing
activity, different barriers prevailed. For example, at the stage
where firms are not motivated to export, attitudinal barriers are
dominant; when deciding how and where to export, informational
barriers are dominant; operations and resource limitations were
felt at the stage where firms are considering feasibility of formalized exporting; when aggressively competing in overseas markets,
firms must deal with foreign buyer resistance; and when involved
in international marketing, firms must overcome foreign competitive factors.

Bilkey and Tesar's work with smaller-sized Wisconsin manufacturing firms tends to confirm this.[20] They categorized firms
as going through stages in the export development process and concluded that until firms reach the stage where they are actively exploring export possibilities they are not affected by internal or
external stimuli (that is, motivated) to enter export markets. At-
tracting the attention and interest of nonexporting firms thus presents a barrier to export marketing. It was also found that nonexporting firms have a higher perception of risk and cost and a
lower perception of profit in exporting than do exporters and are
more overwhelmed by the prospect of getting started, that is, how
to gather information. Firms' greatest needs, regardless of size,
are low-cost specific leads, detailed product-market-oriented
information, and buyer/representative contacts.[21]

SURVEY METHODOLOGY

The purpose of this study is to present an analysis of export
orientation of the Nova Scotia manufacturing firms. The study describes the characteristics of exporters and determines the factors
that differentiate exporting and nonexporting firms. In an attempt
to achieve this objective, a group of Nova Scotia manufacturers with
export orientation and a group of nonexporters were interviewed via
a mail questionnaire from September 1980 through January 1981.

Sample Size

The sample of this study was selected from the <u>Nova Scotia Directory of Manufacturers 1979/80</u>, which was compiled by the Nova Scotia Department of Development. In the list, there were 368 exporters and a total of 1,110 nonexporting firms. All exporters were contacted. For some industries like fishing, all exports are channeled through the head or central office and export activities are performed by the headquarter. In these type of cases, questionnaires were sent only to the head office. A total of 325 active exporters were contacted. For the nonexporter sample, 170 manufacturing firms were randomly chosen from the <u>Directory</u> representing 15 percent of the total companies.

Interviewing

Letters of introduction were sent to all selected exporter and nonexporter firms by the president of Mount Saint Vincent University in advance of the questionnaire, explaining the nature and objectives of the study and soliciting their cooperation.

The questionnaire used in the study was pretested by personal interviews among a group of exporters and nonexporters in the Halifax area. In light of the feedback received, minor adaptations were made and the questionnaires were sent to the sample population. Stamped, self-addressed envelopes were included with the questionnaire to elicit a higher response rate. After a period of four weeks, follow-up letters with additional questionnaires were mailed to some 260 firms who had not responded to the initial request for information. All correspondence was sent to the owner/president of the firm as identified in the <u>Directory</u>. The owner/president was asked either to complete the questionnaire or to refer it to the person primarily responsible for export activity within the firm.

Exporters returned 107 questionnaires, nonexporters returned 85. This represents a 40.3 percent response rate. Nineteen questionnaires were discarded because they were incomplete and hence not usable in the study. The analysis is based on responses from 101 exporting manufacturing firms and 72 nonexporting manufacturing firms.

Product Categories Used

Both exporting and nonexporting manufacturing firms were categorized into eight product groups according to Standard Industrial

Classifications. [22] Eight major product groupings were chosen to reduce classifications to a manageable size for analysis purposes. The group of industries chosen and their total size and the sample selected are indicated in Table 8.1.


Method of Analysis

The method of analysis used in this research study was an R-Factor Analysis on the data on seven variables identified by exporters as initiating the first export activity of Nova Scotia manufacturers. The results of the measurement were initially used to produce correlation coefficients for the attributes. Given the substantial intercorrelations, the scale scores for the attributes were factor analyzed using a principal component factor analysis with varimax rotation. [23] Two significant factors with eigen value greater than one were extracted, which accounted for 79.3 percent of the variance. The loadings of each attribute in the rotated factor structure for exporters are presented in Table 8.2.


SURVEY RESULTS

The general topic of export behavior of firms is very complex and while previous research has enlightened the field in terms of descriptive data, more work is necessary in the area of assimilating the data into a comprehensive framework that can then be applied in more than one situation. Interpretations of the results of the factor analysis is straightforward. The first factor in Table 8.2 deals with those variables that initiate first export activity. Export push was considered to be the most important factor influencing first export activity of Nova Scotia exporters. This factor is heavily loaded on attributes 1 through 5. This factor accounts for about 89.6 percent of the total variation in the data output, which makes it the main factor for initiating first export activity.

The second factor can likewise be identified as export pull. Better opportunities for products in the foreign markets attribute is heavily loaded on this dimension. This factor accounts for 10.4 percent of the total variation in the data.

Generally, decision makers are confronted with one or more stimuli that may result in the consideration of export possibilities. The stimulating factors can be internal or external to the firm. An adequate analysis of the form of the export stimulus should focus on whether stimuli are primarily external, internal, or some combination of the two. As a result of the analysis of the stimuli, an answer could be provided to the question of whether decision makers

TABLE 8.1

Sample of Exporting and Nonexporting Firms

| Product Group | Industry | SIC Codes | Total Number of Firms | Nonexporter Sample | (percent) | Exporter Sample | (percent) |
|---|---|---|---|---|---|---|---|
| I | Food and beverage, and tobacco products | 1011–1530 | 348 | 17 | (23.6) | 18 | (17.8) |
| II | Rubber and plastics | 1623–2499 | 74 | 5 | (6.9) | 17 | (16.8) |
| III | Wood, furniture and paper | 2511–2890 | 429 | 21 | (29.2) | 35 | (34.7) |
| IV | Primary metal | 2910–3090 | 146 | 7 | (9.7) | 13 | (12.9) |
| V | Machinery | 3110–3290 | 151 | 12 | (16.7) | 7 | (6.9) |
| VI | Electrical products | 3310–3399 | 21 | 3 | (4.2) | 7 | (6.9) |
| VII | Minerals and chemicals, and petroleum | 3511–3799 | 122 | 7 | (9.7) | 1 | (1) |
| VIII | Miscellaneous manufacturing | 3911–3999 | 102 | — | | 3 | (1) |
| | Total | | | 72 | (100) | 101 | (100) |

140

TABLE 8.2

Factors Initiating First Export Activity

|  | Factors | |
| Attributes | 1 | 2 |
|---|---|---|
| 1. Saturated Canadian market | .91895 | .11344 |
| 2. Intense competition in Canada | .98198 | .01419 |
| 3. Unfavorable economic climate in Canada | .96500 | .01139 |
| 4. Receipt of an unsolicited order | .88691 | -.13935 |
| 5. Availability of unutilized production capacity | .91288 | .09222 |
| 6. Encouragement by government agencies | .00383 | .18949 |
| 7. Better opportunities for products in foreign markets | -.03312 | .67478 |

Note: Varimax rotated factor matrix after rotation with Kaiser normalization.

systematically initiated investigations of foreign markets or whether exports arose from fortuitous circumstances. Internal stimuli are those that develop as a result of specific action by the firm. In this study, intense competition, excess capacity, and a saturated Canadian market can be considered as internal stimuli. External stimuli came about as a result of no specific or determinable action by the firm. These are better opportunities for products in foreign markets, encouragement by government agencies, and receipt of an unsolicited order.

After delineating the factors initiating first export activity, the importance of foreign markets for Nova Scotia manufacturers was worked out. The responses of exporters and nonexporters are listed in Table 8.3.

The United States ranked first in all categories for both exporting and nonexporting firms. This makes sense since about 80 percent of Nova Scotia exports are to the United States and export trade is facilitated by geographic and psychic proximity. Canada and the United States share similar cultures, language, trade practices, and traditionally trade patterns have emerged on a north-south axis. Nova Scotia's closeness to New England has inevitably meant strong trade relations and export activity.

## TABLE 8.3

The Importance of Foreign Markets for Nova Scotia Manufacturers

| Markets Considered | Exporters | | | | Nonexporters | | | |
|---|---|---|---|---|---|---|---|---|
| | Present Importance | Rank | Future Importance | Rank | Present Importance | Rank | Future Importance | Rank |
| Western Europe | 2.89* | 2 | 2.90 | 2 | 1.29 | 4 | 1.44 | 2 |
| Eastern Europe | 0.09 | 12 | 1.80 | 8 | 1.18 | 7 | 1.25 | 8 |
| Middle East | 1.80 | 6 | 2.13 | 4 | 1.22 | 6 | 1.28 | 7 |
| Africa | 1.78 | 7 | 2.03 | 5 | 1.12 | 9 | 1.29 | 6 |
| United States | 3.80 | 1 | 3.75 | 1 | 2.34 | 1 | 2.51 | 1 |
| Latin America | 2.18 | 3 | 2.26 | 3 | 1.32 | 3 | 1.36 | 3 |
| Far East, excluding Japan | 1.69 | 8 | 1.66 | 9 | 1.11 | 10 | 1.14 | 10 |
| Australia | 1.89 | 4 | 1.92 | 7 | 1.33 | 2 | 1.32 | 5 |
| Japan | 1.80 | 5 | 2.02 | 6 | 1.15 | 8 | 1.24 | 9 |
| China | 1.41 | 9 | 1.66 | 9 | 1.03 | 12 | 1.07 | 12 |
| Soviet Union | 1.26 | 10 | 1.42 | 10 | 1.08 | 11 | 1.10 | 11 |
| West Indies | 1.84 | 5 | 1.92 | 7 | 1.28 | 5 | 1.33 | 4 |
| Others | 0.40 | 11 | 0.28 | 11 | 0.24 | 13 | 0.22 | 13 |

*Mean values of a five-point measurement with 5 = very important, 4 = important, 3 = of some importance, 2 = of little importance, 1 = of no importance.

Exporters perceive that the future importance of the U.S. market will be diminished somewhat with greater emphasis being placed on Western Europe and Latin America. There has been considerable attention paid to developing markets in Western Europe, particularly West Germany, on the part of the Export Development Corporation and the Department of Industry, Trade, and Commerce. Several firms have participated in trade fairs within the past year and Western Europe is anxious to deal with Canadian companies in certain product areas. Latin America has also had a high profile recently, that is, Mexico has had trade missions with Canada and the government has encouraged meetings with Nova Scotia manufacturing firms.

It is interesting that Japan is not foreseen as developing in importance as a foreign market for Nova Scotia products. In the resources industries, the Canadian government has been aggressively trying to stimulate export activity. Yet this study indicates future importance as perceived by exporters to be more heavily concentrated in the Middle East and Africa. Not much activity is expected in the Far East (excluding Japan), the Soviet Union, and China. In the past, these countries have not been very receptive to foreign trade.

Another interesting point is the decreasing relative importance of the West Indies as a foreign market. Size may be a factor here; larger markets are available to be developed offering increased sales to exporting firms.

Nonexporters perceive foreign market potential in a very different way. The United States is perceived as increasing in importance as a foreign market. Of course, as nonexporters begin considering export activity, the first market examined is the U.S. market because of the ease of doing business in a country so closely aligned. Western Europe and Latin America are given emphasis for future direction, again probably because of government intervention and encouragement. However, it is interesting that Australia's relative ranking decreases from second to fifth as a country of future importance. There have been visits from Australian and New Zealand Trade Commissioners to the province recently and the high profile of these countries should manifest itself in higher rankings. Perhaps nonexporting firms are not exposed to meeting with these trade commissioners for a number of reasons and hence do not benefit from increased information. Nonexporters perceive the West Indies and Africa as being more important in the future, possibly because of geographic proximity and accessibility by water. Geographically distant countries were ranked lowest (Far East, Japan, China, Soviet Union); possibly for that reason the distance creates a barrier that nonexporting firms are less likely to overcome.

## MARKETING POLICY IMPLICATIONS

The implications of this study are significant for manufacturers of Nova Scotia who are considering exporting as a major business activity. There exists a consistent type of agreement among Nova Scotia exporters on the factors to be considered in initiating export activity. Based on the results of the empirical study, decision makers of both consumer and industrial product manufacturing firms do not act directly to enter export markets to any large degree.

This study found general agreement on the key markets explored frequently by manufacturers of Nova Scotia. The major obstacles perceived in export marketing of both industrial and consumer goods manufacturers were: government barriers (customs/tariffs), different competitive practices, selecting a reliable distributor, inadequate transportation system, existence of nontariff barriers, and communications with foreign customers.

## NOTES

1. Warren J. Bilkey, "An Integrated Integration of the Literature on the Export Behavior of Firms," Journal of International Business Studies, Spring/Summer 1978, pp. 33-46; Warren J. Bilkey and George Tesar, "The Export Behavior of Smaller Sized Wisconsin Manufacturing Firms," Journal of International Business Studies, Spring 1977, pp. 93-98; S. Tamer Cavusgil, Warren Bilkey, and George Tesar, "A Note on the Export Behavior of Firms: Exporter Profiles," Journal of International Business Studies, Spring/Summer 1979, pp. 91-97; and Michael R. Czinkota, "An Analysis of Export Development Strategies in Selected U.S. Industries," Ph.D. dissertation, Ohio State University, 1980.

2. J. Donald Weinrauch and C. P. Rao, "The Export Marketing Mix: An Examination of Company Experiences and Perceptions," Journal of Business Research, October 24, 1974, pp. 447-52.

3. I. A. Cosini, "Is Exporting Really Too Much Trouble?" Carroll Business Bulletin, Fall 1975.

4. D. A. Tookey, "International Business and Political Geography," British Journal of Marketing, Autumn 1969, pp. 139-40; Michael J. Baker, "Export Myopia," The Quarterly Review of Marketing 4, no. 3 (Spring 1979); and P. C. N. Mitchell and T. R. Ingram, "Export Strategy and the Small Firm," The Quarterly Review of Marketing 4, no. 2 (Winter 1978):17-26.

5. C. L. Simpson, Jr., and Duane Kujawa, "The Export Decision Process: An Empirical Inquiry," Journal of International Business Studies 5 (Spring 1974):107-17.

6. William C. Pavord and Raymond G. Bogart, "The Dynamics of the Decision to Export," Akron Business and Economic Review, Spring 1975, pp. 6-11.

7. Charles S. Mayer and Joy E. Flynn, "Canadian Small Business Abroad: Opportunities, Aids, and Experiences," Business Quarterly 38 (Winter 1973):33-47.

8. Simpson and Kujawa.

9. Bilkey and Tesar.

10. Finn Wiedersheim-Paul, H. C. Olson, and L. S. Welch, "Pre-Export Activity: The First Step in Internationalization," Journal of International Business Studies, Spring/Summer 1978, pp. 47-58.

11. Tamer S. Cavusgil and John R. Nevin, "Conceptualizations of the Initial Involvement in International Marketing," in Theoretical Developments in Marketing, ed. Charles W. Lams and Patrick M. Dunne, Proceedings of the AMA Theory Conference, Phoenix, April 1980.

12. Tamer S. Cavusgil, "On the Internationalization Process of Firms," European Research 8, no. 6 (November 1980):273-81.

13. Bilkey.

14. Paul O. Groke and John R. Kreidle, "Export! Why or Why Not? Managerial Attitude and Action for Small Sized Business Firms," Business and Society 8 (Fall 1967):7-12.

15. Tookey.

16. Samuel Rabino, "An Examination of Barriers to Exporting Encountered by Small Manufacturing Companies," paper presented at the Academy of International Business Annual Meeting, Las Vegas, June 20, 1979.

17. Bilkey and Tesar.

18. C. G. Alexandrides, "How the Major Obstacles to Expansion Can be Overcome," Atlantic Economic Review, May 1971, pp. 12-15.

19. Tamer S. Cavusgil, Joboc D. Moose, and G. Tesar, "Recent Empirical Investigations of Firm's Export Behavior: Implications for Export Stimulation and Promotion Policies," paper presented at the Academy of International Business Annual Meeting, Las Vegas, June 20, 1979.

20. Bilkey and Tesar.

21. Rabino.

22. Nova Scotia Directory of Manufacturers 1979/80 (Halifax: Nova Scotia Development Statistical Services Branch, March 1980).

23. N. H. Nie et al., Statistical Package for the Social Sciences, 2d ed. (New York: McGraw-Hill, 1975).

# PART II
## EXPORT ACTIVITIES OF MULTINATIONAL CORPORATIONS

This section focuses on the export activities of large-sized corporations and on macro exporting issues. Daniel Van Den Bulcke focuses on the export activities of multinational enterprises in Belgium, differentiating between foreign-owned and Belgian-owned companies. He investigates and compares their export propensity, their export mix, and their responsiveness to government programs. Peter Buckley looks on a global scale at the role of exporting in the market servicing policies of multinational manufacturing enterprises and the changes of these policies and identifies main factors that account for these changes. Ravi Sarathy investigates major industrial exporters in Japan and searches for factors that influence export success, paying particular attention to financial issues. Ronald Hoyt examines technology transfers through industrial cooperation between East and West, focusing particularly on the foreign trade policy and development of the Soviet Union.

# 9

## EXPORT ACTIVITIES OF MULTINATIONAL ENTERPRISES IN BELGIUM

### Daniel Van Den Bulcke

Belgians like to boast about the export orientation of their economy. They point out that they export more per capita than any other nation in the world and that Belgium, although only a small country, ranks tenth in the league of world exporters with almost 4 percent of world exports. They generally mention that one out of two Belgians works for exports, although it has been shown—on the basis of an input–output analysis—that only one out of three Belgians is engaged in production that goes to foreign markets.[1] As their country is highly dependent on foreign trade, Belgians are getting worried about their balance of trade, which has been deteriorating since 1974 and will, according to preliminary figures, show a deficit of 200 billion Belgian francs (BFR) in 1980 (about 5 percent of GNP).

In retrospect Belgians seem to be somewhat less happy about the high rate of foreign direct investment into their economy. In 1978 foreign industrial enterprises (defined as having a 10 percent

---

This chapter is partly based on a research project about multinational companies in Belgium, financed by the Belgian Fund for Collective Fundamental Research, which was carried out by the Seminar of Applied Economics at the University of Ghent (Director: Prof. Dr. A. J. Vlerick) and the Research Center of the Economische Hogeschool Limburg (Director: Prof. Dr. D. Van Den Bulcke). The coauthors of the main publication (in Dutch) from this project were Frans Haex and Eric Halsberghe.

foreign ownership in their equity capital) were responsible for almost four out of ten jobs in Belgian manufacturing. [2] In 1958 only one out of ten Belgian industrial employees had been working in a plant controlled from abroad.

During the 1960s, multinational enterprises (MNEs) flocked to Belgium mainly for its central location in the Common Market, its excellent infrastructure and communications with the rest of Western Europe, its flexible labor market (availability of skilled and unskilled workers and high productivity), and its generous policy of government incentives and subsidized loans. [3] When the economic crisis, which started in 1974, resulted in a slowdown of new foreign investment and the withdrawal of a number of foreign MNEs from the Belgian economy, one got the impression that Belgium was at the mercy of the continuing presence of foreign MNEs. [4] The Belgian government accordingly stressed, in a white paper about a "new industrial policy," that measures should be taken to become less dependent upon decision centers located abroad. The government's white paper is not very explicit, however, as to the realization of this objective and should perhaps not be taken too seriously. [5]

To combat the increasing unemployment and to eliminate the adverse balance of trade, the Belgian government has been stressing the need for increased exports. The respective ministers of foreign trade have been urging a reorientation of both the product composition and the geographic spread of Belgian exports and have taken a number of measures to promote sales abroad. In view of the fact that foreign-owned enterprises realized almost 30 percent of Belgian exports in 1968 and that this proportion had probably increased to 45 percent in 1975, it should be interesting to investigate the comparative export performance of foreign MNEs and Belgian enterprises in somewhat more detail. Other important questions are: Have foreign MNEs contributed to the sectoral and geographic diversification of Belgian exports? Are intragroup exports a hindrance or an advantage to the national efforts of export promotion? Do export restrictions within the multinational framework restrict the export chances of multinational subsidiaries in Belgium? How autonomous are decisions about export activities by foreign subsidiaries? What is the effect of the investment abroad of Belgian MNEs on the export performance of Belgium?

EXPORT PROPENSITY OF FOREIGN
AND BELGIAN ENTERPRISES

Previous studies have shown that the export performance of U.S. subsidiaries abroad was better than the national industry as a whole in Great Britain, the Netherlands, and Germany. In New Zealand, Australia, and Canada the export intensity (exports as a percentage of total sales) of foreign and U.S. enterprises was not found to be higher than indigenous firms, however.[6] Many MNEs have located in these latter countries to avoid import restrictions and are therefore more geared to production for the local market. The superior export propensity of U.S. subsidiaries in Great Britain has been explained by the particular influence of certain sectors. Dunning and Moyer have shown that if the sectoral distribution for U.S. firms in Britain would have been the same as for British companies, the differences would be much less pronounced.[7]

Recent data for Belgium indicate that foreign-owned subsidiaries are more export oriented than indigenous enterprises. In 1976 foreign MNEs exported 68 percent of their sales, while uninational Belgian firms sent only half of their production abroad. When Belgian MNEs (export propensity = 67 percent) are included in this comparison, the export ratio for Belgian firms increases to 61 percent (see Table 9.1).* Only in food was the export ratio of uninational Belgian enterprises higher than their foreign competitors located in Belgium. The fact that Belgian enterprises surpass foreign subsidiaries in metal construction is due to the high export ratio of Belgian MNEs.

To eliminate to some extent sectoral and other differences, two methods were used. First, a matched sample of 93 pairs was established. The pairing of the foreign subsidiary and the Belgian firm was based on the precondition of a similarity in subsector, employment category, and age group. Second, by way of simulated totals and averages, the characteristics of foreign-owned enterprises were calculated as if they had the same sectoral distribution as the Belgian uninational enterprises. Both the matched sample and the simulation confirm the results of the global sample, that is, that the export propensity is typically higher in foreign- and U.S.-owned firms.

---

*The data that are used in this study refer to 1976 and are based on a systematic comparison of 231 Belgian indigenous firms (including 30 Belgian MNEs) and 262 foreign subsidiaries. The companies responded to a questionnaire that was sent out by mail but mainly collected by personal interviews. This so-called global sample includes on the one hand 27 percent of all foreign-owned enterprises in Belgium and 40 percent of their total sales and employment, and on the other hand 13 percent of all uninational firms with more than 50 employees and about 20 percent of their total sales and 25 percent of employment. A similar study was conducted in 1968 but did not include comparative information on Belgian indigenous firms.

TABLE 9.1

Export Intensity of Foreign and Belgian Enterprises, 1976

| | Export Intensity* | | Export per Employee | | Average Contribution to Trade Balance | |
|---|---|---|---|---|---|---|
| | Number | Percent | Number | Million BFR | Number | Million BFR |
| Global sample | | | | | | |
| Belgian enterprises | 207 | 61 | 207 | 1.12 | 170 | 372 |
| Belgian uninational enterprises | 185 | 50 | 185 | 0.95 | 151 | 131 |
| Foreign enterprises | 226 | 68 | 226 | 2.21 | 202 | 340 |
| U.S. enterprises | 93 | 67 | 93 | 2.32 | 83 | 400 |
| EEC enterprises | 114 | 67 | 114 | 2.01 | 102 | 256 |
| Matched sample | | | | | | |
| Belgian enterprises | 87 | 51 | 87 | 0.93 | 76 | 80 |
| Belgian uninational enterprises | 81 | 47 | 81 | 0.88 | 76 | 77 |
| Foreign enterprises | 92 | 66 | 92 | 1.44 | 81 | 185 |
| Simulated total | | | | | | |
| Foreign enterprises | | 61 | | 1.53 | | 242 |
| U.S. enterprises | | 71 | | 1.96 | | 512 |
| EEC enterprises | | 59 | | 1.26 | | 146 |

*Exports as percent of sales.

Source: F. Haex, E. Halsberghe, and D. Van Den Bulcke, Buitenlandse en Belgische Ondernemingen in de Nationale Industrie (Ghent: SERUG, 1979), pp. 308, 314, 354.

Table 9.1 indicates that foreign subsidiaries realize not only a higher average export value per employee, with the U.S. enterprises outperforming their European Economic Community (EEC) competitors, but also a higher average contribution to the Belgian trade balance, at least if the Belgian MNEs are not taken into account. Again, the matched sample and simulated averages generally confirm the foreign and U.S. superiority as far as the average export per employee and contribution to the trade balance per enterprise are concerned.[8]

Safarian has tested out if the export ratio of foreign-owned subsidiaries was linked to the total number of subsidiaries of the multinational group.[9] His hypothesis was that the export propensity would diminish with an increase in the size of the network of the MNEs, for example, as a result of market distribution between parent company and subsidiary. He found out, however, that those subsidiaries that belonged to the MNEs with most subsidiaries abroad were relatively more present in the category with the highest export intensity. Our own analysis according to the "degree of multinationality"* did not bring out any differences in export intensity either (both in 1968 and 1976).[10]

## SECTORAL AND GEOGRAPHIC DIVERSIFICATION

### Product Orientation

Larson's analysis of Belgium's trade specialization concluded that exports as of 1976 were still mainly oriented toward standard

---

*A distinction was made between EME (emerging multinational enterprises), which consist of firms that have only one plant abroad and small multinational groups that have only a few subsidiaries in no more than three to five countries; GME (global multinational enterprises), which are the most multinationalized and answer simultaneously to the following quantitative—and to some extent arbitrary—criteria: minimum total sales of 15 billion BFR, manufacturing operations in at least six countries, minimum 25 percent of total activities abroad, and manufacturing establishments in Europe, North America, and developing countries; and MOE (multinational oriented enterprises), which did not fulfill all of the above-mentioned criteria but had sales of at least 10 billion BFR, were located in at least four countries, realized at least 10 percent of their total sales abroad, and controlled subsidiaries in the EEC, European Free Trade Association countries, Southern Europe, and North America.

products. There were some indications, however, that Belgian trade was slowly evolving in the direction of special products. It was also found that Belgium trades standard products up-market to more advanced countries, in particular the United States, and special products down-market to less developed countries.[11] The Belgian National Bank mentioned in its annual report of 1978 that Belgian exports consisted too much of products for which the demand in the OECD (Organization for Economic Cooperation and Development)-countries had not increased since 1974.[12] The minister of foreign trade recently stated that the Belgian export package has to be adapted and should be reoriented toward sectors that are competitive on a world level and research-and-development-intensive.[13]

The calculation of a so-called sectoral concentration coefficient (that is, the ratio of the share in total industrial employment and the share of the employment provided by foreign enterprises located in Belgium) illustrates that foreign MNEs are relatively more present in research-intensive sectors.* For electronics (including miscellaneous metals), chemicals, and transport equipment the concentration coefficients oscillate around 2.0, while rubber, petroleum, and plastics register 1.3, as compared with 1.1 for metals and 0.9 for machine construction and nonmetallic minerals.

Foreign subsidiaries are on the other hand relatively more engaged in the production (and consequently exports) of semifinished products and raw materials than indigenous firms (see Table 9.2). This characteristic, which is probably a consequence of the intragroup trade of MNEs, shows up in both the global and matched samples. Foreign-owned enterprises produce relatively more industrial and investment goods, while local companies concentrate more on durable consumption goods. These differences are mostly sectorally determined, however, and tend to disappear with the calculation of the matched sample.

Thirty percent of the indigenous firms were exposed to a "strong" competitive pressure of imports coming from developing countries as compared with only 15 percent for foreign subsidiaries. The matched sample confirms that Belgian firms are in a weaker competitive position than their foreign counterparts. Foreign (and especially U.S.) MNEs were suffering relatively more than local firms from imports from industrial countries. More than half of

---

*A coefficient that is higher than 1 means that foreign subsidiaries are relatively more present in these sectors than Belgian manufacturing as a whole. A coefficient that equals 1 indicates that the sectoral proportions are equal, while a coefficient of less than 1 points to a relative absence of foreign MNEs.

the indigenous companies complained about an increase in competitive pressure during 1970–76, as compared with only 40 percent of the foreign subsidiaries. About half of the multinational subsidiaries stressed that their belonging to a multinational group offered special competitive advantages through their direct access to the R & D pool of the group, their use of brands from the parent company, and their cheaper imports through global sourcing.[14]

TABLE 9.2

Production of Semifinished Products and Raw Materials
by Foreign and Belgian Enterprises, 1976

| | Semifinished Products | | Raw Materials | |
|---|---|---|---|---|
| | Number | Percent* | Number | Percent* |
| Global sample | | | | |
| Belgian enterprises | 48 | 22 | 11 | 6 |
| Belgian uninational enterprises | 39 | 21 | 12 | 6 |
| Foreign enterprises | 84 | 34 | 37 | 15 |
| U.S. enterprises | 31 | 30 | 15 | 14 |
| EEC enterprises | 46 | 36 | 19 | 15 |
| Matched sample | | | | |
| Belgian enterprises | 22 | 24 | 6 | 7 |
| Belgian uninational enterprises | 19 | 22 | 5 | 6 |
| Foreign enterprises | 35 | 38 | 10 | 11 |

*As percentage of total number of companies.
Source: F. Haex, E. Halsberghe, and D. Van Den Bulcke, Buitenlandse en Belgische Ondernemingen in de Nationale Industrie (Ghent: SERUG, 1979), p. 60.


Geographic Orientation

The ministerial document "A Foreign Trade Policy" (1979) stresses the need for a geographic diversification of Belgian exports. While urging a continuing and more aggressive presence in the markets of the EEC (72 percent of total Belgian exports) and

other industrial countries (14 percent of total Belgian exports),
Belgian ministers of foreign trade have for some time been pointing
out that Belgian exporters should penetrate the markets of developing countries and look for particular formulas to increase trade
with Eastern Europe and Latin America. [15]  Larson concluded that
Belgium has a special stake in trade with developing countries and
that it should develop special products on the basis of its standard
products. [16]

It was apparent from our earlier study that Belgian exports as
a whole were relatively going more to EEC countries than for foreign-
owned subsidiaries. While more than half of the exports of U.S.
subsidiaries in Belgium were sold outside the former EEC market
of the Six, this proportion amounted to only one-third for the global
exports of the Belgian-Luxembourg Economic Union. [17]  Cracco has
concluded from a study about the export activity of firms situated
in Wallonia (the southern part of Belgium) that the adherence to a
multinational group does not necessarily result in a more geographic
diversification but leads to a greater concentration upon the European continent. The same author finds, however, that multinational
subsidiaries export relatively more to Eastern bloc countries and to
Africa. He also notices that foreign subsidiaries export to more
countries than indigenous firms. [18]

Our own analysis indicates that the geographic scope of Belgian companies in general and uninational firms in particular is extremely limited. Foreign-owned subsidiaries export relatively
more frequently to most industrial markets (Table 9.3) and the developing countries (Table 9.4). The differences are small or non-
existent only for the markets of Japan, North America, and the
Netherlands. Foreign subsidiaries are most present in the category
of less than 25 percent of total exports to particular markets. The
higher percentage of exports of 50 percent and more to the Dutch
and German markets is a consequence of the fact that it is mainly
travail à facon. The matched sample confirms the above findings of
the global sample, although the differences between Belgian and foreign enterprises, as to their export activities in Africa and Latin
America, become less pronounced.


SIZE AND CHARACTERISTICS OF
INTRAGROUP EXPORTS

National authorities tend to get uneasy about the intragroup
trade of MNEs as it depends only indirectly on market demand and
is often settled through administrative decisions based upon the
global strategy and the priorities of the multinational group as a

TABLE 9.3

Geographic Spread of Exports to Industrial Countries, 1976
(global sample)

| | France | Nether-lands | West Germany | Italy | Great Britain | Ireland and Denmark | United States and Canada | Norway, Sweden, and Switzerland | Japan |
|---|---|---|---|---|---|---|---|---|---|
| **No exports to** | | | | | | | | | |
| Belgian enterprises | 30[a] | 26 | 38 | 78 | 72 | 84 | 80 | 74 | 95 |
| Uninational Belgian enterprises | 33 | 17 | 40 | 82 | 75 | 86 | 84 | 77 | 96 |
| Foreign enterprises | 27 | 15 | 28 | 59 | 49 | 66 | 78 | 48 | 96 |
| **Exports from 1 to 24 percent[b]** | | | | | | | | | |
| Belgian enterprises | 31 | 40 | 38 | 21 | 25 | 16 | 18 | 24 | 5 |
| Uninational Belgian enterprises | 28 | 37 | 34 | 17 | 22 | 14 | 15 | 22 | 4 |
| Foreign enterprises | 44 | 53 | 43 | 39 | 44 | 23 | 20 | 47 | 4 |
| **Exports from 25 to 49 percent** | | | | | | | | | |
| Belgian enterprises | 17 | 18 | 11 | 1 | 3 | — | 2 | 0.5 | — |
| Uninational Belgian enterprises | 16 | 18 | 12 | 1 | 3 | — | 0.5 | 0.5 | — |
| Foreign enterprises | 20 | 10 | 18 | 2 | 6 | 0.4 | 2 | 3 | — |
| **Exports of over 50 percent** | | | | | | | | | |
| Belgian enterprises | 22 | 16 | 11 | 0.5 | — | — | 0.5 | 1 | |
| Uninational Belgian enterprises | 23 | 18 | 14 | 0.5 | — | — | — | 1 | — |
| Foreign enterprises | 10 | 21 | 9 | 0.4 | — | — | — | 1 | — |

[a] Number of enterprises in the different categories as percent of total number of enterprises.
[b] As a percentage of total exports.

Source: F. Haex, E. Halsberghe, and D. Van Den Bulcke, Buitenlandse en Belgische Ondernemingen in de Nationale Industrie (Ghent: SERUG, 1979), p. 346.

TABLE 9.4

Geographic Spread of Exports to Developing and Third Countries, 1976
(global sample)

| | Middle East and Asia | Africa | Latin America | Eastern Bloc | Other Countries |
|---|---|---|---|---|---|
| No export | | | | | |
| Belgian enterprises | 78[a] | 73 | 91 | 90 | 82 |
| Belgian uninational enterprises | 83 | 77 | 93 | 93 | 84 |
| Foreign enterprises | 69 | 67 | 85 | 77 | 88 |
| Exports from 1 to 24 percent[b] | | | | | |
| Belgian enterprises | 19 | 22 | 8 | 9 | 13 |
| Belgian uninational enterprises | 14 | 17 | 6 | 6 | 12 |
| Foreign enterprises | 28 | 32 | 15 | 22 | 11 |
| Exports from 25 to 49 percent | | | | | |
| Belgian enterprises | 3 | 3 | 0.5 | 1 | 2 |
| Belgian uninational enterprises | 3 | 3 | 0.5 | 1 | 2 |
| Foreign enterprises | 3 | 0.4 | — | 1 | 0.4 |
| Exports over 50 percent | | | | | |
| Belgian enterprises | — | 2 | — | — | 2 |
| Belgian uninational enterprises | — | 3 | — | — | 1.5 |
| Foreign enterprises | — | 1.4 | — | — | — |

[a]Number of enterprises in the different categories as percent of total number of enterprises.
[b]As a percentage of total exports.

Source: F. Haex, E. Halsberghe, and D. Van Den Bulcke, Buitenlandse en Belgische Ondernemingen in de Nationale Industrie (Ghent: SERUG, 1979), p. 346.

whole. A general policy of export promotion might have little effect on the export performance of those multinational subsidiaries and thus limit the scope for an independent export policy. The Canadian Gray report concluded that in view of the high size of intragroup trade in Canada it would be extremely difficult to enlarge its export markets as was stipulated by the government.[19] Intragroup trade also worries fiscal authorities as it facilitates the potential practice of transfer pricing by which profits can surface outside of the country where they were realized and thus diminish fiscal receipts.

In 1976 total intragroup exports had reached 53 percent of the sales abroad of foreign subsidiaries in Belgium. In 1968 this percentage was only 37 percent. This increase in intragroup exports resulted mainly from enterprises that were controlled by a European parent company (Table 9.5). From 1968 to 1976 the relative share of intragroup exports to total exports of EEC subsidiaries went up from 40 to 63 percent. Exports of U.S. subsidiaries to their multinational group changed only slightly from 36 percent in 1968 to 40 percent in 1976. During the same period exports that were directed to the parent company itself became more important for U.S. (from 4 to 12 percent) than for European MNEs (from 38 to 45 percent). Intragroup exports were most important in electronics and clothing (more than 66 percent) on the one hand and machine construction, transport equipment, and food (about 60 percent) on the other hand.

TABLE 9.5

Intragroup Exports of Foreign MNEs in Belgium
in Percent of Total Sales, 1976
(averages)

| | Exports to Parent Company | | Total Intragroup Exports | |
|---|---|---|---|---|
| | 1968 | (percent) 1976 | 1968 | (percent) 1976 |
| Foreign enterprises | 14 | 28 | 37 | 53 |
| U.S. enterprises | 4 | 12 | 36 | 41 |
| EEC enterprises | 38 | 45 | 40 | 63 |

Sources: F. Haex, E. Halsberghe, and D. Van Den Bulcke, Buitenlandse en Belgische Ondernemingen in de Nationale Industrie (Ghent: SERUG, 1979), p. 328; and D. Van Den Bulcke, et al., Les entreprises étrangères dans l'industrie belge (Brussels: Belgian Office of Productivity Increase, 1971), p. 205.

A categorical analysis of intragroup exports (as a percent of total exports) indicates that about 70 percent of foreign subsidiaries send less than one-quarter of their total sales abroad to the parent company and about half of them export less than this percentage to the multinational group (parent company included) (see Table 9.6). Almost one out of five subsidiaries export more than 75 percent to the parent company while one out of three send 75 percent of their exports to the multinational group as a whole. EEC companies (more in particular Dutch and German subsidiaries) export more than 75 percent to the multinational group. These characteristics of the intragroup trade in Belgium had already been noticed in 1968.

Looking upon intragroup exports from the point of view of the degree of multinationality, one finds that a higher multinational maturity implies more intragroup exports in U.S. MNEs only. Exports to the parent company and the total group are relatively higher in European than U.S. MNEs. Geographic proximity and sectoral concentration are the main reasons why intense intragroup trade within the group of emerging multinational enterprises is very high (see Table 9.7).

Fiscal authorities might be interested to know that 86 percent of the intragroup exports that left Belgium in 1968 resulted from export activities of the global multinational enterprises, which represented only about one-third of foreign enterprises in Belgium. The affirmation by Deane—"If governments are concerned that the transfer pricing practices of foreign owned manufacturing enterprises leave something to be desired, a check on the vast bulk of these transactions can be made by an examination of the records of relatively few companies"[20]—appears to be correct.

The subsidiaries that participated in the inquiry were asked to specify if, in view of the specific product characteristics, they could sell their products outside of the multinational group. Only one out of five foreign-owned subsidiaries answered that this was not possible or not allowed. About one out of four of the subsidiaries that were able to sell their products to independent companies thought they could have obtained higher arm's length prices. This proportion applied to both U.S. and non-U.S. subsidiaries.

On the other hand, one out of four respondents specified that they could have sold outside the multinational group only at lower prices. For about one out of two subsidiaries, sales abroad at arm's length pricing would not have affected their prices.

About one-third of the foreign subsidiaries in Belgium are able to decide autonomously about their export prices in intragroup trade. For about half of these (U.S. and non-U.S.) subsidiaries it is the parent company or regional headquarters that decides upon the level of the export prices. As to the basis of the export pricing,

TABLE 9.6

Intragroup Exports of Foreign MNEs in Belgium According to
Country of Origin and Export Category, 1976

| | Trade with Parent Company | | | | | Total Intragroup Trade | | | | |
|---|---|---|---|---|---|---|---|---|---|---|
| | Less than 25 Percent | 25–49 Percent | 50–74 Percent | 75 Percent and Over | Total Number = 100 | Less than 25 Percent | 25–49 Percent | 50–74 Percent | 75 Percent and Over | Total Number = 100 |
| U.S. enterprises | 92 | 6 | 0 | 1 | 79 | 70 | 11 | 3 | 17 | 76 |
| EEC 6 enterprises | 44 | 10 | 8 | 38 | 89 | 33 | 10 | 10 | 47 | 89 |
| Dutch enterprises | 32 | 3 | 8 | 57 | 37 | 14 | 3 | 14 | 69 | 36 |
| French enterprises | 58 | 19 | 6 | 16 | 31 | 55 | 16 | 6 | 23 | 31 |
| West German enterprises | 41 | 9 | 9 | 41 | 22 | 29 | 14 | 10 | 47 | 21 |
| EEC 9 enterprises | 53 | 9 | 7 | 31 | 117 | 41 | 9 | 9 | 41 | 115 |
| British enterprises | 85 | 8 | 4 | 4 | 26 | 69 | 4 | 8 | 19 | 26 |
| Other countries | 93 | 0 | 0 | 7 | 15 | 53 | 7 | 13 | 27 | 15 |
| All enterprises | 71 | 8 | 4 | 18 | 211 | 53 | 9 | 7 | 31 | 206 |

Source: F. Haex, E. Halsberghe, and D. Van Den Bulcke, Buitenlandse en Belgische Ondernemingen in de Nationale Industrie (Ghent: SERUG, 1979), p. 332.

## TABLE 9.7

Intragroup Exports According to Degree of Multinationality, 1976

| | Degree of Multinationality[a] | | | | | |
| | GMEs | | MOEs | | EMEs | |
| Intragroup Exports[b] | Number | Percent | Number | Percent | Number | Percent |
|---|---|---|---|---|---|---|
| U.S. subsidiaries | | | | | | |
| Exports to parent company | 34 | 5 | 28 | 5 | 14 | 0.1 |
| Exports to total group | 34 | 29 | 25 | 25 | 14 | 7 |
| Non-U.S. subsidiaries | | | | | | |
| Exports to parent company | 30 | 29 | 38 | 19 | 51 | 55 |
| Exports to total group | 30 | 49 | 37 | 34 | 51 | 64 |
| All subsidiaries | | | | | | |
| Exports to parent company | 64 | 16 | 66 | 13 | 65 | 43 |
| Exports to total group | 64 | 38 | 62 | 30 | 65 | 52 |

[a]GMEs = global multinational enterprises; MOEs = multinational oriented enterprises; EMEs = emerging multinational enterprises.

[b]As a percentage of total exports.

Source: D. Van Den Bulcke and E. Halsberghe, "Degree of Multinationality and Foreign Headquarter-Subsidiary Relationship in a Belgian Context," paper presented at International Research Symposium, Stockholm, June 2-4, 1980, p. 34.

one-third of foreign MNEs use the market price and another third apply the total cost approach for their intragroup exports. U.S. companies rely relatively more on market prices (46 percent as compared with 27 percent for EEC firms), while EEC subsidiaries more often take total costs as a basis for their calculations (42 percent as compared with 24 percent for U.S. firms).

## CONTROL OVER SUBSIDIARY EXPORT DECISIONS

### Export Decisions in General

In 1976, 44 percent of the foreign subsidiaries in Belgium were completely autonomous to decide about their export contracts. This percentage is only slightly higher than our inquiry for 1968 had shown. In 28 percent of all cases the parent company takes the decision in its own hands (12 percent) or decides after having consulted with the subsidiary (16 percent). In 1968, 24 percent of all subsidiaries were unable to decide about exports. These proportions compare favorably, however, with investment decisions where, in 1976, 66 percent of the subsidiaries were completely dependent on the headquarters as well as 56 percent for financing, 49 percent for product policy, 40 percent for cost price systems, and about 30 percent for pricing and marketing. In wage policy and personnel matters the parent company took the final decisions in one out of five subsidiaries. [21]

It is interesting to notice that a high propensity to export decreases the autonomy of the subsidiary in other fields such as finance and personnel. There is also a clear-cut tendency for more centralization with an increase in intragroup trade. Subsidiaries that did not export to the parent company experienced a decisive influence on investment and personnel decisions in respectively 64 and 27 percent of all cases. Subsidiaries that forwarded all of their production to the parent company had to rely exclusively on the decision making of their headquarters in 91 percent for investment and 56 percent for personnel questions. [22]

An analysis of the autonomy of export decisions according to the degree of multinationality pointed out that relatively more subsidiaries that belonged to the most (GMEs) and to the least multinationalized (EMEs) MNEs were narrowly controlled by their parent company than those in the middle group (MOEs). [23] This was confirmed by the 1976 analysis. One out of four of the MOEs was strongly controlled in the field of exports as compared with one out of three for the EMEs and the GMEs. [24] This result is completely determined, however, by the non-U.S. subsidiaries, of which 40 percent are experiencing a decisive influence from the parent company, as compared with only 17 percent for U.S. subsidiaries (see Table 9.8). U.S. enterprises in Belgium that are members of GMEs are relatively more controlled by the parent company than EMEs. Geographic proximity and type of production are probably the main reasons why emerging European MNEs (especially Dutch and German companies) are very dependent on the parent company.

TABLE 9.8

Decisive Influence by Headquarters on Export Decisions
of Multinational Subsidiaries According to Degree
of Multinationality, 1976

| Degree of Multinationality | U.S. Subsidiaries | | Non-U.S. Subsidiaries | | Total | |
|---|---|---|---|---|---|---|
| | Number | Per-cent | Number | Per-cent | Number | Per-cent |
| GMEs | 10 | 21 | 13 | 42 | 23 | 29 |
| MOEs | 4 | 14 | 12 | 33 | 16 | 25 |
| EMEs | 2 | 9 | 21 | 45 | 23 | 33 |
| Total | 16 | 17 | 46 | 40 | 62 | 29 |

Source: D. Van Den Bulcke and E. Halsberghe, "Degree of Multinationality and Foreign Headquarter-Subsidiary Relationship in a Belgian Context," paper presented at International Research Symposium, Stockholm, June 2-4, 1980, p. 33.

Restrictions of Export Market Penetration

Autonomous decision making in export matters does not necessarily mean that subsidiaries in a particular host country can export all over the world. Certain markets are often inaccessible to the subsidiary as they are reserved for the parent company or other subsidiaries. This limitation of the export potential of subsidiaries has resulted in many adverse reactions in Canada, New Zealand, and Australia and has been considered as the main explanation of the lower export propensity of foreign subsidiaries within these countries.[25]

In 1968 only 18 percent of foreign subsidiaries in Belgium were completely free to export to whatever country they wished. About one out of four subsidiaries could not export to Germany, France, and Italy, while 70 percent had to leave the U.S. market alone. Especially the market of the parent country was typically declared out of reach for the Belgian subsidiary. Table 9.9 lists the export restrictions to the most important markets according to the nationality of the parent company (1976) and generally confirms the previous findings. Almost three out of four U.S. subsidiaries are excluded from the U.S. market, while almost four out of five were not allowed to export to Latin America. European markets are generally much more accessible to U.S. than European subsidiaries, probably because of the proximity of the European parent company. Two-thirds of Dutch subsidiaries cannot export freely to the Netherlands, while almost half did not get permission to sell in West Germany (48 percent) and Great Britain (44 percent). West German MNEs reserve their parent country for only one out of two of their subsidiaries and are also somewhat less restrictive for other markets (generally one out of four subsidiaries do not have access to other markets). French MNEs consider their own market as their exclusive territory in almost two-thirds of all cases, while they insist on priority for the parent or other subsidiaries in the markets of the developing countries for about one-third. British MNEs keep their subsidiaries' exports out of their home markets in two out of three cases and are also very protective about the lucrative U.S. market (60 percent) and the developing and the Eastern bloc countries (from 45 to 50 percent).

Steuer has found that there is a positive and significant relationship between the practice of export restrictions by MNEs and the number of host countries. There was no such correlation however between export restrictions and the size of the network.[26] Table 9.10 presents the restrictions of export markets according to the degree of multinationality, which is partly based on the criteria used by Steuer. Only in the neighboring EEC markets are U.S. GMEs more restrictive that the other typological categories. The MOEs are most restrictive, however, in the industrial markets of Britian and Sweden, the developing continents, and the Eastern bloc countries. U.S. EMEs are most restrictive of their home market. The MOEs are also the most restrictive of the non-U.S. multinationals, although at a higher level for the markets of the industrial countries than the U.S. MOEs. That GMEs make less use of export restrictions seems to indicate that they carry out the international division of labor better than the other stages of multinationality.

TABLE 9.9

Export Restrictions by Multinational Subsidiaries According to Parent Country, 1976
(percentage of firms that are not allowed to cover these markets)

| Export Destination | United States | Netherlands | Parent Country West Germany | France | Great Britain |
|---|---|---|---|---|---|
| United States | 72 | 30 | 20 | 30 | 59 |
| Netherlands | 8 | 67 | 25 | 20 | 23 |
| West Germany | 12 | 48 | 50 | 37 | 32 |
| France | 10 | 37 | 30 | 63 | 29 |
| Great Britain | 24 | 44 | 25 | 30 | 68 |
| Sweden | 17 | 33 | 25 | 23 | 45 |
| Latin America | 57 | 19 | 25 | 27 | 45 |
| Africa | 29 | 22 | 25 | 33 | 45 |
| Asia | 46 | 29 | 25 | 30 | 50 |
| Eastern bloc countries | 15 | 19 | 25 | 20 | 50 |

Source: F. Haex, E. Halsberghe, and D. Van Den Bulcke, Buitenlandse en Belgische Ondernemingen in de Nationale Industrie (Ghent: SERUG, 1979), p. 352.

TABLE 9.10

Export Restrictions According to Parent Country and
Degree of Multinationality, 1976
(percentage of firms that are not
allowed to cover those markets)

| Export Destination | Parent Country and Degree of Multinationality | | | | | |
|---|---|---|---|---|---|---|
| | United States | | | Non-United States | | |
| | GMEs | MOEs | EMEs | GMEs | MOEs | EMEs |
| United States | 58 | 75 | 95 | 39 | 51 | 26 |
| France | 14 | 7 | 5 | 39 | 49 | 36 |
| Netherlands | 12 | 7 | — | 35 | 34 | 33 |
| West Germany | 14 | 10 | 5 | 42 | 40 | 44 |
| Great Britain | 24 | 32 | 9 | 45 | 57 | 31 |
| Sweden | 14 | 32 | — | 32 | 46 | 31 |
| Africa | 31 | 39 | 14 | 32 | 46 | 28 |
| Asia | 38 | 61 | 50 | 32 | 51 | 31 |
| Latin America | 50 | 68 | 59 | 29 | 46 | 26 |
| Eastern bloc countries | 14 | 21 | 5 | 29 | 43 | 20 |

Source: D. Van Den Bulcke and E. Halsberghe, "Degree of
Multinationality and Foreign Headquarter-Subsidiary Relationship
in a Belgian Context," paper presented at International Research
Symposium, Stockholm, June 2-4, 1980, p. 36.

While judging the practices of export restrictions one should
not forget that some of these market reservations may be institu-
tionalizations of a weaker competitive situation in particular regions (for example, because of higher transport costs) and that certain subsidiaries for the same reasons will not use the freedom they
theoretically enjoy. Export restrictions are often linked to licensing agreements, even between independent partners. It should also
be realized that if subsidiaries are prohibited to export to certain
markets, they generally get the assurance that the parent company
or other subsidiaries will not invade their own privileged markets.
In 1968 respectively 80, 60, 40, and 30 percent of foreign subsidiaries in Belgium were attributed to the Belgium Luxembourg
Economic Union, Benelux, European Community of the Six, and
Europe as their exclusive sales area. [27]

## EXPORT PERFORMANCE OF
## BELGIAN MULTINATIONALS

The white paper on industrial policy and trade policy stressed the need for more foreign direct investment abroad in order to increase Belgian exports, mainly of investment goods. It is thought that foreign subsidiaries will increase exports from Belgium and improve and diversify the Belgian trade position abroad. [28]

It has been estimated that the so-called associated exports of semifinished products, parts, and finished products from Belgium to foreign subsidiaries amounted to 14 percent of total exports. Most of these exports were finished products that were sold without any transformation by the subsidiary abroad. An extrapolation from Belgian MNEs that participated in the inquiry (about 30) to the global population of 96 Belgian manufacturing MNEs showed that those associated exports amounted to 25 billion BFR in 1976 (that is, 2.5 percent of Belgian exports). [29]

These exports cannot completely be attributed to Belgian subsidiaries abroad, however. Part of these exports would have been realized even if there had not been any subsidiaries abroad. To estimate this effect it would be necessary to formulate hypotheses about the actual influence. About 55 percent of Belgian MNEs answered that investment abroad had not affected their export performance. One out of three Belgian MNEs thought that exports had increased, and one out of ten claimed that exports had declined because of their subsidiaries abroad. Although these answers by managers of Belgian MNEs are subjective, they indicate that the contribution to exports by foreign subsidiaries should not be exaggerated. [30] It has been mentioned before that the export propensity of Belgian MNEs (67 percent) was higher than for Belgian uninational firms, but not very different from foreign subsidiaries in Belgium.

A study by Jacquemin and Petit has been much quoted as it established a link between increased investment abroad and higher exports. [31] Their regression analysis indicated that the presence of a subsidiary abroad had a positive effect on exports and that the effect declined with an increasing size of the company. These authors inadvertently made no distinction between Belgian MNEs and foreign subsidiaries in Belgium, because they were misled by a wrong phrasing in the questionnaire of the Belgian Office for Foreign Trade, which collected the data. More than 90 percent of the responding firms actually were foreign-owned subsidiaries.

Out of a list of the largest Belgian enterprises Haex and Van Den Bulcke selected 210 companies with sales of at least 200 million BFR (1976). [32] The sample consisted of 83 uninational Belgian firms, 80 foreign subsidiaries, and 47 Belgian MNEs. A regression analysis showed on the one hand a small negative correlation between exports and the possession of an establishment abroad by a Belgian MNE and on the other hand a slight positive correlation between exports and the membership of a foreign multinational group. The multinational character of Belgian enterprises has a negative influence in all sectors, although the relationship is not significant in metals (see Table 9.11). In order to eliminate the effect of heteroscedasticity (concerning sales and exports), the analysis was also carried out according to size of total sales. This calculation pointed to a nonsignificant negative correlation for Belgian MNEs with sales lower than \$50 million and a significant positive effect (at the 0.15 level) for Belgian MNEs with sales of more than \$50 million.

TABLE 9.11

Belgian Multinational Enterprises and Exports:
Regression Coefficients

| | S | $D_1$ | $D_2$ | $R_a^{2*}$ | DW[+] |
|---|---|---|---|---|---|
| Food | 0.3488 $(7.91)^a$ | -5,501 $(0.81)$ | -21,098 $(-2.55)^{a*}$ | 0.78 | 1.11 |
| Textiles | 0.4323 $(8.23)^a$ | 3,731 $(1.07)^b$ | -2,765 $(-1.04)^c$ | 0.71 | 2.32 |
| Chemicals | 0.8466 $(32.85)^a$ | 2,934 $(0.40)^d$ | -15,035 $(-1.53)^b$ | 0.97 | 1.42 |
| Metals | 0.5942 $(23.71)^a$ | 1,943 $(0.20)^d$ | -2,087 $(-0.24)^d$ | 0.89 | 2.08 |
| Total | 0.6270 $(33.69)^a$ | 7,355 $(1.33)^b$ | -7,140 $(-1.05)^b$ | 0.88 | 1.82 |

Note: The regression coefficients are of the relation X = a + bS + cD$_1$ + dD$_2$, where X = volume of exports (1976), S = sales (1976), D$_1$ = dummy—subsidiary of foreign MNE, D$_2$ = dummy Belgian MNE.

*Coefficient of determination adopted to degree of freedom.
[+]Durbin-Watson statistic.
[a]Significant at the 0.01 level.
[b]Significant at the 0.05 level.
[c]Significant at the 0.15 level.
[d]Not significant.

Source: F. Haex and D. Van Den Bulcke, Belgische Multinationale Ondernemingen (Diepenbeek: VWOL, 1979), p. 131.

CONCLUSION

As foreign trade and foreign direct investment are very important in Belgium, it is not surprising that foreign subsidiaries play a significant role in Belgian exports. The global rationalization policy of MNEs does not guarantee the best possible effect on the foreign trade performance of the host country. It is sometimes feared that the centralization at headquarters of the export decisions will not be beneficial to host country exports, especially when some lucrative markets are excluded from the export area that can be covered.

Some of the main findings of this study were: that foreign MNEs on the one hand and Belgian MNEs on the other hand outperform Belgian uninational enterprises as far as export propensity is concerned; that they produce (and export) relatively more industrial and investment goods and are much more active in research-based sectors; and that they export to more industrial countries and developing continents than Belgian firms. They actually answer much better to the repeated pleas by Belgian ministers of foreign trade to diversify the product composition and geographic spread of Belgian exports in order to improve Belgium's competitive position in world markets and to assure continuing exports and more employment.

Belgian authorities should realize that in view of the dominant position of MNEs in their economy, it becomes increasingly expensive to carry out a nondifferentiated policy of export promotion. If one takes into account that about half of the exports of foreign subsidiaries are intragroup exports and are less likely to be sensitive to particular measures of export promotion; that in many cases multinational subsidiaries are not authorized to take independent export decisions; that the home markets of the MNEs and certain other near or distant markets are prohibited territory for the subsidiaries, it comes as a surprise that, notwithstanding these limitations, multinational subsidiaries are generally doing better than indigenous firms. MNEs have achieved an international division of labor on the basis of their global strategy, which seems out of reach for uninational firms. Should the government therefore not concentrate its export promotion efforts on uninational firms? The export propensity of foreign subsidiaries is not very different according to the degree of multinationality and changed only slightly between 1968 and 1975 from 65 to 68 percent. Indigenous firms do not have the intragroup channels of MNEs at their disposal or do not benefit from the international brand names and research and marketing experience of a parent company. A recent study of the province of Limburg in Belgium illustrated that only one out of five firms are experienced exporters that are actively trying to penetrate foreign markets.

Half of those companies were passive exporters that had not acquired the necessary routine in export business.[33]  The Belgian government should spend more time in looking for an appropriate and segmented export policy,[34] taking into account the level of experience and dynamic attitude of uninational firms, instead of squandering funds on multinational subsidiaries that would export anyway or convincing local companies to venture abroad in order to increase exports.  Although it may well be necessary to invest abroad in order to protect or conquer foreign markets, no direct positive link between direct foreign investment and increased exports is to be expected.

If policy makers opt—as they should—for an approach that segments firms according to the stages of international development and the export expertise they have built up in order to determine their needs in terms of export assistance, they should also gather information about the nationality of the parent company and—to a lesser extent—about the degree of multinationality.

## NOTES

1. A. R. Tejano, "Belgian Exports and Employment," Tijdschrift voor Economie en Management, no. 4 (1975), pp. 485, 494.

2. D. Van Den Bulcke and E. Halsberghe, Employment Effects of Multinational Enterprises: A Belgian Case Study, Working paper no. 1 (Geneva: International Labour Office, 1979).

3. D. Van Den Bulcke et al., Les entreprises étrangères dans l'industrie belge (Foreign Corporations in Belgian Industries) (Brussels: Belgian Office of Productivity Increase, 1971), pp. 143-64; F. Haex, E. Halsberghe, and D. Van Den Bulcke, Buitenlandse en Belgische Ondernemingen in de Nationale Industrie (Ghent: SERUG, 1979), pp. 95-99.

4. For more details, see D. Van Den Bulcke et al., Investment and Divestment Policies of Multinational Corporations in Europe (London: Saxon House, ECSIM, 1979), pp. 1-59.

5. L. Tindemans and W. Claes, Communication of the government concerning "Une nouvelle politique industrielle" (A New Industrial Policy), Chamber of Representatives, Session 1977-78 (Brussels, February 22, 1978), pp. 19, 67.  See also D. Van Den Bulcke, "Belgian Industrial Policy and Foreign Multinational Corporations: Objectives versus Performance" (Berlin: International Institute of Management, 1980), paper presented at a Conference on MNC-Government Relations: Policy Issues.

6. J. H. Dunning, American Investment in British Manufacturing Industry (London: Allen & Unwin, 1958), p. 64; F. Stubenitsky, American Direct Investment in the Netherlands Industry (Amsterdam: Rotterdam University Press, 1970), pp. 109-10; Divo-Institut, Amerikanischer Tochtergesellschaften in der Bundesrepublik (American Subsidiaries in the Federal Republic of Germany) (Frankfurt am Main, 1968), p. 315; R. Deane, Foreign Investment in New Zealand Manufacturing (Wellington: Sweet and Maxwell, 1979); D. T. Brash, American Investment in Australian Industry (Cambridge: ANU Press, 1966), p. 220; and H. P. Gray, Foreign Direct Investment in Canada (Ottawa: Queen's Printer, 1972).

7. Dunning, p. 72; and R. Moyer, "Performance of U.S. Operations in Britain," Journal of International Business Studies, Fall 1971, pp. 37-40.

8. For a more detailed analysis, see Haex, Halsberghe, and Van Den Bulcke.

9. A. E. Safarian, Foreign Ownership of Canadian Industry (Toronto: University of Toronto Press, 1966), p. 128.

10. D. Van Den Bulcke, De Multinationale Ondernemingen (The Multinational Corporation) (Ghent: SERUG, 1975), pp. 175-76, and D. Van Den Bulcke and E. Halsberghe, "Degree of Multinationality and Foreign Headquarter-Subsidiary Relationship in a Belgian Context," Paper presented at International Research Symposium, Stockholm, June 2-4, 1980.

11. D. W. Larson, "Manufacturing Production Techniques and the Evolution of Belgian Trade Specialization," International Economics Research Paper, no. 20 (Louvain: KUL, 1978), p. 45.

12. Banque Nationale de Belgique, Annual Report (Brussels, 1978).

13. Een beleid voor de Buitenlandse Handel (A Foreign Trade Policy) (Brussels: Department of Foreign Trade, 1979), pp. 29-32.

14. Haex, Halsberghe, and Van Den Bulcke, p. 133; and "Entreprises multinationales et entreprises nationales. Résultats comparés en Belgique" (Multinational and National Firms. Comparative Results in Belgium), Reflets et perspectives de la vie économique, no. 3/4 (1980), pp. 205-06.

15. Een beleid voor de Buitenlandse Handel, pp. 26-27, 63.

16. Larson, pp. 45-46.

17. Van Den Bulcke et al., Investment and Divestment Policies, pp. 200-01.

18. E. Cracco et al., La politique d'exportation des entreprises wallonnes (The Export Policies of Wallonian Firms) (Louvain: UCL, CRGI, 1977), pp. 11-15.

19. Gray, p. 174.

20. Deane, p. 226.

21. Van Den Bulcke, De Multinationale Ondernemingen, pp. 190-91; and E. Halsberghe and D. Van Den Bulcke, Beleidsautonomie van multinationale dochterondernemingen (Autonomy of Multinational Subsidiaries) (Ghent: SERUG, 1981).

22. Ibid.

23. Van Den Bulcke, De Multinationale Ondernemingen, p. 191.

24. Van Den Bulcke and Halsberghe, "Degree of Multinationality," p. 31.

25. Gray, pp. 163-64; Brash, p. 228; and Deane, p. 320.

26. M. Steuer et al., The Impact of Foreign Direct Investment on the United Kingdom (London: HMSO, 1973), pp. 148-52.

27. Van Den Bulcke, De Multinationale Ondernemingen, p. 190.

28. Tindemans and Claes; and Een beleid voor de Buitenlandse Handel, pp. 17, 32.

29. F. Haex and D. Van Den Bulcke, Belgische Multinationale Ondernemingen (Belgian Multinational Corporations) (Diepenbeek: VWOL, 1979), p. 126.

30. The employment effect of this so-called export stimulation effect was estimated to be situated between 2,650 and 5,300 jobs according to an export percentage via foreign subsidiaries of 20 and 40 (Haex and Van Den Bulcke, p. 143). The total effect was negative because of the "job displacement effect."

31. A. Jacquemin and J. Petit, "Les exportations des entreprises belges: Eléments d'explications structurelles" (The Exports of Belgian Firms: Elements for Structural Explanation), Working Paper no. 753 (Louvain: UCL, CRIDE, 1975).

32. Haex and Van Den Bulcke, pp. 129-33.

33. D. Van Den Bulcke and C. Lambie, "Exportervaring en exportdynamisme van de Limburgse industriële ondernemingen: Classificatiecriteria en beleidsimplicaties," Economie in Limburg, no. 1 (1981).

34. Compare M. R. Czinkota and W. J. Johnston, "Segmenting U.S. Firms for Export Development, "Journal of Business Research 9, no. 4 (1981).

# 10

## THE ROLE OF EXPORTING IN THE MARKET SERVICING POLICIES OF MULTINATIONAL MANUFACTURING ENTERPRISES: THEORETICAL AND EMPIRICAL PERSPECTIVES

Peter J. Buckley

This chapter seeks to examine the role of exports in the market servicing policies of both growing firms and established multinational enterprises (MNEs). The attention that has focused on direct foreign investment has rather deflected interest from the role of exporting, despite its crucial role in the internationalization process and its continuing importance as a means of servicing foreign markets, even in the world's largest firms. The chapter is cast entirely at the level of the individual firm, although reference to macro issues is made where appropriate.

In servicing a foreign market, a multinational manufacturing firm has a choice between three main groups of policy tools: exporting, licensing productive knowledge to a local firm, or foreign direct investment (FDI). In practice, each of these three broad groups covers a variety of contractual arrangements: direct versus indirect (perhaps through a merchanting house) exports, the sale of blueprints to a "turnkey operation," and sales subsidiaries versus production subsidiaries. Indeed the distinctions between the three types blur at the edges.

However, there are distinct analytical differences between the three policies. Exporting is distinguished from foreign licensing and direct investment essentially because production takes place outside the country of consumption—this applies even when "third country" manufacture is involved. Licensing is distinguished from the other two because of the ownership of production changes in the production process—host country ownership replaces the multinational's control of production. Thus an "ownership effect" and a "location effect" separate the three forms of market servicing (Dunning, 1977; Buckley and Casson, 1978).

Final goods markets cannot be considered in isolation from the markets for the intermediate goods involved in the production process. Intermediate goods are also subject to location and ownership effects. In order to service a final product market it may be advantageous to locate different stages of production in different locations. The ownership of "the good" may also change as we move through the process. An example of this is licensing where essential proprietory knowledge is sold from one producer to another. Vertically and horizontally integrated production may involve the export of intermediate goods across national frontiers but internal to the multinational enterprise (Buckley and Casson, 1976, 1978; Casson, 1979).

Exporting therefore may be an internal process, in which case prices will be largely determined by the accounting procedures of the firm in the form of transfer prices. Alternatively, it may be, at an intermediate or final stage, external, in which case prices are determined by the normal elements of supply and demand. One important form of internal export for many multinationals is "offshore production," where semifinished goods are processed, assembled, or finished in a low-cost country—often for export back to the source country (Moxon, 1974; Lall, 1980; Finger, 1975, 1976, 1977).

This exporting is a crucial policy tool not only in final goods markets but also in internal intermediate goods markets linking the various subsidiaries. The establishment and control of such exporting networks are crucial variables in a multinational manufacturing firm's strategy.

When we observe the market servicing strategy of a particular MNE, the picture is a snapshot at a moment in time of a dynamic process. The mix of exporting, foreign licensing, and direct investment constantly evolves under internal and external pressures. The role of time in a market servicing strategy is an important one and it is for this reason that the remainder of the chapter discusses separately the role of exports in the internationalization process and in established multinational firms.


THE ROLE OF EXPORTS IN THE GROWTH AND
INTERNATIONALIZATION PROCESS OF THE FIRM

Several key issues have been identified in the literature relating to the role of exports in the growth and internationalization process of the firm. First, exporting can be seen as an innovative strategy and as the first step in internationalizing; possibly a step that ends in failure. Second, the direction of export growth has come under scrutiny. Third, the role of exports in launching a process of deepening international commitment, possibly leading to direct foreign investment, has been emphasized.

## Exports as the First Step in Internationalization

It is argued strongly by several analysts that export behavior is rooted in the past development of the firm. The exporting process is traced back to preexport behavior. The sequence is envisaged as follows:

- a small firm, geared entirely to local demand, has no extra-regional or international links,
- engages in extraregional expansion, widening its experience and "market consciousness,"
- may fill unsolicited export orders but engages in no serious export planning,
- engages (perhaps prematurely) in an investigation of exporting,
- if successful, becomes an "experimental exporter,"
- if successful, becomes an experienced exporter, and
- diversifies the markets to which it is exporting (Bilkey, 1978; Bilkey and Tesar, 1977; Carlson, 1975; Johanson and Vahlne, 1977; Simmonds and Smith, 1968; Welch and Wiedersheim-Paul, 1980b).

The first six stages of this development are subject to several critical influences. First, a learning or feedback process operates as the firm progresses from one stage to the rest. Severe negative feedback at any stage may retard or prevent progression to the next stage (Welch and Wiedersheim-Paul, 1980a, b; Aharoni, 1966). Consequently when we survey or observe exporters we are looking back over a process and "missing out" those firms that may have traversed the first five stages and regressed. This has important implications for policy: support may be needed for firms at a much earlier stage than the exporting or experimental exporting stages at which it is conventionally given.

Second, external pressures on the firm play an important, perhaps decisive, role in the firm's development. Such "outside change agents" may bring on the export move before the firm is ready or may distort the export development of the firm [examples are potential foreign agents approaching primarily domestically oriented firms (Newbould, Buckley, and Thurwell, 1978)]. Such change agents include unsolicited orders from customers, potential foreign agents, host or even foreign country governments, suppliers or competitors. Threats to existing business seem as powerful a spur in exporting as in other activities (Vernon, 1966, 1971).

Third, studies point to the crucial role of management activity and orientation. Exporting, particularly before it becomes routinized, is a highly management-intensive activity. In small owner-manager firms, managerial capacity may be fully extended on normal "noninnovatory" tasks. Consequently, attention has focused on excess managerial capacity as an important determinant of export success (Penrose, 1969; Wolf, 1975, 1977). Affinity with an international outlook and an awareness of the problems are critical elements in top management perception (Abdel-Malik, 1974; Roux, 1979).

Linking the above three factors is the crucial role of information, which plays a vital role in the feedback process. Shortages of information internal to the firm can lead to excessive reliance on the opinions and judgments of interested parties, often with disastrous results. Shortages of skilled management time can lead to decisions being taken on highly imperfect or fragmentary information with resulting highly uncertain outcomes. Perception of risk in exporting is strongly correlated with available information resources.

Suggestions for improvement of export performance at the level of the firm include:

Greater inputs in market research, training, and selecting foreign intermediaries and increasing stepwise penetration of foreign markets (Khan, 1978);
Concentrating on a small number of key markets and devoting larger numbers of specialist salesmen, replacing agents by sales subsidiaries and allocating more resources to foreign market penetration (ITI Research, 1975).

Both of these sets of suggestions, derived from experience of Swedish and U.K. exporters, advocate increasing international involvement and it seems that in many cases firms require an overseas presence to successfully service particular foreign markets (Newbould, Buckley, and Thurwell, 1978; see also Duguid and Jacques, 1971). The issue then becomes one of judging the timing and the most fruitful markets in the switch from exports to FDI.

Before going on to a formal analysis of the switch from exporting to direct investment in a particular market, it is worthwhile to examine two empirical studies of the route to full foreign production from domestic activities and the intermediate states in this process. Figure 10.1 shows that only two routes through intermediate stages omit the exporting phase (routes A and G) and in a combined sample of 78 direct investors in production facilities, only 12 firms took this route. Over half of these 12 firms were prevented from

FIGURE 10.1

Route to a Foreign Production Subsidiary

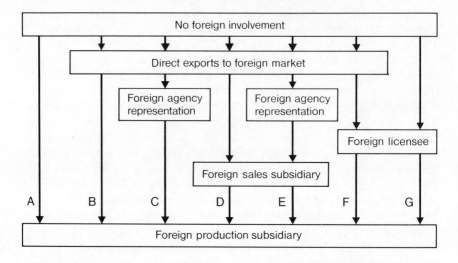

Routes Taken by Two Groups of Direct Investors in Production

|   | UK smaller firm first time direct investors | Continental European direct investors in UK |
|---|---|---|
| A | 7 | 4 |
| B | 9 | 3 |
| C | 20 | 19 |
| D | 2 | 3 |
| E | 5 | 4 |
| F | – | 1 |
| G | – | 1 |
| Total | 43 | 35 |

Sources: Column 1: Newbould, Buckley, and Thurwell (1978); Buckley, Newbould, and Thurwell (1979). Column 2: Buckley, Newbould, and Berkova (1981).

exporting by the nature of their product—transport cost barriers or a high "service" element effectively ruled out exporting as a means of servicing the foreign markets (Newbould, Buckley, and Thurwell, 1978; Buckley, Newbould, and Berkova, 1981).

## The Direction of Exports

On export destination, the "sequentialist" school, particularly associated with the University of Uppsala, argues that exporting tends to begin with the psychologically (or culturally) closest country, extending progressively to countries with increasing psychic distance. Psychic distance is defined as "the sum of factors preventing the flow of information to and from the market" (Johanson and Vahlne, 1977, p. 24). Psychic distance therefore includes language, education, business practice, culture, and industrial development. The economic and cultural links of the exporter's home country play a major role in the direction of outward links.

The exporter behaves by making incremental adjustments to changing conditions of the environment and the pressures upon him to export are likely to be greater the closer are the psychic or informational links between him and the (potential) market. Increasing market commitment leads to increasing involvement with the market. Increasing market knowledge is achieved by search behavior on the part of the exporter—search costs of course being lower the smaller is the psychic distance to the potential market (Wiedersheim-Paul, 1972; Wiedersheim-Paul, Olson, and Welch, 1978).

The problem with this approach arises from the difficulty of in any way quantifying psychic distance. It is reasonably clear, on an intuitive level, which elements constitute psychic distance, but the weighting of the elements to make up one all-embracing measure of the concept is far from clear. To give precision to the concept, a great deal of empirical work is required.

## The Switch from Exporting to Direct Investment

Several approaches have been suggested for the switch from exporting (or licensing) to investment. Two comparative static approaches are given by Horst (1972a,b) and Hirsh (1976). Hirsh's analysis is based on cost minimization and he derives the following inequalities to give firms in country A simple decision rules on the best way to service foreign market B, either from source country A by export or by direct investment in B. (Subscripts a and b indicate location.) Therefore, for firms in A:

$$\text{Export to B if} \quad P_a + M < P_b + K \quad (1)$$

$$\text{and} \quad P_a + M < P_b + C \quad (2)$$

$$\text{Invest in B if} \quad P_b + C < P_b + K \quad (3)$$

$$\text{and} \quad P_b + C < P_a + M \quad (4)$$

Where $P_a$ and $P_b$ are production costs in the two countries, M is the difference between export and domestic marketing costs, C represents the extra costs of controlling a foreign rather than a domestic operation, and K represents firm specific know-how and other intangible income-producing assets. All quantities are present values of costs covering the life span of a specific investment project. The meaning of inequalities (1) and (2) is that exports should be undertaken if costs of domestic production and export marketing costs are below costs of doing business abroad. Inequalities (3) and (4) suggest that investment should be undertaken when total costs of production abroad (including control costs) are below costs of utilizing the firm-specific advantages (K) in production abroad and below the costs of exporting from parent country A.

It should be noted that Hirsh's analysis assumes that demand is insensitive to the location of supply and can therefore be ignored. The analysis is also concerned with an initial investment abroad assuming no excess capacity in parent country A (otherwise this would mean exporting until marginal costs of further exporting exceeded revenues). It is thus applicable to the siting of a new additional production facility. No analysis is given of the generation of K (firm-specific know-how) and thus no idea of relative costs of investing in R & D (to attempt to generate K) versus other types of investment. K is given as a return from a past sunk cost. No light is shed on the timing of the investment and demand factors are removed by assumption.

Horst's (1971) analysis concentrates on the influence of tariff and tax rates in the "invest versus export" decision. Rather than being able to throw up simple rules, Horst shows that the analysis breaks down into special cases according to the conditions under which the firm is operating and the level of taxes and tariffs in home and foreign countries. Horst notes the interesting finding that high tariffs are a mixed blessing for MNEs; on the one hand they make exporting more costly, on the other they enhance the firm's prospects for increasing profits by allowing increased price discrimination between markets. If the price elasticity of demand is lower in the protected market than elsewhere, then an increase in the tariff will allow the firm to raise its price locally, thereby reducing demand and discouraging investment. Investment policy is further influenced by the conditions of production of the firm and market size: the sensitivity of foreign investment to tariff policy being greatest when the marginal cost of production is decreasing with respect to output. If the protected market is a relatively large one, then there is a certain tariff level beyond which it is optimal for the firm to concentrate all production in that market, even if resource costs are higher in the protected market, because saving of tariff costs outweighs additional resource costs. The complexity of decision rules even in this simple model is illuminating. Horst adds industry-specific influences on foreign investment (firm size, R & D intensity, concentration of the industry, and desire for resource control) to the firm-specific factors above in a further study (1972a).

The analyses of Hirsh and Horst highlight different aspects of the foreign investment decision. Hirsh's emphasis on marketing and technological costs is complementary to Horst's inclusion of tariff and tax rates. Both include relative production costs at home and abroad, although Horst emphasizes returns to scale. However, neither approach is particularly concerned with the timing of the switch to FDI, which the following paragraphs explore.

Analyses that are concerned with the dynamics of foreign expansion of the firm should be able to specify those factors that govern the timing of the initial FDI. Aliber (1970, 1971) attempts to do this by reference to the capitalization of returns from the firm's alternatives: exporting, licensing, and foreign investment. Aliber assumes that the firm possesses a "patent" or monopolistic advantage. He argues that the costs of doing business abroad prevent investment from being the preferred strategy until a certain market size. Only at a particular size of market will the higher capitalization ratio, which applies to source-country firms, overcome the cost advantage of a local producer (which can be exploited via licensing the "patent" to a local firm). In Aliber's system, the source-country firm will always be a higher-cost producer than the host-country firm, provided the latter has access to the patent at competitive rates. This limits the analysis by ruling out those situations where the source-country firm (through familiarity with the technology, firmwide economies of scale, and so on) has compensating advantages vis-a-vis host-country competitors.

The dynamics of the switch from exporting to licensing and then to FDI are thus dependent, according to Aliber, on the host country market size and the differentials in capitalization ratios between assets denominated in different currencies. The latter is determined by the currency premium in the capital market—the compensation that investors require so they will bear uncertainty concerning fluctuations in exchange rates. Tariffs are easily incorporated into this framework—an increase in the host country tariff will bias the foreign patent owner toward use of the patent in the host country; the choice between its use in licensing or internally via FDI remains unchanged, the choice depending on whether host market size allows the capitalization factor to outweigh the cost of doing business abroad.

Raymond Vernon in his classic Product Cycle Hypothesis (1966) views the switch from exports to FDI (licensing is ignored) in terms of costs alone:

> As long as the marginal production cost plus the transport cost of the goods exported from the United States is lower than the average cost of prospective production in the market of import, United States producers will presumably prefer to avoid an investment. But that calculation depends on the producer's ability to project the cost of production in a market in which factor costs and the appropriate technology differ from those at home.

This move (in the "maturing" phase of the cycle) can be triggered, or reinforced, by the desire to defend a market established through exports, and most analysts agree that this is best done by a direct investment.

In a recent theoretical paper, Buckley and Casson (1981) provide a model that specifies the optimal timing of a "switch" to direct investment by reference to the costs of servicing the foreign market, demand conditions in that market, and host market growth. The market servicing decision is more complex than it appears at first sight, particularly when the initial costs of setting up a foreign investment are time-dependent.

This analysis of the switch from exporting to FDI leads us to the exporting behavior of "established" multinational firms. Here a subtle change of emphasis occurs: The question is no longer "why do firms not export?" but "why do firms with such resources continue to export rather than servicing the markets via direct investment?"


## THE ROLE OF EXPORTS IN THE MARKET
## SERVICING PATTERN OF ESTABLISHED
## MULTINATIONAL ENTERPRISES

The literature on multinational enterprises concentrates very largely on their role as foreign direct investors (see Horst, 1974).

Consequently the exporting role of multinational firms has been rather neglected. However, multinational firms dominate international trade as well as investment and the internal exports of such firms constitute a large part of world trade. The importance of exporting is linked with the role of locational factors in the theoretical approach to the MNE and to multinationals as special cases of the multiplant firm. Exports in the market servicing strategy of MNEs are important because they allow economies of scale at plant level to be achieved.

It is fair to suggest that location theory elements in the modern theory of the MNE have been neglected. Yet any viable explanation of the growth, pattern, and operations (particularly market servicing policies) must include elements of location theory. Under the general theory of the multinational firm, the MNE can be seen as simply a major vehicle for the transfer of mobile resources (technology, capital, management skills) to areas with immobile (or fixed) complementary inputs (markets, raw materials, labor). The simple dichotomy of transferable ownership advantages (internal to firms) and fixed location-specific endowments is used with great effect in Dunning (1977) to integrate foreign trade and foreign investment in terms of the location of economic activity (see also Dunning, 1979, 1980).

The location-specific endowments of particular importance to MNEs are raw materials, leading to vertical FDI; cheap labor, leading to "offshore production" facilities (Moxon, 1974); and protected or fragmented markets, leading to FDI as the preferred means of market servicing over exporting. Location factors therefore enter the theory not only in their own right, as an influence on the relative costs facing an MNE with a choice of locations, but also provide the motives for FDI.

The important connections between location factors and the (internal) organization of MNEs should however be given due weight. First, the MNE will normally be a multistage, multifunction firm and the location of different stages and functions will be subject to different locational influences connected by (international) flows of intermediate products. Second, the internalization of markets will affect location in two important ways:

The MNE will have an incentive to minimize government intervention through transfer pricing, for instance, to reduce the overall tax liability by imputing high mark-ups in the lowest tax countries and possibly by altering its location strategy completely to take in a low-intervention "tax haven." (For evidence on transfer pricing, see Lall [1973, 1978], and for the nature and amount of intracompany trade and its determinants, see Buckley and Pearce [1979, 1981]).

The increased communication flows in an internal market may bias high communication cost activities toward the "center"—usually toward the source country where critical activities are focused on the head office. (A forceful extension of this argument is given by Hymer [1971]).

In a restatement of the Product Cycle Hypothesis, Vernon (1977a) gives a great deal of weight to the interplay between the stage of the industry's development and the relevant locational influences upon it. The location of research activities (in the center) and the changing locational influences on production provide the dynamic for the theory.

Standard location theory can be shown to be of direct relevance to the strategy of MNEs as illustrated by Dunning's paper on the location of MNEs in an enlarged EEC (1977) and Horst's work on the servicing of the Canadian market by U.S. MNEs (1971). The reduction, removal, or increase of tariffs between nations will alter MNEs' market servicing decisions and cause a restructuring of the location of MNE activities. This area leads into an interesting discussion centered on the relative "comparative advantages" of firms and nations (Lundgren, 1977; Cornell, 1975) and thence to relative bargaining capabilities (Vaitsos, 1974).

Trade Creating and Trade Diverting Investment

From a consideration of location endowments directly, the attempts at integrating trade theory with the theory of the MNE have brought about the investigation of the impact that MNEs have on trade and on national comparative advantage. Kojima (1975, 1978) has suggested that U.S. MNEs have been carrying out "antitrade-oriented" direct investment, while Japanese investment is in those areas where Japan is losing its comparative advantage. It is true that Japanese investment is oriented toward the control of (foreign) raw materials and that it is prevalent also in labor-intensive industries such as textiles where direct investments are made in countries where the wage rate (and pollution regulation) is lower than Japan. Despite a careful integration of investment theory with the theory of comparative advantage (Kojima, 1978), the normative element in Kojima's approach cannot be denied. The labor-intensive FDI of Japan (very similar to other offshore investments) can also replace host-country indigenous industry. Moreover, doubts have been expressed by its progenitors (Vernon, 1971, 1977a and b, 1979) as to the efficacy of the Product Cycle Model on which Kojima relies to obtain his trade-displacing result of U.S.-type FDI. It is also possible to project that Japanese development will bring its FDI much closer to the U.S. pattern. Kojima's model has the virtue of placing location endowments at the center of MNEs' location decisions and thus it moves toward the full integration of trade theory with the theory of the MNE. In addition he points to the influences on MNE behavior that derive from source-country conditions.

Exporting in Multiplant Firms

This avenue of investigation leads us into the area of MNEs as special cases of multiplant firms. The theory of multiplant firms is addressed to the question, "Why should firms operate several plants of suboptimal size rather than a smaller number of plants that would be above minimum efficient scale?" This question is tackled by Scherer et al. (1975) and it is clear that the results are of direct relevance to the choice between exporting and direct investment. Scherer brings together findings from location theory, optimal lot size theory, monetary theory, and physical distribution theory to derive hypotheses concerning "optimal unbalanced specialization paths" for firms. In the international sphere it is clear that many markets are small and do not provide enough scope for even one optimal-size plant. In addition, buyers' desire for choice and variety dictates from the demand side that no one firm, let alone plant, shall dominate individual markets. Third, in many industries long-run unit production cost is relatively flat and cost penalties are not imposed severely on less than optimal plant scales. Finally, multiplant operation is often a rational response to problems of manufacturing highly specialized products with volatile demand or other features requiring close managerial supervision or technologies well suited to low-volume production. These findings can be integrated with the above theory and with location theory to yield a fruitful synthesis. The interplay of plant-level economies and firm-level economies has a major role in the market servicing (exports versus direct investment) decisions of MNEs (Dunning and Buckley, 1977).

Empirical Evidence

The empirical data that follow use information on the market servicing behavior of 523 of the world's largest manufacturing enterprises in 1977 (Buckley and Pearce, 1981). These firms represent a subsample of one made up of the 866 largest industrial enterprises covered by Fortune magazine data in that year. However, since our coverage is most complete among the larger firms, the sales of the 523 firms included here amounted to 78 percent of the sales of the full 866. These data were compiled during a recent study of the world's largest firms (Dunning and Pearce, 1980). The 523 firms were classified by nationality of ownership and by industry.

For the firms included in our main sample we were able to obtain answers to the following questions:

1. What percentage of your worldwide sales for 1977 (or financial year 1976/77) was accounted for by your foreign affiliates or associated companies, where sales of foreign affiliates and associated companies include all goods produced and sold abroad, but exclude finished goods imported from parent company for resale (that is, without any further processing or packaging)?

2. What percentage of the total sales of your domestic operations were exported in 1977 (or in the financial year 1976/77)?

Our major source for this information was a special survey carried out in 1979. This was supplemented by information obtained from company reports; information given in Table IV-1 in UN Commission on Transnational Corporations, Transnational Corporations in World Development (1978); Jane's Major Companies of Europe; and The Financial Times International Business Yearbook.

By applying the percentage figures to the absolute value of worldwide sales of the enterprises in 1977 (obtained from Fortune magazine, May 8 and August 14, 1978), we obtained the following data for each of the 523 companies: total worldwide group sales, total foreign production, total parent company production, and total parent company exports. From this information four market servicing ratios are derived, which are presented in Tables 10.1 and 10.2.

For a further subsample of 196 firms (covering 58 percent of the sales of the 523 firm sample, or 45 percent of those of the original 866), we obtained information (mainly from survey replies, but in some cases from company reports and Jane's Major Companies of Europe) on an additional question:

3. What percentage of total parent exports were exported to affiliate or associate companies?

This figure serves as a further result included in Tables 10.1 and 10.2.

From the information collected we can calculate five market servicing ratios. The first four of these, based on the sample of 523 firms for 1977, are:

## TABLE 10.1

The Average 1977 Values of the Five Ratios, by Area and Major Country

(percentages)

| | 1 Foreign Sales Ratio | 2 Foreign Production Ratio | 3 Parents' Exports Ratio | 4 Foreign Market Servicing Ratio | 5 Internal Exports Ratio |
|---|---|---|---|---|---|
| United States | 34.5 | 29.2 | 7.5 | 84.5 | 45.5 |
| Europe (total) | 57.8 | 37.5 | 32.6 | 64.8 | 29.7 |
| EEC (total) | 56.4 | 36.6 | 31.3 | 64.8 | 29.6 |
| Germany | 49.5 | 18.5 | 38.0 | 37.4 | 34.6 |
| France | 48.8 | 28.6 | 28.4 | 58.5 | 32.2 |
| Italy | 45.2 | 14.7 | 35.7 | 32.6 | 4.9 |
| Netherlands | 62.5 | 29.0 | 47.2 | 46.4 | 12.7 |
| Belgium | 86.7 | 43.9 | 76.3 | 50.6 | 15.2 |
| United Kingdom | 53.6 | 41.8 | 20.2 | 78.0 | 29.6 |
| Other Europe | 66.4 | 43.0 | 41.0 | 64.8 | 29.8 |
| Finland | 39.0 | 3.2 | 37.0 | 8.2 | 1.1 |
| Sweden | 66.0 | 33.1 | 49.2 | 50.1 | 36.1 |
| Switzerland | 93.4 | 82.9 | 61.3 | 88.7 | 53.4 |
| Spain | 10.4 | 0.2 | 10.2 | 2.0 | 0.0 |
| Japan | 29.7 | 6.7 | 24.6 | 22.6 | 17.0 |
| Other countries (total) | 40.6 | 20.4 | 25.3 | 50.3 | 22.8 |
| Canada | 54.1 | 31.8 | 32.7 | 58.8 | 39.3 |
| All country average | 41.6 | 29.5 | 17.1 | 71.0 | 32.8 |

Note: For definitions see text.
Sources: As described in text.

TABLE 10.2

The Average 1977 Values of the Five Ratios, by Industry
(percentages)

| | 1 Foreign Sales Ratio | 2 Foreign Production Ratio | 3 Parents' Exports Ratio | 4 Foreign Market Servicing Ratio | 5 Internal Exports Ratio |
|---|---|---|---|---|---|
| Aerospace | 35.7 | 8.1 | 30.0 | 22.8 | 1.8 |
| Office equipment (including computers) | 46.9 | 42.2 | 8.2 | 89.9 | 91.3 |
| Petroleum | 53.2 | 50.5 | 5.4 | 95.0 | 51.0 |
| Measurement, scientific, and photographic equipment | 46.1 | 33.2 | 19.3 | 72.0 | 58.2 |
| Electronics and electrical appliances | 39.6 | 22.0 | 22.5 | 55.6 | 36.5 |
| Chemicals and pharmaceuticals | 45.5 | 30.8 | 21.2 | 67.7 | 35.0 |
| Total high research intensity | 47.5 | 37.7 | 15.8 | 79.3 | 34.5 |

| | | | | | |
|---|---|---|---|---|---|
| Food | 37.4 | 33.3 | 6.1 | 89.2 | 9.2 |
| Tobacco | 47.5 | 44.0 | 6.2 | 92.7 | 0.5 |
| Paper and wood products | 32.2 | 19.7 | 15.5 | 61.3 | 9.5 |
| Rubber | 32.9 | 29.3 | 5.0 | 89.2 | NA |
| Building materials | 37.4 | 30.5 | 9.9 | 81.6 | 8.7 |
| Metal manufacturing and products | 34.4 | 13.1 | 24.5 | 38.2 | 12.8 |
| Total vertically integrated | 35.9 | 23.6 | 16.1 | 65.8 | 11.7 |
| Industrial and farm equipment | 44.1 | 22.4 | 28.0 | 50.7 | 52.6 |
| Shipbuilding, railroad, and transportation equipment | 46.1 | 4.8 | 43.4 | 10.3 | 0.1 |
| Motor vehicles | 36.6 | 21.0 | 19.8 | 57.3 | 62.4 |
| Beverages | 21.3 | 18.3 | 3.7 | 86.0 | 20.3 |
| Textiles, apparel, and leather goods | 30.2 | 19.2 | 13.6 | 63.6 | 12.8 |
| Publishing and printing | 13.7 | 10.4 | 3.7 | 75.9 | 5.4 |
| Other manufacturing | 16.4 | 6.6 | 10.5 | 40.1 | 5.9 |
| Total other industries | 35.8 | 19.4 | 20.3 | 54.2 | 51.5 |
| All industry average | 41.6 | 29.5 | 17.1 | 71.0 | 32.8 |

Note: For definitions see text.
NA = not available.
Source: As described in text.

The Foreign Sales Ratio, which is sales of foreign affiliates and associated companies (and goods imported from parent for resale) plus parent company's exports, divided by total worldwide sales of the group: $(b + d)/a$.

The Foreign Production Ratio, which is the sales of foreign affiliates and associated companies (and goods imported from the parent for resale) divided by the total worldwide sales of the group, that is, $b/a$ (the answer to question 1).

The Parent's Export Ratio, which is parent company's exports divided by parent company's production, that is, $d/c$ (the answer to question 2).

The Foreign Market Servicing Ratio,* which is the sales of foreign affiliates and associated companies (excluding goods imported from the parent for resale) divided by such sales of foreign affiliates and associated companies plus parent company exports, that is, $b/(b + d)$.

The fifth ratio is the Internal Exports Ratio, which is the exports of a parent firm to its foreign affiliates and associates divided by the parent firm's total exports (that is, the answer to question 3 above). As we have seen, 196 firms were covered in calculating this ratio.

Tables 10.1 and 10.2 give simple averages, by nationality of ownership and industry, respectively, for the five market servicing ratios in 1977. Table 10.1 reveals wide variations by nationality of ownership on each of the ratios. An average of 41.6 percent foreign sales ratio is made up of highly foreign-sales-oriented firms such as Switzerland (93.4 percent) and Belgium (86.7 percent) and much more home-market-oriented firms like Spain (10.4 percent) and Japan (29.7 percent). A more marked variation occurs in the foreign production ratio. Foreign production as a percentage of worldwide sales varies from 82.9 percent (Switzerland) to 0.2 percent (Spain) and 6.7 percent (Japan). Belgian firms have the highest ratio of parent exports to parent production (76.3 percent) and, interestingly, U.S. firms have the lowest among the groups we identify separately (7.5 percent). The foreign market servicing ratio (column 4) is greater, the higher the extent to which the firm meets its foreign market by foreign production rather than exports. Nationalities of firms relying most on foreign production are Switzerland (88.7 percent) and the United States (84.5 percent). The most export-oriented countries (in relation to foreign production) are

---

*For 9 of the 523 firms, which had no overseas production or parent's exports, this ratio could not be calculated.

Spain (2. 0 percent), Finland (8. 2 percent), and Japan (22. 6 percent). The internal exports ratio shows the importance of intrafirm exports in total exports and varies from 0. 0 percent (Spain) and 1.1 percent (Finland) to 45. 5 percent (United States) and 39. 3 percent (Canada).

Table 10. 2 analyzes the same ratio by industry and industry grouping. High foreign sales industries such as petroleum (53. 2 percent), which of course represents sales outside the firm's country of ownership, contrast with largely home-based sales industries, printing and publishing (13. 7 percent) and other manufacturing (16. 4 percent). Foreign production ratios vary more widely by industry from 50. 5 percent (petroleum) to 4. 8 percent (transportation equipment), 6. 6 percent (other manufacturing), and 8. 1 percent (aerospace). Exporting from the parent-country firm is most extensive in transportation equipment (43. 4 percent) and least common in beverages (3. 7 percent) and publishing and printing (3. 7 percent). The importance of foreign production rather than exporting is very pronounced in a number of industries as the foreign market servicing ratio shows: office equipment, petroleum, food, tobacco, rubber, and beverages all account for over 85 percent of market servicing by foreign production, whereas in aerospace the foreign market servicing ratio is as low as 22. 8 percent and in transport equipment 10. 3 percent, illustrating the low levels of foreign production. Internal exports as a proportion of total exports are extremely important in office equipment (91. 3 percent) and insignificant in aerospace, tobacco, and transport equipment.

Tables 10. 1 and 10. 2 provide partial evidence for the view that we can adduce a nationality effect and an industry effect in the analysis of market servicing policy. We can also begin to detect effects arising from the skills of individual firms (ownership effect) and from particular locations.

CONCLUSIONS

Foreign market servicing by multinational manufacturing firms evolves under the influence of several important factors. Changes in the foreign market servicing policy can be explained to a large extent by reference to the size of firm, to main industry of operation, and its nationality of ownership.

The fascination of shifting market servicing policies by multinationals arises in the identification of the pressures that bring about such changes. Several elements can be isolated. First, the interplay of location factors, immobile and specific to particular locations and countries, with "ownership factors," mobile and under

TABLE 10.3

The Structure of British Trade Abroad, 1965–77
(£ million)

|  | 1965 | 1968 | 1971 | 1974 | 1977 |
|---|---|---|---|---|---|
| Total foreign sales (X + L + I) | 13,708 | 18,376 | 23,553 | 38,475 | 74,527 |
| Manufactured exports (X) | 4,752 | 6,244 | 8,926 | 16,091 | 32,025 |
| Licensed sales (L) | 536 | 962 | 1,293 | 2,149 | 4,072 |
| Direct investment sales (I) | 8,420 | 11,171 | 13,334 | 20,236 | 38,430* |
| Exports as percent of total foreign sales | 34.7 | 34.0 | 37.9 | 41.8 | 43.0 |

*1978.

Source: Adapted and updated from Peter J. Buckley and Howard Davies, "The Place of Licensing in the Theory and Practice of Foreign Operations," University of Reading Working Papers in International Investment and Business Studies, no. 47 (1979).


TABLE 10.4

The Structure of Four Countries' Trade Compared

|  | Finland | West Germany | Sweden | United States |
|---|---|---|---|---|
| Exports as percent of total foreign sales, 1969 | 91.5 | 73 | 57 | 17 |

Source: Reijo Luostarinen, "Internationalization Process of the Firm," Working Papers in International Business, 1978/1, Helsinki School of Economics, 1978.

the control of individual enterprises, exercising a powerful influence on observed behavior. The uneven distribution of natural materials, final markets, labor, and other inputs induces inward investment to exploit such immobile endowments. The internalization of flows of information, knowledge, and intermediate product markets enable multinational firms to combine such mobile resources with locationally fixed inputs in order to achieve an optimum locational mix of productive facilities. The outcome of this process is the observable admixture of exporting and foreign production. Internal export flows of information and intermediate goods correspond to this locational pattern across industries and nationality of firms. Second, there is an interesting interplay between plant economies of scale, which encourage single-location production, combined with worldwide export of products, versus firm-level economies of scale such as spreading of research costs, splitting production on vertical lines so as to achieve optimum location of each stage of production, and expanding local demand by establishing a presence in a market. Third, there are cultural and sociopolitical elements, arising particularly from nationality of ownership, which encourage interpenetration by investment: unusual isolation over time may discourage outward investment, close cultural and political links will encourage foreign investment.

We have shown above that market servicing policies are not static but change over time in response to changing external conditions.

To turn finally and briefly to macro issues, Tables 10.3 and 10.4 show exports to continue to be an important proportion of total foreign involvement (defined as exports, plus sales related to foreign investment, plus foreign licensed sales produced abroad). The study of exporting behavior, both in the internationalization process and as a strategic tool for multinational enterprises, thus merits further continued research. As most trade between advanced countries is carried out by large, multinational firms (Lall, 1978) and is intratrade (trade between countries within the same industries) rather than traditional intertrade (between countries specializing in particular industries [Meyer, 1978]), new theoretical frameworks are necessary for such research, involving the issues alluded to above.

REFERENCES

Abdel-Malik, T. Managerial Export Orientation. London, Ontario: University of Western Ontario, 1974.

Aharoni, Y. The Foreign Investment Decision Process. Cambridge, Mass.: Harvard University Press, 1966.

Aliber, R. Z. "A Theory of Direct Foreign Investment." In The International Corporation, edited by C. P. Kindleberger. Cambridge, Mass.: MIT Press, 1970.

Aliber, R. Z. "The Multinational Enterprise in a Multiple Currency World." In The Multinational Enterprise, edited by J. H. Dunning. London: Allen & Unwin, 1971.

Bilkey, W. J. "An Attempted Integration of the Literature on the Export Behaviour of Firms." Journal of International Business Studies 9, no. 1 (Spring/Summer 1978).

Bilkey, W. J., and Tesar, G. "The Export Behaviour of Smaller Sized Wisconsin Manufacturing Firms." Journal of International Business Studies 8 (Spring 1977).

Buckley, P. J., and Casson, M. The Future of the Multinational Enterprise. New York: Macmillan, 1976.

Buckley, P. J., and Casson, M. "A Theory of International Operations." In European Research in International Business, edited by J. Leontiades and M. Ghertman. Amsterdam: North-Holland, 1978.

Buckley, P. J., and Casson, M. "The Optimal Timing of a Foreign Direct Investment." Economic Journal 91, no. 361 (March 1981).

Buckley, P. J., and Davies, H. "The Place of Licensing in the Theory and Practice of Foreign Operations." University of Reading Discussion Papers in International Investment and Business Studies, no. 47 (1979).

Buckley, P. J., Newbould, G. D., and Berkova, Z. "Direct Investment in the United Kingdom by Smaller Continental European Firms." Work in progress, University of Bradford, 1981.

Buckley, P. J., Newbould, G. D., and Thurwell, J. "Going International—The Foreign Direct Investment Behaviour of Smaller UK Firms." In Recent Research on the Internationalization of Business, edited by L. G. Mattsson and F. Wiedersheim-Paul. Stockholm: Almquist and Wicksell, 1979.

Buckley, P. J., and Pearce, R. D. "Overseas Production and Exporting by the World's Largest Enterprises—A Study in Sourcing Policy." Journal of International Business Studies 10, no. 1 (Spring 1979).

Buckley, P. J., and Pearce, R. D. "Market Servicing by Multinational Manufacturing Firms: Exporting Versus Foreign Production." University of Reading Discussion Papers in International Investment and Business Studies, 1981.

Carlson, S. How Foreign Is Foreign Trade? University of Uppsala, 1975.

Casson, M. Alternatives to the Multinational Enterprise. London: Macmillan, 1979.

Cornell, R. A. "Trade of Multinational Firms and Nations Comparative Advantage." In Multinational Corporations and Governments, edited by P. M. Boarman and H. Schollhammer. New York: Praeger, 1975.

Duguid, A., and Jacques, E. Case Studies in Export Organisation. London: Her Majesty's Stationery Office, 1971.

Dunning, J. H. The Location of International Firms in an Enlarged EEC, An Explanatory Paper. Manchester: Manchester Statistical Society, 1972.

Dunning, J. H. "Trade, Location of Economic Activity and the MNE: A Search for an Eclectic Approach." In The International Allocation of Economic Activity, edited by B. Ohlin, P. O. Hesselborn, and P. M. Wijkman. London: Macmillan, 1977.

Dunning, J. H. "Explaining Changing Patterns of International Production: In Defence of the Eclectic Theory." Oxford Bulletin of Economics and Statistics 41, no. 4 (November 1979).

Dunning, J. H. "Towards an Eclectic Theory of International Production." Journal of International Business Studies 11, no. 1 (Spring/Summer 1980).

Dunning, J. H., and Buckley, P. J. "International Production and Alternative Models of Trade." Manchester School 65, no. 4 (December 1977).

Dunning, J. H., and Pearce, R. D. The World's Largest Companies 1962-78. Farnborough: Gower Press, 1980.

Finger, J. M. "Tariff Provision for Offshore Assembly and the Exports of Developing Countries." Economic Journal 85, no. 338 (June 1975).

Finger, J. M. "Trade and Domestic Effects of the Offshore Assembly Provision in the U.S. Tariff." American Economic Review 66, no. 4 (1976).

Finger, J. M. "Offshore Assembly Provisions in the West German and Netherland Tariffs: Trade and Domestic Effects." Weltwirtshaftliches Archiv 113, no. 2 (1977).

Hirsh, S. "An International Trade and Investment Theory of the Firm." Oxford Economic Papers 28, no. 2 (July 1976).

Horst, T. O. "The Theory of the Multinational Firm: Optimal Behavior under Different Tariff and Tax Rates." Journal of Political Economy 79 (1971).

Horst, T. O. "Firm and Industry Determinants of the Decision to Invest Abroad, An Empirical Study." Review of Economics and Statistics 14 (1972a).

Horst, T. O. "The Industrial Composition of U.S. Exports and Subsidiary Sales to the Canadian Market." American Economic Review, March 1972b.

Horst, T. O. "The Theory of the Firm." In Economic Analysis and the Multinational Enterprise, edited by J. H. Dunning. London: Allen & Unwin, 1974.

Hymer, S. H. "The Multinational Corporation and the Law of Uneven Development." In Economics and the World Order, edited by J. W. Bhagwati. New York: World Law Fund, 1971.

ITI Research (for the Royal Society of Arts). Concentration on Key Markets. London, 1975.

Johanson, J., and Vahlne, J. E. "The Internationalization Process of the Firm—A Model of Knowledge Development and Increasing Foreign Market Commitments." Journal of International Business Studies 8, no. 1 (Spring/Summer 1977).

Khan, M. S. A Study of Success and Failure in Exports. University of Stockholm, 1978.

Kojima, K. "International Trade and Foreign Investment: Substitutes or Complements." Hitotsubashi Journal of Economics 16, no. 1 (June 1975).

Kojima, K. Direct Foreign Investment: A Japanese Model of Multinational Business Operations. London: Croom Helm, 1978.

Lall, S. "Transfer Pricing by Multinational Manufacturing Firms." Oxford Bulletin of Economics and Statistics 35 (1973).

Lall, S. "The Pattern of Intra-Firm Exports by U.S. Multinationals." Oxford Bulletin of Economics and Statistics 40 (August 1978).

Lall, S. "Offshore Assembly in Developing Countries." National Westminster Bank Quarterly Review, August 1980.

Lundgren, N. "Comment on Professor Dunning's Paper." In The International Allocation of Economic Activity, edited by Ohlin et al. London: Macmillan, 1977.

Luostarinen, R. "Internationalization Process of the Firm." Working Papers in International Business, 1978/1, Helsinki School of Economics, 1978.

Meyer, F. V. International Trade Policy. London: Croom Helm, 1978.

Moxon, R. W. "Offshore Production in the Less Developed Countries." The Bulletin, no. 98-9, Institute of Finance, New York University, July 1974.

Newbould, G. O., Buckley, P. J., and Thurwell, J. Going International—The Experience of Smaller Companies Overseas. London: Associated Business Press, and New York: Halstead Press, 1978.

Penrose, E. T. The Theory of the Growth of the Firm. Oxford: Basil Blackwell, 1969.

Roux, E. "The Export Behavior of Small and Medium Size French Firms: The Role of the Manager's Profile." In Recent Research on the Internationalisation of Business, edited by L. G. Mattsson and F. Wiedersheim-Paul. Stockholm: Almquist and Wicksell, 1979.

Scherer, F. M. et al. The Economics of Multi-Plant Operation— An International Comparisons Study. Cambridge, Mass.: Harvard University Press, 1975.

Simmonds, K., and Smith, H. "The First Export Order: A Marketing Innovation." British Journal of Marketing, Summer 1968.

Vaitsos, C. V. Intercountry Income Distribution and Transnational Enterprise. Oxford: Oxford University Press, 1974.

Vernon, R. "International Investment and International Trade in the Product Cycle." Quarterly Journal of Economics 80 (1966).

Vernon, R. Sovereignty at Bay. London: Pelican, 1971.

Vernon, R. "The Location of Economic Activity." In Economic Analysis and the Multinational Enterprise, edited by J. H. Dunning. London: Allen & Unwin, 1977a.

Vernon, R. Storm Over the Multinationals: The Real Issues. London: Macmillan, 1977b.

Vernon, R. "The Product Cycle Hypothesis in a New International Environment." Oxford Bulletin of Economics and Statistics 41, no. 4 (November 1979).

Welch, L. S., and Wiedersheim-Paul, F. "Domestic Expansion— Internationalization at Home." South Carolina Essays in International Business, no. 2 (December 1980a).

Welch, L. S., and Wiedersheim-Paul, F. "Initial Exports—A Marketing Failure." Journal of Management Studies 17, no. 3 (October 1980b).

Wiedersheim-Paul, F. Uncertainty and Economic Distance. Uppsala Studies in International Business, Uppsala University, 1972.

Wiedersheim-Paul, F., Olson, H. C., and Welch, L. S. "Pre-Export Activity: The First Step in Internationalization." Journal of International Business Studies 9, no. 1 (Spring/Summer 1978).

Wolf, B. M. "Size and Profitability among U.S. Manufacturing
     Firms: Multinational vs. Primarily Domestic Firms." Journal
     of Economics and Business 28 (Fall 1975).

Wolf, B. M. "Industrial Diversification and Internationalization:
     Some Empirical Evidence." Journal of Industrial Economics 26,
     no. 2 (December 1977).

# 11

## THE FINANCIAL BASIS OF EXPORT SUCCESS: AN ANALYSIS OF JAPAN'S MAJOR INDUSTRIAL EXPORTERS

Ravi Sarathy

Much attention has been devoted in recent years to examining reasons for Japan's phenomenal export success.[1] The reasons advanced include technological leadership—economic and regulatory conditions in Japan are deemed to stimulate high rates of capital spending[2] and the purchase of the latest machinery, resulting in high-quality mass-produced goods with which it is hard to compete. A related factor is the assembly-line control of quality in production. High labor productivity is cited as another cause, such productivity arising because of Japan's permanent employment system and because of loyalty to one's firm based on Japan's cultural emphasis on belonging to and being responsible to one's group.[3] A third explanation points to Japan's low-cost advantage, rooted in lower wage rates on an international scale,[4] as well as in the Japanese system of subcontracting, whereby affiliates and small suppliers work at wages lower than the national average and bear the brunt of profit squeezes that might result because of demand conditions, both in the domestic and international markets.[5]

Yet another line of reasoning suggests that pricing policy provides Japanese companies with a competitive edge; specifically, the use of market penetration pricing and experience curve economies yet to be achieved, allowing a pricing policy that undercuts competition. Japanese business strategy thus relies on market share increases to provide increased volume that would compensate for the low profit margins and yield acceptable returns on investment. This policy has often been described as dumping, both in the United States and the European Economic Community (EEC). An extension of this explanation leads to the postulation of a longer time horizon for decision making in Japanese firms,[6] which allows for low profit

200

margins on sales on the assumption that profits from volume sales will provide a satisfactory return on investment over the product life cycle. Japan's industrial structure can be viewed as a supportive element under this approach; the longer time horizon for decision may be promoted by the concentration of shareholding in the hands of banks, life insurance companies, and friendly corporations, often members of the same economic group, a phenomenon referred to as stabilized shareholding. Such a distribution of shares reduces the need to demonstrate short-term performance allowing policy making to concentrate on long-term issues.[7]

This study is an attempt to trace the influence of some of the factors described above on the export success of Japanese firms. Specifically, a sample of 77 of the largest industrial exporting firms in Japan is examined in this study. These 77 firms are those with the largest absolute amount of exports for the fiscal year ending between March 1979 and March 1980. For these 77 firms, the variable of interest is export performance, operationalized as the percentage of sales that are represented by exports.

The study consists of two parts: exports as a percentage of sales is the dependent variable in a multiple regression study, with independent variables consisting of some of the factors outlined above; second, a concept of dependence on exports is derived and the 77 firms are divided into two groups, one more and the other less dependent on exports; then, discriminant analysis is used to examine the differences between the two groups; these differences in turn throw some light on the variables influencing export performance in the sample Japanese firms.

## METHODOLOGY

The 100 largest exporters were first identified. Of these, 23 were initially discarded for being commercial firms. As is well known, much of Japan's exports are made through giant trading companies. These firms are generally divided in Japan into general and special trading companies, depending on the range of goods exported. These sogoshosha have been recently studied;[8] furthermore, their operations, being of a wholesale nature, are not directly comparable to those of industrial firms. Hence it was considered best to exclude the large exporters whose operations were primarily concentrated in the wholesale trading area.

### Dependent Variables

For the remaining 77 firms, two dependent variables were set up:

EX%, being exports as a percentage of total sales, and
EXDEP, being a measure of dependence on exports.

Export dependence was measured in relation to break-even sales.
It was reasoned that if a firm's domestic sales were below break-
even, then it was dependent on export sales to bring it above break-
even and show a profit. Hence, data were collected on the fixed
costs and contribution margins for the industrial firms in the same. [9]
From these figures, the break-even sales volume was derived.

If (Break-Even Volume + Exports) greater than Total Sales,
EXDEP = 2; else, EXDEP = 1.

Thus, the largest exporters were divided into two categories whose
characteristics could be further analyzed. This concept of export
dependence derives from the view that firms that must export in order to show a profit are at an extreme point, and their profile is
likely to indicate those characteristics that have a large impact on
attaining export success.

Independent Variables

Next, several independent or explanatory variables were developed:

INT%SAL, being interest expense as a percentage of sales;
MTHREC, being the number of months outstanding of receiv-
ables;
MTHINV, being the number of months of inventory on hand.

These three variables represent aspects of working capital and have
considerable influence on costs; for example, interest expense in
the conduct of exporting is often subsidized by official export credit
organizations. In 1980 Japan's export bank provided $5.4 billion
for export financing, with official funds financing 39 percent of Japanese exports.[10] Similarly, the length of credit provided may be a
selling point, as also the immediate availability of goods.

%CONTR, being the contribution margin percentage per yen
of sale;
BRKEVN%, being the percentage of total sales represented
by break-even volume.

The above two variables are interesting for the light they throw on
the nature of cost structure and pricing policies adopted in the sample.

VALAD%, being the percentage that value-added in a firm
bears to sales;
PROD, being the amount of value-added per employee;
CAPSP, an index derived by dividing capital expenditure by
depreciation.

The three variables outlined are measurements of industrial structure, with value-added being a surrogate for industrial dualism.
This refers to the divisions within the Japanese economy that enable large firms to exploit the lower wages and smaller scale of
secondary firms in a subcontracting relationship. For our purposes, value-added is here defined as operating profit + personnel
expenses + rent + taxes + depreciation + net interest charge. Productivity is measured in terms of value-added per employee and
clearly bears on export competitiveness, while the index of capital
spending is designed to measure the rate of modernization of technology, thus being a proxy for technological leadership. The assumption here is that firms spending more than the depreciation on
gross capital spending are modernizing technology. To the extent
that inflation increases replacement cost of assets well above his-
toric levels, the index may not truly reflect technological leadership.

PR%, being the percentage of net profit after taxes to sales;
NOEMP, being the number of employees, a measure of size;
TAXRAT, being the percentage of taxes levied on profits;
BKLOG%, being the percentage of backlog to total sales.

The backlog variable is particularly interesting in that a large backlog may be an indicator of product quality, attractiveness of price,
and the general state of demand for the product.
It should be pointed out that several other variables were also
formulated and tested. For example, several forms of profitability
indicators were derived, and as is to be expected, the gross profit
rate, the operating profit rate, and pretax profit rate were all highly
correlated with the net profit rate. Similarly, a second indicator of
productivity, sales per employee, was highly correlated with value-
added per employee. An attempt was made to develop an indicator
of dumping, using as a surrogate the relationship of exports to the
break-even volume. It was posited that if exports exceeded the
break-even volume, perhaps some indication of predatory pricing
might exist. However, such was the case for only four of the firms
in the sample and hence, statistically, the information from this
variable was inadequate, therefore being discarded.

The Sample

Table 11.1 represents a summary of the information further analyzed in this study, being the mean values for the sample for each of the variables. For comparison purposes, mean values for all companies listed on the Tokyo Exchange, excluding financial and insurance companies, are presented (1,301 companies).

TABLE 11.1

Selected Statistics: Sample and All Industrial Firms

| Variables | Mean Values Sample (77) | All Industrial Firms (1,301) |
|---|---|---|
| INT%SAL (percent) | 1.302 | 1.44 |
| MTHREC | 3.464 | 2.94 |
| MTHINV | 2.177 | 1.53 |
| %CONTR | 27.6 | 19.39 |
| NOEMP | 16049 | 2842 |
| EX% | 34.6 | 15.6 |
| PR% | 2.8 | 1.3 |
| VALAD% | 23.8 | 15.15 |
| PROD (VALAD/NOEMP) (million yen) | 9.141 | 8.54 |
| CAPSP | 1.559 | 1.81 |
| TAXRAT (percent) | 49.6 | 54.0 |
| BKLOG% (N = 35) | 78.5 | 15.8 |
| Sales (million yen) | 595222 | 160355 |
| BRKEVN% | 78.26 | 84.41 |

Table 11.1 indicates that certain differences seem to exist between large exporters and the average Japanese firm. The sample firms tend to offer more liberal credit terms to customers and carry larger inventories. Their contribution margin is higher, perhaps reflecting greater technological intensity, a higher level of fixed costs. They are much larger, as is to be expected, with about eight times the average number of employees.

Exports are about twice as important to them when compared to the average, and they are twice as profitable. Their value-added within the firm is about 1.5 times the average, while productivity is slightly higher. Paradoxically, the capital spending index is somewhat less for the sample firms. Backlog is more than five times the average, perhaps implying the greater demand for the products of the sample firms. The break-even volume is somewhat lower, indicating the slightly greater margin of safety in the face of sales fluctuations for the sample firms. Of course, the size difference is reflected in the average sales volume, being about five times the average. All in all, the large exporting firms are somewhat healthier than the average firm.


ANALYSIS

Regression Results

Table 11.2 sets out the correlation coefficients for key independent variables used in the multiple regression studies. As mentioned earlier, only some of the previously defined independent variables are included in later analysis; some are excluded because of missing information, and some are left out because of multicollinearity. Even so, some interrelationship does exist between the independent variables, as for example in the correlation between PR% and VALAD% of .6588. What this means is that the individual regression coefficients of each independent variable entering into the regression equation would not be completely stable.

Table 11.3 sets out in summary form the results of a multiple regression with EX% as the dependent variable. The coefficient of determination is .27 and is significant at the .01 level. As for the independent variable regression coefficients, only two are significant, and these are the capital spending index and the number of months receivable. This seems to indicate that export success is most related to modernization of plant and equipment and to credit terms offered. However, the sign of the coefficient is negative. This suggests that successful exporting firms reduce receivables by substituting official or external export credits for firm-financed credit, thus extending working capital and underwriting export expansion.

Table 11.4 consists of regression results for the same dependent variable, EX%, but using a slightly different set of independent variables. The difference is the substitution of the effective tax rate by the backlog variable. The results show a dramatic improvement, with backlog and credit terms being the two key independent variables, both significant, with the overall coefficient of determination being .59, also significant at the .01 level. However, one caveat is in

TABLE 11.2

Correlation Coefficients, with Significance Levels

| | MTHREC | PR% | VALAD% | PROD | CAPSP | TAXRAT |
|---|---|---|---|---|---|---|
| INT%SAL | 0.3852<br>P = 0.000 | -0.4058<br>P = 0.000 | 0.1968<br>P = 0.051 | 0.2228<br>P = 0.032 | -0.3772<br>P = 0.000 | -0.1147<br>P = 0.170 |
| MTHREC | 1.0000<br>P = 0.000 | -0.3225<br>P = 0.002 | 0.0068<br>P = 0.477 | -0.2069<br>P = 0.041 | -0.2503<br>P = 0.014 | -0.3401<br>P = 0.002 |
| PR% | -0.3225<br>P = 0.002 | 1.0000<br>P = 0.000 | 0.6588<br>P = 0.000 | 0.0127<br>P = 0.458 | 0.3640<br>P = 0.001 | -0.1205<br>P = 0.155 |
| VALAD% | 0.0068<br>P = 0.477 | 0.6588<br>P = 0.000 | 1.0000<br>P = 0.000 | -0.1352<br>P = 0.129 | 0.0529<br>P = 0.330 | -0.1330<br>P = 0.138 |
| PROD | -0.2069<br>P = 0.041 | 0.0127<br>P = 0.458 | -0.1352<br>P = 0.129 | 1.0000<br>P = 0.000 | 0.1400<br>P = 0.120 | 0.3685<br>P = 0.001 |
| CAPSP | -0.2503<br>P = 0.014 | 0.3640<br>P = 0.001 | 0.0529<br>P = 0.330 | 0.1400<br>P = 0.120 | 1.0000<br>P = 0.000 | 0.0009<br>P = 0.497 |
| TAXRAT | -0.3401<br>P = 0.002 | -0.1206<br>P = 0.155 | -0.1330<br>P = 0.138 | 0.3685<br>P = 0.001 | 0.0009<br>P = 0.497 | 1.0000<br>P = 0.000 |

## TABLE 11.3

### Regression Equation No. 1, Summary

| Dependent Variable | EX% | | |
|---|---|---|---|
| Multiple R | 0.51574 | F | 3.05437 |
| R square | 0.26599 | | |
| Standard error | 0.18596 | | |
| significant at .01 level | | | |

#### Variables in the Equation

| Variable | Beta | F | |
|---|---|---|---|
| PROD | -0.25378 | 2.356 | |
| CAPSP | 0.25001 | 4.099 | sig. at .05 level |
| MTHREC | -0.25279 | 3.577 | sig. at .10 level |
| VALAD% | 0.34513 | 1.743 | |
| TAXRAT | -0.10083 | 0.486 | |
| INT%SAL | -0.19411 | 0.712 | |
| PR% | -0.21821 | 0.619 | |
| (Constant) | 0.4491819 | | |

## TABLE 11.4

### Regression Equation No. 2, Summary

| Dependent Variable | EX% | | |
|---|---|---|---|
| Multiple R | 0.76999 | F | 4.16083 |
| R square | 0.59288 | | |
| Standard error | 0.12679 | | |
| significant at .01 level | | | |

#### Variables in the Equation

| Variable | Beta | F | |
|---|---|---|---|
| BKLOG% | 0.96992 | 16.100 | sig. at .01 level |
| MTHREC | -0.56745 | 3.178 | sig. at .10 level |
| PR% | 0.00959 | 0.001 | |
| CAPSP | -0.32333 | 2.188 | |
| INT%SAL | -0.36457 | 0.845 | |
| VALAD% | 0.16046 | 0.249 | |
| PROD | 0.14612 | 0.207 | |
| (Constant) | 0.4296749 | | |

order: Sample size is rather small, since backlog information was not available for all 77 firms. As a result, sample size for this particular configuration was only 35.

Having said this, one might infer that backlog is the predominant indicator of export success and is probably a surrogate for product quality. It is also interesting that credit terms shows up again as an explanatory variable, and again with a negative sign. The other variable of some importance is the index of capital spending. To summarize, backlog levels, the index of capital spending, and the reduction of receivables are correlated with high levels of exports.

Table 11.5 presents a third set of multiple regression results, this time with EXDEP as the dependent variable. It should be remembered that the dependent variable can take on only two values, indicating greater or lesser reliance on exports for profitability. The overall coefficient of determination is .32, significant at the .01 level. The break-even percentage was the only significant regression coefficient and is somewhat intriguing. It indicates that firms that are more reliant on exporting have a higher break-even point. This most likely is explained by price squeezes, resulting in lowered profit and contribution margins. An alternative is the existence of higher fixed costs, which might imply greater capital intensity and technological innovation.

## Discriminant Analysis of Export Dependence

The next set of results presents the findings of an application for discriminant analysis. The two groups are defined by their values for the variable EXDEP. To recapitulate, this variable measures the extent of reliance on exports, with firms more dependent on exports being those that would not achieve the break-even point if it were not for exports.

Table 11.6 sets out the group means for key independent variables for each of the two groups, as well as the means for the total sample. It should be noted that insufficient information was available for five firms, leaving a sample of 72, of which 19 were classified as less dependent on exports (EXDEP = 1), with the rest being classified as more dependent (EXDEP = 2). It is interesting that a vast majority of the largest exporters have to export in order to break even and show profits. Exporting is thus not a sideline activity, but the central activity of these firms.

Analyzing Table 11.6, it can be seen that there are differences between the two groups in interest expense, inventory levels, contribution margins, and value-added per employee. Of course, it is

## TABLE 11.5

### Regression Equation No. 3, Summary

| Dependent Variable | EXDEP | | |
|---|---|---|---|
| Multiple R | 0.56187 | F | 3.3473 |
| R square | 0.31570 | | |
| Standard error | 0.40075 | | |
| significant at .01 level | | | |

### Variables in the Equation

| Variable | Beta | F | |
|---|---|---|---|
| BRKEVN% | 0.41736 | 4.880 | sig. at .05 level |
| VALAD% | 0.43095 | 2.645 | |
| PROD | -0.14623 | 0.760 | |
| MTHREC | -0.17875 | 1.751 | |
| CAPSP | 0.11455 | 0.907 | |
| PR% | -0.24795 | 0.619 | |
| TAXRAT | -0.05325 | 0.140 | |
| INT%SAL | -0.08357 | 0.139 | |
| (Constant) | 0.6645098 | | |

## TABLE 11.6

### Discriminant Analysis, Group Means

| EXDEP | INT%SAL | MTHINV | %CONTR |
|---|---|---|---|
| 1 | 0.72000 | 1.30947 | 0.22918 |
| 2 | 1.37750 | 2.21104 | 0.29615 |
| Total | 1.19104 | 1.95537 | 0.27716 |

| EXDEP | PROD | EX% | PR% |
|---|---|---|---|
| 1 | 12.26647 | .18532 | .03312 |
| 2 | 8.19219 | .41551 | .02813 |
| Total | 9.34758 | .35024 | .02954 |

to be expected that the group less dependent on exports would also exhibit a lower percentage of exports to sales. More precisely, the dependent group's exports amount to nearly 42 percent of sales, while the corresponding figure for the less dependent group is only 18 percent. There is also some slight difference in profit margins, with the less dependent group being slightly better off.

Table 11.7 summarizes the results of the discriminant analysis, with three variables—contribution margin percentages, profit rates, and value-added per employee—being the distinguishing variables. This implies that Japanese firms that export the most do so at reduced contribution margins, by lowering profit margins and by reducing value-added, that is, by considerable subcontracting. Thus, export success in Japan is partly brought about by low prices, by assuming more fixed costs and, hence, one assumes, greater capital intensity, and by taking advantage of the industrial dualism in Japan, which means using cheap subcontracting.

TABLE 11.7

Discriminant Analysis, Summary

| Step | Action Entered | Action Removed | Vars In | Wilks' Lambda | Sig. |
|---|---|---|---|---|---|
| 1 | PROD | | 1 | 0.874648 | 0.0033 |
| 2 | MTHINV | | 2 | 0.816512 | 0.0015 |
| 3 | %CONTR | | 3 | 0.787450 | 0.0017 |
| 4 | PR% | | 4 | 0.735559 | 0.0007 |
| 5 | | MTHINV | 3 | 0.744069 | 0.0003 |

Discriminant
function: Z = .96853 %CONTR −.82210 PR% − .57646 PROD
Group centroids: EXDEP = 1, −.91816
EXDEP = 2, .36344

The canonical correlation coefficient obtained for the discriminant function is .5059, indicating that a fair degree of separation between the two groups was achieved; the relative percentage of the eigenvalue associated with the function was .34396, also pointing to a fair degree of separation. Finally, the Wilks' lambda of .744 was significant at the .001 level.

Table 11.8 presents the results of using the discriminant function to classify the sample firms. Of the sample firms, 75 percent were correctly classified using the discriminant functions, which is another criterion of the usefulness of the discriminant function.

TABLE 11.8

Discriminant Analysis, Classification Results

| Actual Group | Number of Cases | Predicted Group Membership | |
|---|---|---|---|
| | | 1 | 2 |
| Group 1 | 19 | 14 73.7% | 5 26.3% |
| Group 2 | 53 | 13 24.5% | 40 75.5% |

Percent of "grouped" cases correctly classified: 75.00%

Finally, Figure 11.1 is a territorial map of the sample firms, using their Z scores as derived from the discriminant function. It may be considered as a histogram of the distribution of sample firms along the discriminant function. It provides visual reinforcement of the discriminant function derived and it is plain to see that there is indeed a difference between the two groups of exporting firms.

Having described the results, some caveats are in order. Factors influencing export performance have been isolated through an examination of Japan's largest exporters. If all Japanese firms were to be studied, the results might be somewhat different. Second, data analyzed pertain to the period March 1979 to March 1980. Again, financial data for earlier periods may yield different results. Third, in concentrating on export success, no examination has been done of the relationship between export success and firm profitability, measured perhaps through return on equity. Finally, results obtained from a study of Japanese companies may not be completely extendable to firms operating in other export-oriented economies. It is planned to extend the study in these directions and thus increase the applicability of the findings.

FIGURE 11.1

Canonical Discriminant Function 1,
All Groups Histogram

```
  SYMBOLS USED IN PLOTS
  SYMBOL  GROUP  LABEL

     1       1
     2       2

                     ALL UNGROUPED CASES

                  8 +                                                                                  +
                    .                                                                                  .
  F                 .                                                                                  .
  R                 .                                                                                  .
  E               6 +                                                                                  +
  Q                 .                                                  2                               .
  U                 .                                                  2                               .
  E                 .                                     2     2 2 2  2                               .
  N               4 +                                     2     2 2 2  2                               +
  C                 .                                     2 22  2 2 2  2   2     2                     .
  Y                 .                                     2 22  2 2 2  2   2     2                     .
                    .                                   222122 22 2 21 2   2     2                     .
                  2 +                                   222122 22 2 21 2   2     2                     +
                    :1       1      1    1       1 1111121122212212211 222 22 2  2  22                 .
                    .1       1      1    1       1 1111121122212212211 222 22 2  2  22                 .
                   OUT..........+.........+.........+.........+.........+.........+.........+........OUT
                               -3        -2        -1          0         1         2         3
  CLASSIFICATION      11111111111111111111111111111111111111222222222222222222222222222222222222222222
                                                                  2
  GROUP CENTROIDS                                      1
```

NOTES

1. Japan's overall exports increased by 113 percent over the period 1970-79, and its manufacturing exports increased 122 percent during the same period. See Study of U.S. Competitiveness (Washington, D.C.: Trade Policy Staff Committee, U.S. Department of Labor, July 1980).

2. See "Business Brief, Japan's Gentle Persuaders," The Economist, January 17, 1981.

3. Rodney Clark, The Japanese Company (New Haven, Conn.: Yale University Press, 1979).

4. Hourly compensation in U.S. dollars for Japan in 1979 was $5.58, compared to $9.09 in the United States. See C. M. Slater, "Shifts in Relative Costs, Exchange Rates Strengthen U.S. Trade Competitiveness," Business America, September 22, 1980.

5. Yasukichi Yasuba, "The Evolution of Dualistic Wage Structure," in Japanese Industrialization and Its Social Consequences, ed. Hugh Patrick (Berkeley: University of California Press, 1976).

6. See M. Y. Yoshino, Japan's Managerial System (Cambridge, Mass.: MIT Press, 1968).

7. R. J. Ballon, I. Tomita, and H. Usami, Financial Reporting in Japan (Tokyo: Sophia University, 1976), pp. 20-24.

8. See Y. Tsurumi, Sogoshosha (Brookfield, Vt.: Renouf USA, 1980); also Alexander Young, The Sogoshosha (Boulder, Colo.: Westview Press, 1979).

9. The Analysts Guide (Tokyo: Daiwa Securities Co. Ltd., 1980).

10. See "Business Brief, The High Cost of Export Credit," The Economist, February 14, 1981.

# 12

## A PURPOSIVE EVALUATION
## OF TECHNOLOGY TRANSFERS
## THROUGH INDUSTRIAL COOPERATION

### Ronald E. Hoyt

It is often assumed that the foreign firm exploits the host
country in which it carries on direct investment.[1] Over the years,
various measures have been brought to bear that seek to curtail exploitation of the host economy, real or perceived. Taxation, legal
restrictions, and expropriation are a few examples of the methods
used. Despite these attitudes of host countries toward direct foreign investment on their soil, even the most autarkic political systems accept the principle that certain important benefits are derived
from a foreign presence. One of these benefits is the process of
implanting advanced technologies developed, tested, and proven
elsewhere—technologies that the host government views as desirable
for its own economic development or growth.

During the decade of the 1970s, the Soviet bloc countries and
later China began a major effort to acquire selected foreign technologies. It was not the first time that the Soviet Union had bought
turnkey plants, or technical specifications for certain industrial
products.[2] What was different in the massive buying program of
the 1970s, which was generally referred to as "industrial cooperation," was the requirement that the foreign firm be involved in the
implantation of the new technology and later also in the management,
quality control, and distribution of end products.[3] In effect, although
the specific rights of ownership of property, plant, and equipment

A previous version of this chapter was presented to the International Business section of the Administrative Sciences Association of Canada in Halifax, Nova Scotia.

were not allowed (although even this was permitted in a joint venture form in Hungary, Romania, and Czechoslovakia), most of the characteristics of a direct investment were present. The foreign firm incurred a liability for the repurchase of product; bore risk relating to markets, inflation, and distribution; and participated on a regular basis in a management capacity (frequently through management consulting contracts), all of which bore a strange resemblance to the essence, even though not the traditional Anglo-Saxon form, of a direct investment. [4]

An evaluation of the Soviet planners' perceptions of the benefits to be derived from the transfers of Western technologies can be drawn from two aspects of these transactions—the magnitude and the forms of transfer employed. In arranging for a portion of the end product to be resold to the Western firm, with the remainder being sufficient to justify transfer costs, the technology transfer was perceived as cheaper in time or rubles than developing the processes themselves. [5] Presumably another reason for the foreign involvement was the view of Soviet planners that it was a necessary ingredient of trade to assure that the large debts they were incurring would be liquidated. Most of the debt burden was placed in Western financial institutions and, although it was guaranteed by the Soviet banks, buyback contracts served as a practical technique to assure that the debts would be liquidated. The central point remains that the scale of technology transfer was much greater than anything attempted previously.

## MODIFIED AUTARKY

One of the early tangible indicators of a major shift in the autarkic policies of the Soviet Union was a trend of marked expansion in trade with industrial nations. The Soviet-U.S. trade agreements signed during the early 1970s by the Nixon administration in the United States were a reflection of general trade expansion already underway with Canada, Japan, and Western Europe. While the magnitude of growth was heralded as detente, the composition of trade and the forms of trade did not necessarily represent a radical shift in Soviet policy or planning as might have been expected. Nor did the Eastern bloc countries approach trade from the same perspective. The deviation from an autarkic development model was really only slight when the forms of trade are examined closely. Always carried out through State Trading Organizations under full control of the Central Plan administrators, the agreements provide goods not destined for profit-making ventures but uniquely to fill certain needs of the State Plan. Certain needs are short term, for consumption or to alleviate bottlenecks in the integrated production network. Other needs are longer term and involve acquisition of new technologies, development of natural resources, or construction of manufacturing capacity. A large proportion, then, of the growth in dollar volume of sales to Eastern Europe shown in Tables 12.1 and 12.2 represents technology transfer and not goods for consumption or resale.

TABLE 12.1

Trade between Industrial Countries and Eastern
Europe for Selected Years, 1969-79
(U.S. dollars, in millions)

|  | 1969 | 1972 | 1976 | 1979 |
|---|---|---|---|---|
| Exports of industrial countries | | | | |
| Total USSR and Eastern bloc | 4,814 | 8,484 | 24,475 | 35,700 |
| Total USSR, China, Eastern bloc | 6,112 | 10,317 | 30,396 | 45,860 |
| Imports of industrial countries | | | | |
| Total USSR and Eastern bloc | 4,971 | 7,349 | 18,076 | 33,240 |
| Total USSR, China, Eastern bloc | 5,853 | 8,894 | 22,099 | 39,420 |

Source: Bureau of Statistics, Direction of Trade Statistics Yearbook, International Monetary Fund, Washington, D.C., pp. 2-7, 1976, 1977, 1980.

TECHNOLOGY PROCUREMENT PRIORITIES

Very little verifiable data are available for analysis of Soviet growth and development strategies; those data that are generally available are often incomplete. One of the better surveys of technology transfers to the USSR was done in the late 1970s at Stanford Research Institute in Washington, D.C. Approximately 270 companies having one or more transactions during the 1973-76 period were included in the data base. A brief description is given of the type of technology and dollar amounts in many instances. Tables

## TABLE 12.2

Trade between the United States and Eastern Europe for Selected Years, 1969–79
(U.S. dollars, in millions)

| | U.S. Exports | | | | U.S. Imports | | | |
|---|---|---|---|---|---|---|---|---|
| | 1969 | 1972 | 1976 | 1979 | 1969 | 1972 | 1976 | 1979 |
| Czechoslovakia | 14 | 50 | 149 | 309 | 26 | 30 | 40 | 51 |
| East Germany | 32 | 18 | 65 | 391 | 9 | 11 | 15 | 33 |
| Hungary | 7 | 23 | 63 | 86 | 5 | 13 | 53 | 110 |
| Poland | 53 | 114 | 623 | 872 | 104 | 147 | 339 | 423 |
| Romania | 32 | 69 | 250 | 501 | 9 | 34 | 218 | 325 |
| USSR | 106 | 542 | 2,308 | 3,968 | 55 | 101 | 239 | 822 |
| Total | 244 | 816 | 3,458 | 6,127 | 208 | 336 | 904 | 1,764 |

Source: Bureau of Statistics, Direction of Trade Statistics Yearbook, International Monetary Fund, Washington, D.C., pp. 2–7, 1976, 1977, 1980.

12.3-12.5 are based on these data, which have been reclassified into 25 categories representing their probable or known end use.*

The first level of analysis deals with the timing of acquisitions. An assumption is made that higher priority items will tend to be acquired first. In Table 12.3 the number of transactions recorded by quarter and year are shown for each end use category. Soon after lifting the embargo, agreements were signed in the areas of oil/gas development, transportation, chemicals, and services.

Another approach to identification of priorities is to observe the relative dollar amounts paid for goods in each category. The most noteworthy categories are chemicals, oil and gas, transportation, and electronics. It should be mentioned that a different classification of the chemical fertilizer agreement in 1973 could be to food production. Other early priorities included consulting services (advanced management computer systems), medical supplies and technology (lasers for eye surgery; enzyme plants), pumping equipment for oil and gas development, and manufacturing equipment (molding machines, automatic forging machines, hydraulic presses). Other miscellaneous items include metal detection equipment (used by airports to detect hijackers), X-ray systems, and the first direct satellite communication "hotline" U.S.-USSR.

In the second year, a major effort began to acquire equipment for the Kama River truck plant (transportation); large oil/gas development contracts were signed; and substantial purchases in the area of electronics and computers were made. The industrial sectors (items 3, 4, 6 in Table 12.3) show a steady level of investment in years two and three, as does food processing. The third order set of priorities seem to be consumer (5), air/water (7), construction (12), timber (14), weather (19), mining (20), and textiles (23) (see Table 12.4).

A third evaluation of technology transfer priorities is based on the average dollar value per transaction.† Average dollar value

---

*It should be noted that the data base is fairly comprehensive for U.S. trade, although dollar amounts were not available for a number of transactions. Several limitations that should be recognized are these: the sample is not necessarily representative of all trade, since U.S. exports were only 20 percent of total exports to the USSR in 1976; the total dollar amounts are reports of contracts, some of which involved periods of 10 to 20 years and are therefore useful for the present analysis of priorities and structure, but do not necessarily match trade figures in Tables 12.1 and 12.2.

†Due to data limitations, the figures shown in Table 12.4 include only those transactions for which dollar amounts were available.

TABLE 12.3

Technology Transfer Agreements Classified by Year, Quarter, and End Use, 1973-75

| Categories | 1973 | | | | | 1974 | | | | | 1975 | | | | | Total by Category |
|---|---|---|---|---|---|---|---|---|---|---|---|---|---|---|---|---|
| | 1 | 2 | 3 | 4 | T* | 1 | 2 | 3 | 4 | T | 1 | 2 | 3 | 4 | T | |
| 1. Food sales | | | | | | | | 1 | 1 | 2 | | | | 1 | 1 | 3 |
| 2. Medical | | | | 2 | 2 | | | 1 | 1 | 3 | | 1 | 1 | | 2 | 7 |
| 3. Metal production | | | | 1 | 1 | | 1 | 2 | | 4 | | 1 | 1 | 1 | 4 | 9 |
| 4. Metal products | | | | 2 | 2 | | 1 | 2 | | 3 | | | 1 | 1 | 2 | 7 |
| 5. Consumer | | | | | | 1 | | | | 1 | 1 | 1 | 1 | 2 | 5 | 6 |
| 6. Manufacturing equipment | | | | 2 | 2 | 1 | 2 | 3 | | 9 | 1 | 1 | 2 | 2 | 8 | 19 |
| 7. Air/water | | | | | | | | | | | 1 | 1 | 1 | | 3 | 3 |
| 8. Oil/gas | 2 | | | | 2 | 3 | 3 | 7 | 3 | 17 | 1 | 1 | 3 | 3 | 10 | 29 |
| 9. Transportation | | 2 | | 3 | 5 | 3 | 3 | 8 | 4 | 23 | 3 | 3 | 6 | 5 | 23 | 51 |
| 10. Chemicals (natural) | | | | 1 | 1 | | 1 | 1 | 1 | 3 | 1 | 1 | 2 | 1 | 6 | 10 |
| 11. Chemicals (synthetic) | | 1 | | 2 | 3 | | 1 | | 1 | 2 | 1 | 2 | 3 | 2 | 10 | 15 |
| 12. Construction | | | | | | | | 1 | 1 | 2 | | 1 | 1 | 1 | 3 | 5 |
| 13. Electronics and computers | | | | 1 | 1 | | 2 | 2 | | 4 | 1 | | 1 | 1 | 3 | 8 |
| 14. Timber | | | | | | | | | | | 1 | 1 | 1 | 1 | 4 | 4 |
| 15. Food production | | | | | | | 1 | 2 | | 4 | 1 | 1 | 2 | 1 | 6 | 10 |
| 16. Food processing | | | 1 | | 1 | | 1 | | 1 | 2 | 1 | 1 | 1 | | 3 | 6 |
| 17. Electricity (energy) | | | | | | 1 | | | | 1 | | | | | | 1 |
| 18. Leisure | | | | | | | 1 | 1 | | 2 | | | | 1 | 1 | 3 |
| 19. Weather | | | | | | | | | | | | | 1 | | 1 | 1 |
| 20. Mining | | | | | | | | 1 | | 1 | 1 | 1 | 2 | 2 | 7 | 8 |
| 21. Paper | | | | | | | | | 1 | 1 | | | | 1 | 1 | 2 |
| 22. Office equipment | | | 1 | | 1 | | | 1 | | 1 | | 1 | | | 1 | 3 |
| 23. Textiles | | | | | | | | | | | | 1 | 1 | 1 | 4 | 4 |
| 24. Instruments | | 1 | | | 2 | 3 | | | 1 | 5 | | | | | 1 | 8 |
| 25. Services | | | 1 | 1 | 2 | | | 1 | 1 | 4 | | | | | | 6 |
| Total by quarter | 2 | 4 | 3 | 15 | 25 | 12 | 17 | 34 | 15 | 94 | 14 | 19 | 31 | 27 | 109 | 228 |

*T = Total number for the year including those transactions identifiable by quarter.

Source: Stanford Research Institute, Trade Data, Strategic Studies Center, Washington, D.C., 1977.

TABLE 12.4

Value of Technology Transfer Agreements Classified by Year and End Use, 1973-75
(in millions of U.S. $)

| Categories | 1973 | 1974 | 1975 | Total by Category |
|---|---|---|---|---|
| 1. Food sales | 0 | 0 | 0 | 0 |
| 2. Medical | 20.040 | .012 | 0 | 20.052 |
| 3. Metal production | 1.000 | 89.310 | 96.420 | 186.730 |
| 4. Metal products | 10.215 | 45.830 | 44.000 | 100.045 |
| 5. Consumer | 0 | .100 | 86.450 | 86.550 |
| 6. Manufacturing equipment | 30.000 | 20.650 | 28.004 | 78.654 |
| 7. Air/water | 0 | 0 | 7.903 | 7.903 |
| 8. Oil/gas | 26.000 | 1,344.700 | 17.500 | 1,388.200 |
| 9. Transportation | 8.888 | 409.061 | 531.785 | 949.734 |
| 10. Chemicals (natural) | .515 | 269.300 | 508.439 | 778.254 |
| 11. Chemicals (synthetic) | 8,000.000 | 33.000 | 84.500 | 8,117.500 |
| 12. Construction | 0 | 8.000 | 93.300 | 101.300 |
| 13. Electronics and computers | 2.400 | 285.000 | 17.620 | 305.020 |
| 14. Timber | 0 | 0 | 29.500 | 29.500 |
| 15. Food production | 0 | 8.130 | 7.500 | 15.630 |
| 16. Food processing | 2.700 | 27.000 | 24.000 | 53.700 |
| 17. Electricity (energy) | 0 | 4.000 | 0 | 4.000 |
| 18. Leisure | 0 | .200 | 0 | .200 |
| 19. Weather | 0 | 0 | 10.000 | 10.000 |
| 20. Mining | 0 | 12.500 | 103.900 | 116.400 |
| 21. Paper | 0 | 0 | 1.000 | 1.000 |
| 22. Office equipment | 18.000 | 0 | 40.000 | 58.000 |
| 23. Textiles | 0 | 0 | 36.000 | 36.000 |
| 24. Instruments | .750 | 1.008 | .800 | 2.558 |
| 25. Services | 180.000 | 0 | 0 | 180.000 |
| Totals, by year | 8,300.508 | 2,557.801 | 1,768.621 | 12,626.930 |

Source: Stanford Research Institute, Trade Data, Strategic Studies Center, Washington, D.C., 1977.

TABLE 12.5

Average Contract Value of Technology Transfer Agreements, 1973–75
(in millions of U.S. $)

| Categories | 1973 | 1974 | 1975 | Average by Category |
|---|---|---|---|---|
| 1. Food sales | 0 | 0 | 0 | 0 |
| 2. Medical | 10.020 | .012 | 0 | 6.684 |
| 3. Metal production | 1.000 | 22.328 | 32.140 | 23.341 |
| 4. Metal products | 5.108 | 15.277 | 22.000 | 14.292 |
| 5. Consumer | 0 | .100 | 21.613 | 17.310 |
| 6. Manufacturing equipment | 30.000 | 4.130 | 4.667 | 6.555 |
| 7. Air/water | 0 | 0 | 2.634 | 2.634 |
| 8. Oil/gas | 13.000 | 134.470 | 3.500 | 81.659 |
| 9. Transportation | 2.222 | 18.594 | 27.989 | 21.105 |
| 10. Chemicals (natural) | .515 | 89.767 | 127.110 | 97.282 |
| 11. Chemicals (synthetic) | 8,000.000 | 16.500 | 21.125 | 1,159.643 |
| 12. Construction | 0 | 8.000 | 31.100 | 25.325 |
| 13. Electronics and computers | 2.400 | 95.000 | 5.873 | 43.574 |
| 14. Timber | 0 | 0 | 7.375 | 7.375 |
| 15. Food production | 0 | 2.033 | 3.750 | 2.605 |
| 16. Food processing | 2.700 | 13.500 | 8.000 | 8.950 |
| 17. Electricity (energy) | 0 | 4.000 | 0 | 4.000 |
| 18. Leisure | 0 | .200 | 0 | .200 |
| 19. Weather | 0 | 0 | 10.000 | 10.000 |
| 20. Mining | 0 | 12.500 | 17.317 | 16.629 |
| 21. Paper | 0 | 0 | 1.000 | 1.000 |
| 22. Office equipment | 18.000 | 0 | 40.000 | 29.000 |
| 23. Textiles | 0 | 0 | 18.000 | 18.000 |
| 24. Instruments | .750 | .202 | .800 | .365 |
| 25. Services | 180.000 | 0 | 0 | 180.000 |
| Average by year | 436.869 | 37.070 | 22.969 | 76.527 |

Source: Stanford Research Institute, Trade Data, Strategic Studies Center, Washington, D.C., 1977.

221

indicates the types of commitments made for a particular purpose. Certain size effects are apparent. The Kama River truck plant was broken down into a large number of subcontracts, ostensibly in order to guard against leaking information about a sensitive sector. By contrast, the contracts in chemical production are dominated in 1973 by a single large ($8 billion) contract arranged by Occidental Petroleum to furnish chemical fertilizer plants (see Table 12.5).

In addition to being an indicator of sensitive industries when the required level of investment is large, average dollar values also show the size of transactions available to foreign companies. One aspect of contract size is, of course, sales volume and potential profit; a second aspect that many of the transfer agreements have in common is financing. Here the strategy of breaking down a major project into subprojects facilitates the spreading of financing among a larger number of Western firms and their banks.

CONCLUSION

There are several types of explanations that may be offered for the priorities in technology transfer discussed above. The most obvious is that we have here an example of the Soviet-type development strategy involving central plans, emphasis on basic industries, and mobilization of resources. [6] A second type of explanation may be a conscious effort to alleviate bottlenecks that are chronic in centralized planning systems. [7] A third possibility that is currently receiving attention focuses on a strategy to control scarce natural resources. The most probable explanation, however, is that Soviet planners are attempting to cope with lagging productivity and declines in the growth rate of the labor force through substitution of advanced technologies supplied by foreign loans.

There are two areas in which these technology transfers could have far-reaching effects as far as external trade is concerned. First, the method of financing (involving buyback arrangements) allows the Soviet products to become integrated into Western supply systems. This integration guarantees debt repayments and also future sources of hard currency—expanding their potential for foreign trade. The second area is competition for Third World markets. Although product quality is generally a problem for Soviet-made goods, price incentives can make these products attractive in developing countries. Based on past trends, it would not be unreasonable to expect the Soviet Union to play a greatly expanded role in trade with developing countries in future decades.

NOTES

1. Richard N. Farmer, however, argues the opposite point in Benevolent Aggression (New York: David McKay, 1972). See, for example, Chapter 12, "Expropriation," pp. 175-83.

2. For example, Dr. Armand Hammer's activities in the sale and transfer of technology to the Soviet Union span the years from Lenin to the present. See Robert Considine, The Remarkable Life of Dr. Armand Hammer (New York: Harper and Row, 1975).

3. John Holt, Paul Marer, and Joseph C. Miller, East-West Industrial Cooperation: The U.S. Perspective, a Report to the Bureau of East-West Trade, U.S. Department of Commerce, May 1976.

4. Ronald E. Hoyt, "Soviet-United States Industrial Cooperation: An Analysis of the Compensation Agreement in East-West Trade," D.B.A. dissertation, International Business Department, Indiana University, 1978.

5. Ronald E. Hoyt, "Profit Measurement in East-West Trade and Industrial Cooperation," The International Journal of Accounting, Spring 1978, pp. 119-44.

6. Robert W. Campbell, The Soviet-Type Economies, 3d ed. (Boston: Houghton Mifflin, 1974).

7. Robert W. Campbell, Soviet Economic Power, 2d ed. (Boston: Houghton Mifflin, 1966).

# PART III
## EXPORT PLANNING
## AND STRATEGY

This section consists of four contributions that focus on the marketing planning for export. David Ford, Anna Lawson, and J. F. Nicholls examine the development of international marketing strategies by investigating the processes by which industrial companies develop their international operations through the establishment of overseas sales subsidiaries. Their study is carried out on an international basis comparing subsidiaries in Germany, France, the United States, Italy, and Abu Dhabi. Charles Green examines the effectiveness of marketing planning for exporting, with particular focus on main concerns for firms that export from abroad to the U.S. market. David Ford and Philip Rosson develop a model of the relationships between export manufacturers and their overseas distributors and test the model empirically by examining pairs of companies from Canada and the United Kingdom. Tamer Cavusgil reviews and interprets pertinent literature drawn from studies of international decision making in different environments for the purpose of developing a coherent understanding of export activities.

# 13

## DEVELOPING INTERNATIONAL MARKETING THROUGH OVERSEAS SALES SUBSIDIARIES

David Ford
Anna Lawson
J. F. Nicholls

This chapter examines the processes by which industrial companies develop their international operations through establishing overseas sales subsidiaries. Many companies initially develop their export sales via agents or directly from their headquarters. For these companies, the establishment of an overseas sales subsidiary marks a significant change. Unlike sales via agent or directly from headquarters, a sales subsidiary involves the company in direct investment of resources overseas. It involves a commitment to a major development of sales in a particular market. This commitment may mean that the company concentrates on selling to one or a few markets via owned subsidiaries. This contrasts with the common policy of selling widely via agents, or directly. Inevitably, the decision to concentrate on fewer markets imposes demands of research, market selection, and a willingness to undertake an investment. Perhaps because of this there is evidence of unwillingness among many exporters to make a major change in operations and invest in an overseas sales subsidiary.[1] Also, the authors' previous work in companies has indicated that firms often experience difficulties when they do set up sales subsidiaries.

There has been virtually no empirical work that has examined the problems faced by companies in establishing overseas sales subsidiaries and how these problems may be overcome. This

---

An earlier version of this chapter was presented at the European Academy for Advanced Research and Marketing, Annual Conference, Edinburgh, March 1980.

contrasts with the wealth of literature on the motivations, problems, organization, and operations of exporters,[2] as well as the overall process by which firms move through different stages of development as exporters.[3] Additionally, the wider process of internationalization has been explored, whereby firms develop from being a national to a multinational company.[4] Also, the operations of multinational companies themselves have received considerable attention in the literature.[5]

The research reported here is part of the IMP Project that has investigated many aspects of the international marketing and purchasing of industrial products.[6] The aim of this part of the research was to examine the issues facing industrial companies in establishing overseas sales subsidiaries. Specifically, it aims to shed some light on the following questions:

Why are sales subsidiaries relatively little used?

What are the problems faced by companies in setting up sales subsidiaries?

Are the problems that companies anticipate before establishing subsidiaries the same as the ones they actually face during the process of establishment?

What are the reasons companies give for setting up subsidiaries?

Are these reasons the ones that actually lead to such a move?

What are the companies' expectations in setting up subsidiaries?

How are subsidiaries set up?

Are sales subsidiary decisions taken as part of overall policy or on an ad hoc basis?

How do companies organize themselves for the operation of sales subsidiaries, both at their headquarters and in the sales subsidiaries themselves?

What are the functions of the sales subsidiary and the extent of headquarters' control?

What do companies learn through operating a sales subsidiary? Can these lessons be applied elsewhere?

The research was intended to examine the establishment of sales subsidiaries by companies of a wide range of size, operating in different industrial markets and different countries. Additionally, it was planned to provide managers with descriptive information about how companies move toward, establish, and operate subsidiaries. These requirements pointed to the value of a case study approach. Approximately 25 firms were visited and cases have been written on companies with a wide variety of experiences. It is planned that a number of these cases will be published shortly with accompanying text in book form.

## LITERATURE REVIEW

This study has developed from previous work in three areas: the internationalization process, buyer-seller relationships in international markets, and export development and sales subsidiaries.

### The Internationalization Process

A number of studies have argued that the development of international marketing is essentially a process involving a number of identifiable stages. Thus Bilkey and Tesar have identified stages in the export development process as follows:

1 Unwilling exporter
2 Fulfills unsolicited orders
3 Explores the feasibility of exporting
4 Exports experimentally to one or a few markets
5 Experienced exporter to those markets
6 Explores the possibilities of exporting to additional markets[7]

A number of Swedish studies have considered internationalization as a wider process than that of simply export development.[8] Four stages of this process were suggested:

1 No regular export activity
2 Establishment of overseas agents
3 Establishment of overseas sales subsidiaries
4 Overseas manufacture

These studies concluded that the use of sales subsidiaries was preceded in virtually all cases by selling via overseas agents. Similarly, local production is generally preceded by the use of sales subsidiaries.[9]

Johanson and Vahlne suggest that internationalization develops from a series of incremental decisions. For example, the experience gained through operation at the stage of selling through agents alters the firm's perceptions, expectations, and its managerial capacity. Thus the firm's perceived risk of further commitment to a market is reduced and this leads to a decision to move

to the next stage in the process. Further internationalization is
stimulated by the increased need to control sales and the increased
exposure to offers and demands to extend the operations. [10]

### Buyer-Seller Relationships in International Industrial Markets

The Swedish studies emphasize the effects on internationalization of the firm's experience, its perception of risk, its commitment to international markets, and the "distance" that exists
between the seller and buyer markets. This "distance" is defined
as the sum of factors preventing flows of information between seller
and buyer. Distance has several elements; geographic, cultural,
social, technological (between the respective technologies of the
two companies), and time (between the time of initial negotiation
and potential delivery of product). [11] The dealings between the
buying and selling companies can be seen as a process of mutual
adaptation to cope with each other's requirements and to bring
their respective production technologies closer together. The
establishment of sales subsidiaries can be regarded as a way of
reducing the distance between buyer and seller. Not only is the
geographic distance reduced, but also the improved interaction
between the companies reduces the problems raised by the social
and cultural distance that exists between them. [12]

A buying company's judgment of the quality or value of its
relationship with a supplier is likely to be strongly influenced by
the extent of that supplier's adaptations to meet the customer's
requirements. These adaptations may include modification of
product, service, procedure, price, and so on. They are an important indication of the supplier's commitment to his relationship
with the buying company. More generally, a selling company can
demonstrate its commitment by investing resources into an overall
market, rather than an individual relationship. A powerful demon-
stration of commitment to a market, and incidentally to a relationship, is the establishment of a sales subsidiary by the seller in
that market. [13]

Some care must be exercised in generalizing from Swedish
experience to other countries having different economic structures
and imperatives toward international trade. Additionally, these
studies have concentrated on the reasons for movement through the
stages and the incremental decisions involved in changes from one
form of international operation to another. There has been relatively less attention paid to the process of making changes between
stages and the problems faced by companies in making them.

Export Development and Sales Subsidiaries

A number of studies have examined the extent to which exporters employ sales subsidiaries as opposed to dealing through independent agencies or selling direct. A 1975 study of 270 U.K. exporting companies indicated that less than 20 percent of them had overseas offices and that in 60 percent of these cases the subsidiaries accounted for less than one-quarter of their export sales. On the other hand, sales via agents or distributors accounted for over three-quarters of export sales in 74 percent of the companies.[14]

Tookey has discussed the supposed advantages of a sales subsidiary when compared to other exporting methods. He argues that they provide a base in a market for the elaboration of marketing operations and the carrying of stock. They provide an improved means of contact with customers. This is particularly valuable where a continuing relationship with customers is necessary and where the provision of spares and after sales service is required. Sales subsidiaries also provide an opportunity for the joining together in a single organization of the firm's own employees and foreign nationals. In this way they allow the sharing of policy making and tasks.[15]

Tookey points out that there is little value in setting up a sales subsidiary and continuing to take all policy decisions centrally. He argues that the subsidiary will build up a knowledge of the market that will enable it to plan its own marketing operations within the framework of corporate policy. However, it would be unwise to generalize to what extent marketing decisions should be delegated to subsidiaries or remain centralized. This will depend upon the overall strategy of the company and the extent to which there is value in common product or pricing policies.

## CASE STUDIES

Space considerations mean that only eight of the cases that were written are presented here. However, some of the analysis draws on other cases where appropriate. The cases presented were selected from a variety of industries and describe companies or divisions with little or no previous experience of setting up sales subsidiaries. The cases have been summarized under headings that relate to the questions posed at the beginning of the chapter and provide for ease of comparison. Case C has been included as an example of separate first and second attempts to establish a subsidiary in the same market.

The cases can now be analyzed under the 12 headings that have been used for their presentation.

| | COMPANY A—COUNTRY OF SUBSIDIARY: GERMANY | COMPANY B—COUNTRY OF SUBSIDIARY: FRANCE |
|---|---|---|
| 1 Company characteristics | Processor of speciality chemicals. Five divisions each serving major customer industry. Turnover 1969 = £1.8 million; 1978 = £25.0 million. | Division of major chemicals manufacturer. Divisions serving separate market segments. Growth by acquisition, new companies integrated into divisions. |
| 2 Prior experience | Extensive direct exports. Successful agency network throughout world. No overseas sales subsidiaries. | Unsuccessful subsidiary in Belgium in 1950s. No recent experience of subsidiaries. Other divisions' experience not considered transferable. |
| 3 Overall policy to overseas subsidiaries | Prefers to keep agents unless unsuccessful. Preference to appoint small, exclusive agents. | Tend to use agent until thoroughly dissatisfied. Subsidiary operations should be autonomous. |
| 4 Reasons for subsidiary | Agent a specialist in one product and unable to cope with whole product range—not exploiting all market segments. | Agent not coping with product range. Newly developed products making no impact. Agency management about to pass to "new generation." |
| 5 Stimuli | German national working in industry approached headquarters (HQ) at the time company was considering new representation. | Acquisition of U.K. company coincidentally using and dissatisfied with same agent. Joint business in market justified establishment of sales subsidiary. |
| 6 Expectations | Not quantified, but expected newly developed product range to be successful. | Not quantified. |
| 7 Headquarters organization | One man in each product division is responsible for liaison with subsidiary. Subsidiary reports to marketing director. | Organized for extensive technical support for subsidiaries. HQ-based accountancy personnel work for subsidiary. |
| 8 Sales subsidiary | German national manager and sales representatives. Subsidiary also responsible for sales agent. | U.K. national manager on short-term contract. Local national as deputy. National salesman. |
| 9 Difficulties | "Nationalistic" feelings in some customer industries. Need to upgrade some products to meet German specifications. Supply shortages from United Kingdom. | Misunderstanding by HQ of appropriate status for personnel leading to tax and social security complications. Choice of right location and size of subsidiary. |
| 10 Outcomes | Subsidiary has grown so that each product division has its own technical salesmen within the subsidiary. | Broke even in one year. Subsidiary now achieving 400 percent of business that company had in market three years earlier. |
| 11 Company learning | Importance of quality of subsidiary manager to success of subsidiary. | This subsidiary has formed the basis of future company policy. HQ had not previously been aware of the inadequacies of its agent. |
| 12 General approach | Kept agents for its specialist products. Subsidiary handles other products. Provided continuity of supply to German market during shortages. Emphasized flexibility to customer needs. | Use former HQ man with experience in chemicals and marketing as manager, supported by French national to establish subsidiary. Increased contact frequency with customers. |

COMPANY C—COUNTRY OF SUBSIDIARY: UNITED STATES

| | First Attempt, 1971 | Second Attempt, 1975 |
|---|---|---|
| 1 Company characteristics | Produces equipment for construction industry. Private company. Subsidiary legally part of one company but represents whole of groups product range. | Group has complex structure of independent companies. |
| 2 Prior experience | No direct exports to United States. Had recently opened French subsidiary, considered successful. | Earlier disappointing U.S. results. Successful subsidiary in France. |
| 3 Overall policy to overseas subsidiaries | General expansion by sales subsidiaries is important because of need for servicing and spares stockholding. | General expansion by sales subsidiaries is important because of need for servicing and spares stockholding. |
| 4 Reasons for subsidiary | U.S. market equal to half world market. | Importance of U.S. market. Management reorganization in HQ with facilities to support subsidiary. |
| 5 Stimuli | Intuitive feeling by company chairman and senior personnel that company should enter market at that time. | Need to reorganize present subsidiary. Market research department proposed new form. |
| 6 Expectations | Not quantified. | Developed an annual budget and five-year plan for the market. |
| 7 Headquarters organization | No involvement; company not organized for foreign markets. | Established department to support subsidiaries. |
| 8 Sales subsidiary organization | U.S. national manager and sales staff, selling to whole U.S. market. | French national as manager. Market through an established network of complementary product distributors. |
| 9 Difficulties | Lack of market information. Different commercial norms for hiring equipment. Huge geographic market. | Establishing dealer network. Local designs very different from those in United Kingdom. |
| 10 Outcomes | Sales of products (units): 1971 = 32; 1972 = 11; 1973 = 157. Considered unsatisfactory by company | Sales (units): Negligible sales 1974 = 75; 1976 = 95; 1978 = 800; 1979 = 1,200. |
| 11 Company learning | The needs to modify product design to suit the requirements of an overseas market. The problems of trying to cover the whole of the U.S. market in the early stages of a subsidiary. The need for strong liaison with HQ to aid in policy formation. | Benefits of an initial large investment to get established quickly. Importance of right man with drive. Regional approach needed United States. |
| 12 General approach | Attempted to duplicate structure of successful French company-dealer networks, and so on. | Transferred French manager to United States. Used distribution network of complementary manufacturer. Concentrated on selected products only. |

| | COMPANY D—COUNTRY OF SUBSIDIARY: UNITED STATES | COMPANY E—COUNTRY OF SUBSIDIARY: FRANCE |
|---|---|---|
| 1 Company characteristics | Manufactures mining equipment for a specific mining technique. Part of a much larger U.K. group. Company turnover £40 million approximately. | Machine tool manufacturer. Turnover £2 million. Sub-contract work undertaken to produce components from own machine tools. |
| 2 Prior experience | Export experience plus U.S. licensee. Subsidiary existed in United States of another division. Experience not considered transferable. | Few direct exports. Agents in France and Sweden. Only minor involvement in overseas sales. |
| 3 Overall policy to overseas subsidiaries | Believes that physical presence needed in some markets as evidence of commitment. | None |
| 4 Reasons for subsidiary | Managerial/organizational HQ changes had enabled company to consider overseas expansion. Dissatisfaction with existing licensee. Recognition of market potential. | Dissatisfaction with agent—sold at high mark up and was unable to undertake subcontract work. |
| 5 Stimuli | Recently promoted manager in HQ set up research department and advocated move into United States. | Visit by H.Q. personnel to agent led to decision to change representation. Employee within agency eager to manage subsidiary. |
| 6 Expectations | Not quantified; expected long lead time to first orders. | Market expectations developed on basis of extent of subcontract work. |
| 7 Headquarters organization | Market research and considerable technical support from HQ. Financial control of subsidiaries initially through another division's U.S. subsidiary, but otherwise reporting to HQ. | No formal management organization. Subsidiary reports directly to chairman. Introduced small technical support in HQ after subsidiary established. |
| 8 Sales subsidiary organization | U.K. nationals as manager and deputy with clerical support. Subsidiary carries out servicing, spares holding, and now does product modifications. | Manager: French national. His wife provided clerical support. Workshop in which manager can do modifications and demonstrate machinery with subcontract work. |
| 9 Difficulties | Cultural difficulties experienced by U.K. nationals in United States. Customers unaccustomed to product and techniques by which it was used. | HQ delayed establishing subsidiary due to lack of finance. Minor problems with technical standards. |
| 10 Outcomes | Subsidiary has 30 percent of market for this type of equipment. Developed to assembly and part manufacture. | Subsidiary lost £3,000 in first full year. Expected to break even in second year. |
| 11 Company learning | Learning not easily transferable. Learning re heavy duty specifications useful elsewhere. | Ease with which subsidiary could be established. Lower costs involved than had been expected. |
| 12 General approach | Used U.K. nationals from the company. Geographically located in center of their industry, not near sister division's subsidiary. "Systems selling" including complementary products. Product trial facilities. | Use of demonstration machinery to stimulate sales and to produce components on subcontract. Learned higher European technical standards that were then applied to all machinery. |

| | COMPANY F—COUNTRY OF SUBSIDIARY: ABU DHABI | COMPANY G—COUNTRY OF SUBSIDIARY: ITALY |
|---|---|---|
| 1 Company characteristics | Group turnover approximately £250 million; five divisions. Division is wholesaler of building materials. | Division (turnover £12 million) of group (turnover £60 million), manufactures heavy-duty rectifiers and semiconductors. |
| 2 Prior experience | Almost none. Modest exports, but no overseas sales subsidiaries. | Other divisions had established sales subsidiaries in France and Canada. |
| 3 Overall policy to overseas subsidiaries | None, overseas sales subsidiary was opportunistic. | None stated. |
| 4 Reasons for subsidiary | Apparent attractive opportunities in the area. | Small level of existing business in Italy. Wish to use sales subsidiary as basis for entry into different market segment and East European market. |
| 5 Stimuli | Impetus came from directors in wholesaling division. | Existing sales operation of competing company offered for sale. |
| 6 Expectations | Break even in 18 months, by persuading medium-sized companies to buy local company stocks rather than import. | Not quantified. |
| 7 Headquarters | Substantial back-up on purchasing/specifications in United Kingdom. Close monitoring of specifications and budgets. | Divisional director made responsible for subsidiary. HQ provided financial management and technical support. Little involvement. |
| 8 Sales subsidiary organization | Locally recruited English manager plus two ex-U.K. salesmen, based in rented accommodation/warehousing in Middle East. | Management, Italian national. Sales staff and small workshop. No HQ staff at subsidiary. |
| 9 Difficulties | Manager's lack of sales experience. Some communication difficulties with local partner, and organization of legal/fiscal structure. | Extensive HQ re organization followed acquisition. This reduced support that could be given to subsidiary shortly after establishment. |
| 10 Outcomes | Break even in two years after appointment of new manager with builders wholesaling experience. Turnover now over £2.5 million with attractive profits. | Progressed to joint manufacturing subsidiary. Break even after four years. |
| 11 Company learning | Now confident about all Middle East business aspects. Three subsequent operations in the region all broke even faster. | Importance of manager. Dangers in overreliance on one man. Importance of HQ support. |
| 12 General approach | Exploit their extensive product knowledge. Obtain exclusive agencies for commonly specified products. Save customer's time by local stockholding. | Changed previous local management. Supplied technical back-up. Initial reasons for sales subsidiary became less valid due to change in objectives following HQ reorganization. |

## Prior Experience

The companies selected for inclusion here were those that had little or no previous experience of sales subsidiaries. However, in some cases sister divisions had subsidiaries overseas or, in the case of Company B, a sales office had been set up in one country 20 years before. However, in all of these cases the company found this experience difficult to utilize and felt that they were essentially "starting from scratch."

Most of the companies had prior experience in the market in which the sales subsidiary was established, as had most of the companies in the total sample. Usually there had been operations via a sales agent. On the other hand, three companies had little previous market experience (C, D, and F). We will point to the significance of this for these companies shortly.

## Policy toward Overseas Sales Subsidiaries

Many of the companies described here lacked an explicit policy covering the timing or conditions that would lead them to establish sales subsidiaries. Some of the companies did relate their decisions to the level of business being obtained in a market, although usually the criteria that would lead to a decision to establish a sales subsidiary were unquantified. More frequently, decisions were based on individual circumstances and an intuition that the "time was right." A move toward sales subsidiaries was often related to problems the company was experiencing in providing service and spares stockholding.

Some of the companies (for example, A and B) clearly preferred to use agencies overseas and would set up a subsidiary only when an agent had been thoroughly unsatisfactory. Additionally, a number of companies were quite clear that the establishment of a sales subsidiary was not part of any development toward overseas manufacture. Rather, sales subsidiaries were an end in themselves and intended to lead to the fuller utilization of U.K. manufacturing capacity. Thus, the companies did not have a view of a general internationalization process and did not think further ahead than the initial decision to establish the sales subsidiary.

## Reasons and Stimuli

One of the questions posed earlier in the chapter concerned the reasons given by firms for establishing sales subsidiaries, and

whether these reasons were actually responsible for the final decision to set up the subsidiary. The case presentation has separated
the reasons that were given by the firm from other factors that we
have termed "stimuli." Companies in all of the cases appeared to
be able to give more than adequate reasons for their setting up of a
sales subsidiary. Dissatisfaction with an existing agent or licensee
figured prominently in the reasons for change. This dissatisfaction
was often over specific issues. For example, the agent may have
been unable to cope with new products or penetrate different market
segments. The more effective exploitation of an available market
potential was given as a prime reason for establishing a subsidiary
in four of the cases.

However, the companies had not gone ahead with establishing
a sales subsidiary even though these reasons had existed for some
time. Instead, it was apparent that some additional or fortuitous
stimuli was necessary before the sales subsidiary decision was
taken. In five of the cases presented, this stimuli was external
for the firm. For example, Company A was approached by a
German national who stressed the market opportunities in that
country that were currently unexploited. Company B acquired a
U.K. company that was in difficulties with the same agent as itself.
This led to reexamination of its own agency relationship. In the
remaining three cases presented, the stimulus was internal to the
firm. These included the initiative of a recently promoted manager, the lobbying of a particular department, a visit to the market,
an inherited responsibility, or a chance to purchase an existing
sales operation.

The dichotomy between external and internal stimuli is
reminiscent of earlier research on the initial decision to export.
This has contrasted those companies that export because of unsolicited orders from those where exporting has been an internal
management decision.[16]

In the majority of the cases we studied, there was a complete
lack of market research available before the sales subsidiary decision was taken. More frequently, research into a market was
undertaken after the establishment decision had been taken.

Market Expectations

The market expectations of the companies presented here
were largely unquantified and quite surprising in their vagueness.
However, Company F had a clearly stated expectation of break-
even within 18 months. Apart from this, companies appeared to
make a commitment to the sales subsidiary operation on the basis

of a generalized expectation of "success," which they did not choose to elaborate on . This may have been because their lack of experience made it difficult for them to construct more explicit yardsticks for the sales subsidiaries.

## Headquarters Organization

There was considerable variation in the cases presented here in the systems used for reporting back from sales subsidiary to head office. It was noticeable that some companies had nominated headquarters' staff to be responsible for detailed liaison with the subsidiary. Similarly, there was a variation in the level of involvement of headquarters in subsidiary operations. In most cases, considerable autonomy was granted over local issues—for example, in conditions of work and accommodation. On the other hand, little discretion was allowed over product range sold or the key question of product specification. However, more discretion was allowed in pricing, often on the basis of a previously agreed "floor price." In the majority of cases there was at least some element of technical back-up and support, and in some of the companies this was quite extensive.

## Sales Subsidiary Organization

The relatively small scale of the initial organization is noticeable in most of the cases described here. This is particularly so in view of the fact that the subsidiaries were often carrying out other functions in addition to selling. A "typical" subsidiary would be started with a manager, a sales representative, possibly a service engineer, and one clerical assistant. Headquarters' staff were used to manage the subsidiary in only a minority of cases. It is noteworthy that these companies using a headquarters manager did report a lower level of difficulties than did some of the other companies. There was no evidence from this study that sales subsidiaries need to achieve a "critical mass" in size in order to be effective, or that a minimum staffing level of perhaps eight people is required for a worthwhile sales subsidiary, as has been suggested elsewhere. [17]

Most of the companies rented office and warehousing accommodation for their subsidiaries, often at modest costs. Their investment in the subsidiary tended to be more in terms of headquarters management time than in capital expenditure.

Difficulties

Many of the difficulties reported by the companies were related to the subsidiary's operations in the market rather than being caused by the setting up of the sales subsidiary itself. In only three cases (C, F, and H) could the problems be regarded as serious. In all of these cases, the companies reported that difficulties with the subsidiary manager played an important part in their problems. The company's lack of experience in the market or in the operation of sales subsidiaries were contributory factors. Those companies that experienced difficulties with the technical aspects of their products appeared to learn from these difficulties and ultimately benefited by applying these technical improvements in other markets.

Generally, the difficulties actually experienced by the subsidiaries did not appear to be those the companies had anticipated. The companies' initial concerns centered on problems of geographic distance between headquarters and the subsidiary, potential cultural clashes with employees from other countries, and the issues of monitoring and controlling subsidiary performance.

Outcomes

The cases presented here were selected from those studied as being companies that considered their sales subsidiary ventures successful. Two of the cases have progressed to manufacture in the country concerned, while others have gone on to set up similar subsidiaries elsewhere. However, three of the companies achieved success in their subsidiaries only after initial setbacks that required management or locational changes, or indeed a "fresh start."

Learning

We now turn to some of the lessons that the companies felt they had learned through establishing the subsidiary. First, many of the companies emphasized the importance of the ability of the subsidiary manager to the success of a sales subsidiary. At the same time, they were aware of the dangers of being overdependent on one man for the success of an operation. The key element in manager selection appeared to be entrepreneurial ability, followed by a grasp of company's products and background. Nationality appeared to be of relatively less importance. For example,

Company C eventually sent its French subsidiary manager, who was a French national, to rescue its U.S. subsidiary. It should be noted, however, that the majority of the cases reported here are subsidiaries established in Western countries. It would be unwise to generalize on the factor of manager nationality in other areas of the world. The companies' experience with a first sales subsidiary led to the recognition that some subsidiaries may require fairly long lead times before significant market penetration is achieved. Many managers have come to expect lead times of the order of four to five years for achievement of satisfactory profits in their later subsidiaries.

Many of the companies in the sample emphasized the importance of the different, and often higher, specifications that were required in particular national markets. They stressed the value to the company as a whole of working toward these standards and the effect on their general production and marketing operations of the increased sophistication in their products. Many of the companies noted the value of the specific location of a sales subsidiary in a market. They emphasized the importance of location in the "center of gravity" of a market rather than a financial or commercial center or where a sister division might have its offices. The establishment of a company's first sales subsidiary frequently highlighted the inadequacy of the service that the company had been receiving from a previous agent. This inadequacy was highlighted in the improved market information that the company enjoyed, its more rapid sales growth, and the improvement in the satisfaction of its customers.

The learning the company achieved about the more general aspects of international business and their own operations appeared to be more valuable to many companies. This was more so than the specific market intelligence they acquired through a sales subsidiary operation. However, at least one company only fully understood the scale and complexity of the U.S. market after establishing a subsidiary there.

Perhaps the most important lesson felt by many managers was the relative ease and low cost involved in the exercise of establishing a sales subsidiary when compared with their expectations of these difficulties and costs.

## CONCLUDING REMARKS

The cases briefly outlined here are of firms or divisions making their first or one of their early investments in overseas sales subsidiaries. Subsidiaries can be regarded as a crucial stage in the internationalization process of the firm. They mark a commitment to a market and hence an important adaptation to the requirements of customers in that market. A subsidiary is also a step involving the company in its first significant investment overseas. A subsidiary reduces the distance that exists between buyer and seller companies caused both by geographic separation and the intermediary of an agent.

The cases presented here illustrate how some of the companies have progressed to the sales subsidiary stage from previous agency arrangements and have gone on to manufacturing or other sales subsidiaries. This is in line with the ideas on the internationalization process as discussed earlier. However, it is clear that the impetus to make this progression is not present in all companies at the time of the sales subsidiary decision. Many do not look for further development beyond that of sales subsidiaries. It may be expected that a considerable time lag would occur before a decision to move to the next stage of overseas manufacture would occur, if at all. Perhaps more importantly, the cases have demonstrated the importance of stimuli in triggering the move to sales subsidiaries as a further stage in internationalization. These stimuli appear to be necessary even when companies are conscious of clear reasons for subsidiary establishment that may have existed for some considerable time. The importance of stimuli relates clearly to the role of external stimuli (change agents) in the initial export decision that has been demonstrated by previous research.[18]

The cases also provide indications about the issue of nationality of sales subsidiary staff. The possession of entrepreneurial ability by the manager of a sales subsidiary appears to transcend the importance of the manager's nationality. Thus, some sales subsidiaries were successfully managed by local nationals, some from the headquarters' country, and some from third countries. In contrast, the sales staff in nearly all of the companies in our sample were of local nationality. Generally, companies did not attempt to transfer sales staff from the headquarters to the subsidiary country. It was the employment of local sales personnel that formed the major means for overcoming cultural differences between the exporter and the export customer. However, companies were able to provide technical support in the areas of product modification and applications engineering with their own nationals. Thus it appears that companies are able to transfer their technology from host to importing country via their own nationals. On the other hand, their commercial activities are less readily transferable and need to be provided by personnel from the host country.

A number of governments have recognized the value of overseas sales subsidiaries in the international development of their small- or medium-sized companies. This has led to a number of government-backed schemes to aid the establishment of subsidiaries. For example, the Market Entry Guarantee Scheme of the British Overseas Trade Board provides capital assistance on a loan basis for establishing subsidiaries. These loans are subject to repayment only if the subsidiary is successful. Nevertheless, it may be that the availability of aid for setting up subsidiaries may not be sufficient inducement to encourage many firms to establish subsidiaries. Thus, government assistance may simply make it easier to those firms that were planning to set up a sales subsidiary anyway. Our research has indicated that some companies may have used government assistance _after_ taking the initial decision to establish a subsidiary. This means that governments face a promotional task in convincing management of the value of establishing subsidiaries. One of the main reasons advanced for managers to start exporting is their diffuse impression of the attractiveness of exporting as an abstract ideal. This impression cannot be formed until the feasibility of exporting has been explored.[19] Many of the managers in our study found that establishing sales subsidiaries was less costly and troublesome than they initially thought. This indicates the need for governmental education of managers as to the true cost and difficulties of establishing sales subsidiaries. The fact that these may be significantly less than initially thought may be a stronger inducement to new subsidiaries than conventional governmental assistance.

## NOTES

1. A. Duguid and E. Jacques. "Case Studies in Export Organization," Department of Trade and Industry (London: Her Majesty's Stationery Office, 1971).

2. W. J. Bilkey, "An Attempted Integration of the Literature on the Export Behavior of Firms," Journal of International Business Studies, Spring/Summer 1978, pp. 33-46.

3. W. J. Bilkey and G. Tesar, "The Export Behavior of Smaller-Sized Wisconsin Manufacturing Firms," Journal of International Business Studies, Spring/Summer 1977, pp. 93-98.

4. J. Johanson and J. Vahlne, "A Model of the Internationalization Process of the Firm," Working Paper, University of Uppsala, Sweden, 1975.

5. For an example of a general work in this area, see M. Z. Brooke and H. Lee Remmers, The Strategy of Multinational Enterprise (London: Pitmin, 1978).

6. See International Marketing and Purchasing of Industrial Goods: A European Study, IMP Group, H. Hakannson, ed. (New York: John Wiley, forthcoming).

7. Bilkey and Tesar.

8. Johanson and Vahlne.

9. J. Johanson and F. Wiedersheim-Paul, "The Internationalization of the Firm—Four Swedish Cases," Journal of Management Studies, 1975, pp. 305-22.

10. Ibid.

11. For further discussion of the concept of distance, see I. D. Ford, "Developing Buyer-Seller Relationships in Export Marketing," Organization Marknad och Samhälle 16, no. 5 (1979): 291-307; and L. Hallen and F. Wiedersheim-Paul, "Psychic Distance and Buyer-Seller Interaction," in ibid., pp. 308-24.

12. Ford.

13. I. D. Ford, "The Development of Buyer-Seller Relationships in Industrial Markets," European Journal of Marketing 14, no. 5/6 (1981):339-53.

14. BETRO Trust Committee, "Concentration of Key Markets—A Development Plan for Exports" (London: Royal Society of Arts, 1975).

15. D. Tookey, Export Marketing Decisions (London: Penguin, 1975).

16. C. L. Simpson and D. Kujawa, "The Export Decision Process: An Empirical Enquiry," Journal of International Business Studies, Spring 1974, pp. 107-17.

17. S. Beeth, "International Management Practice" (Chicago: American Marketing Association, 1971).

18. G. Tesar, "Empirical Study of Export Operations Among Small and Medium Sized Manufacturing Firms," Ph.D. dissertation, University of Wisconsin, Madison, 1975.

19. Bilkey.

# 14

## EFFECTIVE MARKETING PLANNING FOR EXPORTING TO THE UNITED STATES

### Charles H. Green

The variety of studies presented in this book is a reminder of the extraordinary complexity of issues facing a company or country that chooses to export. An exporter must take into account issues of tariffs, the complexity of international financing and currency fluctuations, national export policies and incentives, and a myriad other technical issues not facing the nonexporting firm. All of these issues are crucial for the success of an export venture; and all of them are very likely unfamiliar to all but the most active exporting firms. In fact, for a beginning exporter, perhaps the only aspect of international business that remains constant is the traditional business management function, particularly that of marketing.

Ironically, the fact that any company in business has at least some awareness of the marketing function can lead to complacency. With all the critical issues uniquely associated with exporting it is easy to take for granted that the business and marketing functions for an exporter are the same as for a company operating in its home market.

There is considerable risk attached to this presumption. The fact is that an effective marketing plan in a company's home country may result in total failure when applied to an export situation. Effective marketing planning must often undergo significant transformations when the marketing plan crosses country boundaries. If the standard business and marketing assumptions are not questioned by an exporter, the effect can be to jeopardize all the special efforts extended in the other areas uniquely associated with exporting.

My expertise in this field is through the Management Analysis Center (MAC), a general management consulting firm based in

Cambridge, Massachusetts. As an international consulting firm, it deals with many international clients and addresses a broad variety of strategic issues—including assistance to companies seeking to export, primarily into the U.S. market. MAC's experience suggests that business and marketing assumptions developed in a foreign country do not transplant well when carried into the U.S. market, and this chapter will center on how non-U.S. companies can achieve business success when exporting to that market.

## CREATING A MARKETING PLAN

The key to business success for an exporter is the same as that for a company operating in its home country—namely, the creation of an effective marketing plan. There are six elements that are essential to creating such a plan. The first is an accurate assessment of the exporter's objectives in entering the U.S. market, and the unique capabilities it can bring to that market. The second element is an informed understanding of the competitive situation facing the exporter within the U.S. market. Third, it is necessary to have an understanding of how much market need exists for the products the exporter is contemplating bringing into the market. A creative approach to customer segmentation is the fourth element. The combination of these four elements is summed up in the concept of "positioning"—that is, a marketing strategy, which is the fifth element. The sixth and final element of an effective marketing plan is a tactical component—the marketing mix—consisting specifically of product characteristics, pricing, promotional activities, and distribution. By using examples from MAC's consulting experience and from the business world at large, I will discuss each of the six elements of effective market planning in succession.

### Objectives and Capability

The first element—a clear understanding of objectives and capability—can be summarized in two questions: What do you want to achieve? and What do you offer to the marketplace? All too often we have found an implicit objective in the motivations of some would-be exporters. That implicit objective is "going to America." Unfortunately, "going to America" is not a very useful objective. A useful objective is one that implies specific business actions. As a result, useful and valuable objectives tend to be more complex. One possible exporter objective centers on the importance of the U.S. market to the producer's product line in general. One exporter might have an objective of off-loading marginal production, for instance. Another exporter might have an objective of achieving stand-alone success within the U.S. market. For example, a European producer of wood-burning stoves, when it first entered the market several years ago, perceived the U.S. market as a valuable place for absorbing extra production. As the company gained success in the U.S. market, its objectives changed to the point where today its stove business in the United States is perceived as having stand-alone importance.

These different objectives will have different tactical implications. An exporter whose objective is to off-load marginal production might choose to export into the United States by means of a U.S. importer. On the other hand, a company whose objective is clearly to see the U.S. market in stand-alone terms will probably opt for a more direct means of sales and distribution.

Another possible objective for an exporter is to establish a beachhead in the U.S. market through the use of a particular product. For example, another European company had developed an innovative approach to tire chains for improved driving in snow conditions. While the product itself may not have been initially justified in profit terms, the company perceived this as a good entry product to be followed by other product lines into the U.S. market. Such an objective—that of establishing a product beachhead—also has tactical implications. A company using a "beachhead strategy" may, for instance, opt to price low. On the other hand, if a company's objective is clearly to make money on the product in question, and that product happens to be superior, an approach of premium pricing is probably called for.

A third type of objective centers around technology. One company may set access to U.S. technology as its objective, while another company may have as an objective the exploitation of its own unique technology in the U.S. market. In the former case, it may be advantageous for the exporter to locate some manufacturing facilities in the Unted States in order to gain access to technology. If, on the other hand, the company wants to market its own technology, it may be that it can best protect its own technological advantage by maintaining manufacturing capacity in its own home market.

Objectives not only imply particular business actions, they can potentially imply conflicting business actions. In the previous examples, some objectives suggest low prices and use of an importer; other objectives may suggest high prices and a more direct presence in the U.S. market. If an exporter is not clear about its own objectives, the implementation of its exporting strategy will almost certainly be muddled and the results disappointing.

Capabilities also require self-examination; there are several types of capability that an exporter might bring to the U.S. market. One type is a specific advantage in, for example, labor, materials, or technology. The U.S. domestic market has high wage rates in some industries, creating labor cost advantages for foreign producers in industries such as home electronics, textiles, or shoes. Although the United States is relatively self-sufficient in materials, it does not possess all the advantages of some other countries; a good example is the interest the paper manufacturing industry has shown in the availability of fast-growing trees in South America.

A second type of cabability an exporter might bring to the U.S. market is that of brand image. A Mercedes automobile in this country, for instance, conjures up very specific images of quality, performance, and status. A third type of capability is manufacturing or marketing expertise. U.S. producers and the U.S. public are often guilty of thinking that the United States has an edge in both these areas. At present, however, the U.S. steel industry clearly has a manufacturing disadvantage, and the success of the Timex Watch Company some years ago came as a total shock to the then-dominant watch producers.

A fourth type of capability—and the most seductive to an exporter—is simply that of a better product. A better product may be better with respect to design, quality, or performance. On a recent visit to the Robert Mondavi vineyards in California, I was informed by the tour guide that the winery continued to pay very high prices to import French oaken barrels for the purpose of aging its wine. He explained that although there is a domestic barrel-producing industry, it has historically been oriented toward creating barrels for the production of whiskey. Apparently a good whiskey barrel is not necessarily a good wine barrel. This is but one example of a business in which U.S. producers are simply not producing equivalent product quality.

The above examples of capabilities have referred to tangible advantages on the part of an exporter. All too often, an exporter thinks—wishfully—that it offers real advantages, and these advantages turn out to be ephemeral. A European tobacco producer, for instance, developed a new kind of chewing tobacco that was tightly compressed into the shape of a small candy and was suitable to be individually wrapped. The thought of the producer was that this approach to chewing tobacco would eliminate some of the most disagreeable aspects of chewing tobacco as it presently exists in the U.S. market—the necessity to carry around large quantities of dirty, bulky, loose-leaf chewing tobacco—thereby appealing to people who are offended by the "nonpolite" aspects of chewing tobacco. Unfortunately, it is probably those very characteristics about chewing tobacco—that is, that its use is dirty, messy, and often considered impolite—that draw the tobacco-chewer to the product in the first place. The chewer is choosing to make a statement about himself. The lesson here is that a product characteristic, or a success in the home market, does not necessarily translate into competitive advantage or capability in the U.S. market. As was the case with objectives, the exporter must specify the exact nature of the capabilities he brings to the market.

### Competitive Situation

The second characteristic of a successful marketing plan has to do with the competitive situation. There are two general rules about competition in the U.S. market. The first is to avoid it whenever possible. Failing that, the second rule is to understand it. The avoidance of competition is important for an exporter for three reasons. First of all, the U.S. market is highly competitive simply because its size, relative to other countries, can and does support a great number of competitors. The United States is also historically a more competitive market than that found in many exporters' home countries, for reasons of public policy: Historically the U.S. government has supported, and with some success, the encouragement of competition. The third reason for avoiding competition is simply that this is sound business strategy. At the root of a great many business successes is an ability to identify market opportunities in ways the competition has not noticed and hence has not addressed. To the extent that the exporter cannot avoid competition it must at least strive to understand it.

The first elements of a competitor that an exporter should strive to understand are exactly those about which it must achieve self-understanding—that is, the competitor's objectives and capabilities. A U.S. competitor's objectives will differ almost by definition, for a U.S. company is functioning in its home market while an exporter into the U.S. market is functioning outside its own market. Second, the exporter may find itself in competition with companies whose portfolio of businesses, technological skills, marketing experiences, and so on, differ, greatly from those of the exporting company. An exporting company can heighten its understanding of its own objectives and capabilities by forcing itself to contrast those objectives and capabilities with those of its U.S. counterparts.

### Market Needs

The third element of an effective marketing plan is a sound understanding of market needs. By market needs, I mean simply the matching of a given product to a defined set of customer needs. Customer needs may be simple, such as the needs for food and shelter. Or they may be, and often are, more complex, like the need for status or for entertainment.

Exporters have been responsible for some dramatic successes due to successful identification of market needs. Exporters were, for example, the first to discover an enormous untapped need for fuel-efficient automobiles. Similarly, exporters were at least partially responsible for recognizing a market need for a product that the U.S. industry assumed had died out years ago—that of the wood-burning stove.

In fact, exporters come to the U.S. market with the advantage of perspective. They have in their own home market a number of fully developed product ideas, which suggest, in highly specific form, certain exporting possibilities. However, the existence of developed products in an exporter's home market cannot be automatically assumed to meet the same market needs in the U.S. market that they meet in the exporter's home market. The fact is that needs change dramatically as they cross national borders.

Certain assumptions about industrial infrastructure are often easily made by exporters. In fact, infrastructural characteristics such as transportation capabilities and communications systems can dramatically affect the business assumptions made by exporters. The regulatory environment, of course, can vary dramatically, not only by country but on an industry-by-industry basis. As a general rule, an exporter will encounter less regulation in the U.S. market than in its home market. (The nuclear power industry, on the other hand, is probably an example of the reverse.)

Differences in national culture are a source of delight to the tourist, but a very real source of very expensive errors to the exporter. A sample of the risks inherent in assuming constant market needs across national borders is provided by a South American company in the horticultural business. The company, in the business of selling flowers in South America, noticed an intriguing fact: Per capita flower purchases in the United States were dramatically lower than those found in South America and Europe. Upon further examination, another fact became apparent: It was also relatively difficult to buy flowers in the U.S. market because of their lack of availability. In contrast to the number of street-corner stores and vendors in other countries, the U.S. consumer often had to go far out of his way to purchase flowers. The South American company put two and two together and decided that the cause of low flower consumption in the United States was the low availability of flowers. In retrospect, it is likely that the reason for low consumption is not low availability. One might simply speculate that U.S. men are less romantic than their South American neighbors.

Customer Segmentation

Customer segmentation is the fourth element of successful market planning. Having identified a market need, the next task is to segment that particular market in a productive way. Segmentation consists of identifying variations in buyer needs so that product variations can be addressed to those specific buyer needs. Within the automobile market, for instance, we may think of buyer needs, and therefore segments, for two-seat or four-seat cars; for fast or slow cars; for expensive or inexpensive cars; and so forth. Buyer needs can vary tremendously by country.

It is instructive to examine the market for beer in the United States and Canada, two countries that, on the surface, are very similar. Yet in the Canadian beer market there is a substantial segment that prefers ales, which tend to be stronger tasting and have more body. In the U.S. market, on the other hand, one of the fastest growing segments is that of light beer—a particularly non-heavy and nonfull-bodied product. The needs of the typical Canadian ale purchaser clearly differ in subtle but significant ways from those of the U.S. light beer purchaser.

In fact, the identical physical product may meet very different needs depending on the country in which it is sold. In South America and in Southern Europe, for example, the moped is a popular mode of transportation. It performs a vital function as an inexpensive, accessible vehicle for a variety of people. In the United States, however, buyers of mopeds are frequently teenagers, whose basic transportation needs would seem to be adequately fulfilled through a combination of bicycles, buses, and the family station wagon. A foreign exporter of mopeds who chose to segment the U.S. moped market by concentrating on blue-collar workers might very quickly discover that a scheme that works in another country will not work here.

It is difficult to formulate rules about how to segment a market or define buyer needs. There are a number of classic approaches to segmentation—by sex, age, income, and the like—but more creative approaches to segmentation are often required. A good example is provided by the women's lingerie business, in particular bras. It is possible to segment the bra market on the basis of product characteristics, such as the size of the bra, be that girth or cup size. Another segmentation scheme may be that of age. A third, and more creative, segmentation approach is to distinguish between unmarried and married women; unmarried women tend to be more frequent purchasers of lingerie. An English company, however, discovered that the most effective approach to segmentation in the bra industry was to distinguish between fashionable bras and functional bras. The distinction between functional and fashionable bras, while it encompasses some of the differences uncovered by segmentation on an age or marriage scheme, is a segmentation approach more directly aimed at the buying motivation of the purchaser. As a result, it more effectively suggests distinct marketing approaches. The most basic characteristic of an effective segmentation scheme is that it highlights differences in buyer motivation, which in turn suggest distinct business approaches.

## Marketing Strategy or "Positioning"

A combination of the preceding four elements makes up the fifth element. Called "positioning," which is another term for market strategy, it is a combination of tangible concepts, such as product characteristics and outlets, with intangible concepts, such as buyer image or needs. The goal is to appear distinctive to a specific market segment.

These elements must, of course, be combined in a coherent and consistent manner. A good example is provided by the U.S. market strategy of Mercedes-Benz. The clearly defined objective of Mercedes in the United States is to serve as a high-profit secondary market for the company. Mercedes seems also to have a clear conception of its capabilities—the combination of a well-respected image and high performance. With respect to the competitive situation, it is equally clear that Mercedes has elected not to play a game of dollars or volume against General Motors. This is sensible, because General Motors is by far the larger of the two companies. Mercedes fills a market need within the automobile industry for an automobile that conveys an image of status, elegance, and performance. While the apparent U.S. competitor of Mercedes would probably be Cadillac, Mercedes has developed a very effective customer segmentation scheme: It has succeeded in bringing to market a product that is distinct from Cadillac in that it appeals to status without conveying the "crassness" sometimes associated with material wealth. This has proved to be an effective segmentation scheme because a Cadillac, in the public's eye, is associated with both status and money. Mercedes has succeeded in isolating the segment that prefers to make a statement about its status and downplay a statement about money.

## Marketing Mix

Successful market planning must also encompass implementation. If the concept of positioning sums up the strategic elements of market planning, the tactical elements of market planning are contained in the notion of the marketing mix. There are four parts to the marketing mix: the product itself, price, promotion, and distribution. These can be illustrated by returning to our example of the bra industry.

Products: The marketing mix appropriate to a functional bra product line differs considerably from that appropriate to the fashion bra business. First, the products themselves vary. In addition to distinct product characteristics, functional bras are typically sold in boxes, while fashion bras utilize what is called a "hang sell" approach; that is, a bra is displayed on a hanger.

Price: Pricing, the second element of the marketing mix, also differs. Functional bras tend to be lower priced, because the model life of a functional bra is relatively long and does not change over time. Fashion bras, however, because they are fashion-oriented, frequently change, causing costs, and therefore prices, to be higher. In addition, a high price tag on a fashionable bra may carry a connotation of quality; a high price tag on a functional bra is more likely to carry a connotation of being overpriced.

Promotion: The third part of the marketing mix is promotion. The typical advertising or graphics for a functional bra tend to highlight the bra itself. Typically, a model is portrayed wearing only the bra, and talking about the features of the product. A different approach is used to promote fashionable bras. For this type of product, a model is typically portrayed in full fashion dress and engaged in some "fashionable" activity. The overt message is that of fashion itself; the covert message is that the bra is a necessary part of that fashion image.

Distribution: Given the three preceding parts of the marketing mix, it is clear that different distribution methods are also appropriate for the functional and fashion segments. Appropriate distribution channels for functional bras would include mail-order houses, discount stores, mass merchandisers, none of which, incidentally, offer changing room facilities. Fashion bras, on the other hand, are appropriately sold in specialty shops or department stores. These types of channels are equipped with changing rooms that facilitate the trying-on of various fashion products.

An exporter will certainly be familiar with the parts of the marketing mix in the exporter's own home market. The exporter may not, however, be familiar with the presence or absence of constraints on the use of those marketing mix elements in a country like the United States. In fact, marketing mix elements may vary considerably by country.

To return to the beer industry example, the ability to use the marketing mix elements varies tremendously between two countries so similar as the United States and Canada. I have already referred to differences in the product itself—that is, to the relative importance of ales and light beers. In the U.S. market, pricing is a significant marketing mix variable for a producer. High prices are clearly identified with premium beers, and vice versa. In fact, a beer intended to be perceived as premium by the market can lose its premium image if the price is set too low. In the Canadian market, on the other hand, pricing levels are essentially fixed by government and regulatory authorities. As a result, pricing as a tactic for differentiating competitive products is greatly reduced in potential impact.

Promotional activities by beer companies in the United States, furthermore, include heavy expenditures on mass media advertising and point-of-purchase promotion. In Canada, federal and provincial governments impose strict guidelines on the quantity and content of beer advertising, as well as on point-of-purchase activities. As a result, promotional activities in the Canadian beer market tend to center around brand proliferation. In the U.S. beer market, beer is typically sold through independent retail channels, be that liquor stores, supermarkets, or whatever. In Canada, beer is sold through government-owned outlets. As a result, two major activities of U.S. producers—efforts to "sell" a retailer and efforts to gain shelf space—are not encountered in the competitive environment in Canada.

To tie together the six elements of effective market planning, it is useful to look at a case example. The case is that of a European electrical equipment manufacturer. One of the company's products was a large piece of equipment that buffers large computers from fluctuations or outages in the electrical power supply. The company had been successful in Europe, had noticed strong growth in the U.S. market, and consequently had become interested in the possibilities of exporting to the United States.

As it began to examine the U.S. market, the management had certain preconceptions; but as a result of a rigorous analytic approach to the six elements inherent in effective market planning, it uncovered hidden assumptions and new facts that led it to revise these preconceptions. Initially, one of the company's objectives was to gain access to U.S. technology. The company was, however, unclear about its own capabilities relative to those of competitors in the U.S. market. The company felt that the U.S. market was, although competitive, a "wide-open" market lacking in dominance by any major supplier. Management also suspected that the major basis for competition in the U.S. market was technological capability of the product, which was a highly complex and expensive piece of machinery.

Based on its European experience, the company thought the market need the product was serving was that of cleaning "dirty power," because fluctuations in the quality of electric power, depending on the country, are quite common in Europe. The company also felt it had strong evidence that the market was growing rapidly in the United States. With regard to segmentation, the company thought it had a viable segmentation scheme in the distinction between batch users and real-time users. The company contemplated entering the U.S. market through use of either an importer or a U.S. sales company.

When these assumptions were examined, several key observations emerged. First, the industry was dominated by three major producers. It appeared that the basis for competitive success in the U.S. market was not technological capability, but rather the ability to point to a long record of successful installation and dependable service. While it was true that a buyer was interested in "clean power," the real motivating need is better defined in terms of "disaster prevention." That is, the consequences, from the user's point of view, of dirty power manifest themselves in severe operational consequences. In effect, the product was analogous to a purchase of insurance more than to a purchase of hardware. This suggested that a technology-based sales strategy would probably be ineffective.

It also became apparent that, although the U.S. market had in fact been growing quite rapidly, there were reasons to expect the growth to slow dramatically. The product in question was purchased primarily by owners of very large computers. While the computer market as a whole continues to grow rapidly in the United States, as well as elsewhere in the world, rates of growth vary within the industry. In fact, in recent years the very large computer segment has slowed dramatically. The same was not true of, for example, the European or South American markets. This suggested that future growth of the product in question would be much less dramatic in the United States than in other markets.

The company's hypothesis about real-time users as the key market segment was true insofar as it went. However, this did not truly reflect buyer motivations. A better segmentation scheme is that of the critical nature of the application. Most of the highly critical applications in the U.S. market had already been protected through the purchase of this sort of equipment. This indicated that future sales would be more difficult.

Based on the above facts, the manufacturer revised its tentative plans. First of all, it became clear that access to technology would be gained only by close proximity to the U.S. market in terms of manufacturing or joint development. Second, the U.S. market appeared less attractive than did Europe or South America. Third, although the producer had not thought clearly about its competitive capabilities, it became clear that it did in fact have some. In particular, it already had experience selling across national boundaries in a number of countries in Europe. The U.S. producers, having sold primarily into the U.S. market, had gained little international exporting experience. As a result, the European company offered better international marketing capabilities than did its U.S. competitors, and in a relatively attractive market. The combination of these facts suggested a different business strategy, one of cultivating a cooperative relationship with a U.S. firm to jointly explore overseas markets. Without having rigorously examined the six elements of effective market planning as they applied to the U.S. market, it is quite possible that the manufacturer could have made highly risky decisions.

CONCLUSION

Much of this discussion has focused on the risks inherent in not rigorously developing a marketing plan. The lack of a concentrated effort in this area can in fact be an Achilles heel for a would-be exporter. Again, market planning is a function that an exporter is accustomed to doing in its own home market. In the midst of all the critical activities that must be undertaken specifically for exporting, it is all too easy to let some critical factors go unexamined. The risk lies in carrying embedded business preconceptions from one market to another.

And yet I don't intend my message to sound pessimistic. There is, in fact, tremendous up-side potential for exporters looking at the U.S. market. There are numerous examples of exporters successfully segmenting markets in the face of U.S. competition, and even of massive new identifications of fundamental market needs. The United States remains a relatively "open" market.

In looking at the U.S. market, exporters have two unique advantages. U.S. producers tend to be highly insular. They are accustomed to working in a single market that is broad enough to support an array of activities, to dealing in a single language and to working under a generally homogeneous set of cultural norms. This can easily lead to ossification of creative marketing thought. The other advantage an exporter has is simply the reverse side of this coin. Companies from non-U.S. countries most frequently begin their entry to the U.S. market with greater international marketing experience than their U.S. competitors. A clear benefit of this international experience is a sensitivity to unspoken assumptions and unexamined needs. Another is the wealth of ready-made and well-developed business examples from other countries and other cultures, some of which—if coupled with creative examination of the market—can be successful in the United States.

# 15

## THE RELATIONSHIPS BETWEEN EXPORT MANUFACTURERS AND THEIR OVERSEAS DISTRIBUTORS

David Ford
Philip J. Rosson

The use of overseas distributors* is an important way for many manufacturers to develop their foreign markets (Business International, 1970; Duguid and Jacques, 1971; Tookey, Lea, and McDougall, 1967). This is particularly the case with small- or medium-sized companies that may not have the necessary scale of operations, financial resources, or experience to operate more directly in foreign markets (Duguid and Jacques, 1971; Tookey, 1975). Two issues in the use of overseas distributors have received considerable attention in the literature. First, a number of writers have examined those circumstances where distributor use may be appropriate (Brady and Bearden, 1979; Daniels, Ogram, and Radebaugh, 1976; Tookey, 1975). A second issue that has been dealt with is that of the selection of the most suitable overseas distributor. Various authors (Bickers, 1971; Heck, 1972; McMillan and Paulden, 1974) provide guidance on how to approach the selection decision. Further, Ross (1972) attempted to relate selection factors and distributor attributes to varying situations that might confront the manufacturer in overseas markets.

A third issue concerns the nature of the association between manufacturer and overseas distributor once the relationship has

---

*The term "distributor" is used here in the sense defined by Miracle and Albaum (1970, p. 356). They distinguish between distributors and agents as follows: "a distributor is a merchant middleman and as such, he is the customer of the exporter. An agent, on the other hand, is a representative who acts on behalf of the exporter; he is not a customer."

been established. There is a lot of advice in the literature on how these relationships should be managed (Beeth, 1973; Bickers, 1971; Terpstra, 1972). However, this advice lacks a real empirical base, for few studies have investigated how manufacturers do manage their overseas distributor relationships, or whether performance is associated with certain practices (Mechanical Engineering EDC, 1968; ITI Research, 1975; Cunningham and Spigel, 1971; Business International, 1970; Rosson and Ford, 1980a, 1980b).

This chapter develops a model of exporter–overseas distributor relationships by drawing upon writings in the fields of interorganizational relations and buyer–seller relationships in industrial marketing. This model is then tested empirically through examining data on 21 pairs of companies, that is, 21 Canadian exporters of industrial goods and their U.K. distributors. Finally, the results are discussed and recommendations are made about the management of manufacturer–overseas distributor relations.

## THEORETICAL BACKGROUND

Two sources of useful writing on manufacturer–overseas distributor relationships were mentioned above. Marrett (1971), an organizational theorist, provides a good starting point for discussion of the question, "How do organizations relate to each other?" Based on her review of a number of field studies of health and welfare agencies, Marrett proposed four dimensions for the analysis of interorganizational relations. Each of these four dimensions are defined below, together with an indication of the relevance of the dimension in the manufacturer–overseas distributor context.

Formalization: This refers to the extent to which the relationship is agreed upon and made explicit. In the exporting context, distributor relationships come into being when two organizations agree to work with each other. Such an agreement, however, may vary with regard to its explicitness and importance. For example, some agreements involve verbal undertakings, whereas others may involve a legal contract.

Intensity: This is the level of contact and resource exchange between the parties. Resource exchange (for example, sales aids, stock held) is an important dimension of a distributor relationship, while the export literature places great emphasis on the level of interfirm contacts as contributors to the efficiency of these business relationships (ITI Research, 1975; Cunningham and Spigel, 1971).

Reciprocity: This is the extent to which the two parties are both involved in decision making, despite the traditional domains of each. The formation of a distributor relationship implies that a certain division of labor will occur. Thus, product design decisions would tend to be the prerogative of the manufacturer, while deployment of the sales force in the overseas market tends to be that of the distributor. However, certain decisions (for example, shipping and delivery scheduling) may require joint efforts. A similar joint involvement may be experienced when the party with major responsibility for a decision area accepts advice from the other. For example, the distributor may have a perspective on the market that allows him to make useful comments regarding the manufacturer's new product program. If both dyad members are involved in decision making and if the involvement is of a constructive and selfless kind, it can be termed reciprocal. In contrast, joint involvement may be less balanced than that implied above, for decision making provides an arena for the exercise of power. (For a discussion of manufacturer-distributor power relationships, see Wilkinson, 1973.)

Standardization: This is the extent to which the established roles and routines of the relationship are adhered to, for example, on the basis of a manufacturer's standard procedure. Continuing transactions in these relationships require that the roles of each party are understood and that routines are established that permit effective operation. From time to time, roles and routines may need modification. This may be externally induced (for example, strikes at the port of entry leading to revised shipping routine) or internally induced (for example, poor distributor product servicing leading to the manufacturer taking over the servicing role).

Marrett's four dimensions—formalization, intensity, reciprocity, and standardization—have been tested empirically by Aldrich (1976) and Schmidt and Kochan (1977). In the latter case, further items were included "to capture dimensions of conflict processes, namely incompatible goals, tension, conflict and influence" (p. 225). The inclusion of conflict as a dimension for study in the manufacturer-overseas distributor setting has merit. Stern and Reve (1980, p. 58) have argued that relations in distribution channels are of a "mixed-motive" kind, and numerous studies have shown that conflict frequently exists between manufacturer and distributor (see, for example, Ford, 1978).

A second source of insight regarding manufacturer-overseas distributor relationships is provided by Ford (1980). Whereas Marrett's approach is static, that is, "What are the dimensions of interorganizational relations?" Ford's is dynamic, that is, "How do intercompany relations change?" This growth model proposes five stages in such relationships: prerelationship, early, development, long-term, and final stages. It suggests that the nature of the relationship between buying and selling companies changes through these stages over time. The stages are described in terms of the experience, uncertainty, commitment, and mutual adaptation of the two parties as well as the distance that exists between them.

Experience here refers to each party's corporate and individual knowledge of the relationship and the other company. The uncertainty faced by the two companies concerns the possible costs and benefits of the relationship with the other party. This uncertainty is likely to be particularly great at the start of a relationship or when changes have been introduced, or where the relationship has deviated from the expectations of either company. Commitment is a measure of the importance of a relationship to a company in terms of the "durable transaction-specific investments" (Williamson, 1979) that it is prepared to make in it. These investments can be seen most clearly in such things as a supplier's development of a special product for a customer, or a buyer's modification of payment procedures to suit the financial requirements of a supplier. Additionally, companies may be involved in "human capital investments" (Williamson, 1979) in a relationship (for example, alterations and procedures, special training or allocation of managerial resources to the relationship).

The investments by companies mark major adaptations by them to the relationship. These adaptations can be formal as in the case of contractual agreements, or companies may make informal adaptations to cope with each other's requirements as circumstances arise. The use of the terms "commitment" and "adaptation" provide a useful link with the export literature, for this contains numerous references to the need for commitment and adaptability if manufacturers are to achieve overseas success (see, for example, Cunningham and Spigel, 1971; Keegan, 1969; Tookey, 1964). Finally, the distance between buyer and seller is defined as the sum of factors preventing flows of information between seller and buyer. It includes elements of geographic, cultural, and social distance (Hallen and Wiedersheim-Paul, 1979; Johanson and Wiedersheim-Paul, 1975).

In summary, in Ford's (1980) model the development of a buyer-seller relationship is seen as a process of increasing experience and commitment as transactions take place. This process is marked by a reduction in uncertainty as the two companies learn more of each other, the nature of the relationship, and its potentialities. Additionally, the process of social exchange between the companies is seen as a means of reducing the distance between them. The model stresses the importance of informal adaptation as a way of demonstrating commitment to the relationship. Additionally, it points out the potential dangers of the developed experience to the relationship. This danger is that companies may allow their dealings with each other to become overly standardized or based on routine or institutionalized practices. In this way the company may appear unresponsive or uncommitted in the eyes of its partner. This is one of the ways in which the model suggests that the relationship may fail to progress. Other factors are the inability of either of the parties to fulfill the requirements of the other, or to achieve suitable rewards for their investments in their relationship. However, this model does not explicitly diagram the failure of a relationship to grow, nor does it detail the characteristics of declining or static relationships.

THE RESEARCH MODEL

The model presented in Figure 15.1 shows how the views of Marrett (1971) regarding relationship dimensions and Ford (1980) regarding relationship development can be integrated and extended. The integration of these separate strands is made explicit in the discussion that follows. The model shown in Figure 15.1 has three main parts: relationship dimensions, participant dimensions, and relationship development states.

FIGURE 15.1

A Model of Manufacturer-Overseas Distributor Relationships

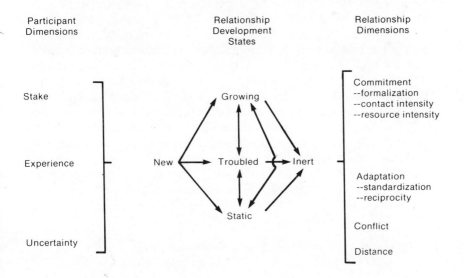

Relationship Dimensions

Marrett's (1971) four relational dimensions are adopted in this study and supplemented by the dimensions "conflict" and "distance." A connection is seen between Marrett's four dimensions and two mentioned by Ford (1980). Thus, the latter's dimension of commitment to the relationship clearly encompasses Marrett's dimensions of intensity of the relationship, and the formalization of the parties' responsibility to it. Similarly, the degree of standardization in intercompany dealings, and of reciprocity in decision making, can be held to be indicators of the adaptability of the two parties. In this manner, Marrett's four dimensions can be accommodated under two of Ford's.

Finally, the geographic and cultural separation between manufacturer and overseas distributor creates distance (Ford, 1980; Hallen and Wiedersheim-Paul, 1979; Johansson and Wiedersheim-Paul, 1975), and provides an opportunity for tension and disagreement, and, thus, contributes to the overt conflict that may exist between the companies (Schmidt and Kochan, 1977).

Participant Dimensions

The model used three dimensions to describe the participants in the manufacturer-overseas distributor relationship: stake, experience, and uncertainty. Thus, the behavior of companies in the relationship is to be likely shaped by the knowledge (or experience) that the firms have of each other (Van de Ven, 1976), as well as their uncertainty about the future of the relationship (Etgar, 1977; Goodnow and Hansz, 1972; Hirsch, 1972; Williamson, 1975).

Stake is defined as "what a party (or the parties) stands to lose if the relationship is terminated." A number of studies suggest the importance of this variable in buyer-seller relationships (ITI Research, 1975; Rosenberg, 1969; Terpstra, 1972). In particular, it has been asserted that the degree of importance of the exporter to the distributor (stake) determines the leverage or control the former has over the latter (Business International, 1970). In summary, the stake, experience, and uncertainty of both manufacturer and overseas distributor are regarded as connected to behavior within such a relationship, and, indeed, the development of the relationship. This point is raised again below.

Relationship Development States

The modeling approach here considers relationships as being in one of five possible "states" of development. Unlike earlier work, the only assumption made here regarding progression is that dyads move from being "new" toward being "inert." Between this beginning point and end point, three relationships states are possible, namely, growing, troubled, or static. In the middle relationship period, any sequence of states may be experienced. For example, the "growing" state might be followed by "troubled" to be followed by a "growing" state again. In this way, the model accommodates fluctuations in relationships.

New relationship states are those where an agreement to work together has been made, but where there is little experience of interaction or transactions. The growing state may describe relatively new or well established dyads, for it simply means that reasonable growth is being achieved. The troubled state may be one in which sales growth is being experienced, but where there is uncertainty for other reasons. Alternatively, the uncertainty may relate to sales inadequacy. Relationships may also be in the static state. Here sales might show little variation from year to year because of lack of potential and/or because of an unwillingness of the parties to increase their stake in it. Finally, the inert state characterizes those relationships that, while still in existence, can scarcely be justified. Termination may be considered, or the association may continue because there is no wish to end it.

The five relationship states have a heavy performance emphasis. This is natural since there are real benefits expected by both parties from their association, and any shortfall from expectations will normally be reviewed and remedial action considered. The dynamic of the relations will thus sharply reflect the extent to which the association currently meets the expectations of the dyad members.

The research model shows a potentially useful way in which previous work can be integrated and extended. The work of Marrett (1971) and others on interorganizational relations is meshed with Ford's (1980) ideas about relationship development to produce a framework for understanding manufacturer-overseas distributor relations in exporting. Next, attention turns to examining the following two propositions (P1 and P2), which flow from the discussion above:

P1: Five relationship development states are found in manufacturer-overseas distributor exporting arrangements: new, growing, troubled, static, and inert.

P2: Different relationship characteristics will be found in the three middle period*—growing, troubled, static—development states.

## RESEARCH METHODOLOGY

The study data were collected through personal interviews in the spring and summer of 1978. Initially, interviews were conducted in 21 Canadian firms that exported industrial goods to the United Kingdom, using an overseas distributor in that market. The interviewee in each case was the person responsible for business with the U.K. firm. Once the Canadian fieldwork was completed, interviews were conducted with each Canadian firm's U.K. distributor. The respondent here was the person responsible for business with the Canadian manufacturer, that is, the Canadian respondent's U.K. contact.

As far as possible, interviews followed a standard format, guided by a questionnaire pretested in two companies. Interviews in Canada averaged 1.75 hours, while those in the United Kingdom averaged 1.5 hours. In each case, the interviewer completed the questionnaire and (in all but two cases) recorded the interview on cassette tapes. The transcribed tapes provided very full information and were used for data coding purposes.

A large amount of information was collected, some of which is reported here. For the most part,[†] the data reported here are summed, that is, the response of manufacturer and overseas distributor is added. In this way, the response of both parties is reflected in the data.

The resulting sample of companies showed considerable variety as to products (sole leather to electronic equipment), exporting and importing experience (2 to 50 years and 1 to 30 years, respectively),

---

*Attention is focused on the three middle period relationship states, as these appear of most importance, that is, few relationships remain new or (hopefully) inert for long, but the period between these states may be very protracted and potentially profitable.

[†]In two cases that are indicated in Table 15.1, single responses were recorded.

level of U.K. sales ($6,000 to $1.5 million per year), and size (manufacturers: 28 to 930 employees; distributors: 5 to 1,409 employees).

PROPOSITION TESTING

Proposition 1

It has been argued that three participant dimensions largely determine the development state the manufacturer–overseas distributor occupies. Therefore, questionnaire data covering these dimensions were used to categorize the 21 dyads to a development state. The questionnaire items were as follows:

| Dimension | Item | Scale or measure |
|---|---|---|
| Stake | Sales trend over last 3 years | 5 point scale, range: (1) declining quickly, to (5) growing quickly |
| Experience | Length of manufacturer–overseas distributor relationship | Years of association |
| Uncertainty | Plans for the future of the relationship | 4 point scale, range: (1) end relationship, to (4) work together more closely |

Categorization proceeded as follows. All three items provided data but these were not equally weighted. For example, the "growing" and "static" state memberships were based on sales trend information. The "troubled" state members were categorized either because their sales were in decline, or because future plans were very uncertain (even though sales growth had been experienced). The two dyads in the "inert" category were so categorized after inspection of both sales trend and future plans. Finally, "new" state membership resulted from considering the length of association.

The categorization of dyads by development state is shown in diagrammatic form in Figure 15.2. Since it was possible to realistically categorize the dyads in this way, the proposition is regarded as supported in this study.

FIGURE 15.2

Categorization of Dyads by Development State

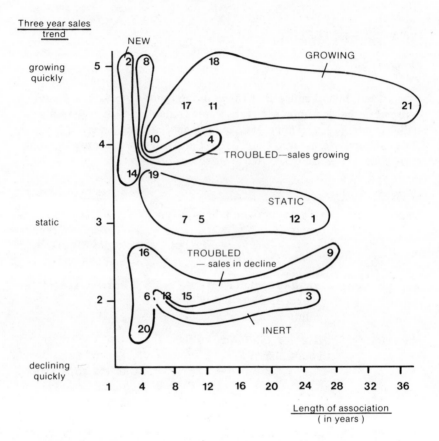

Note: Read as follows: Dyads 10, 11, 17, 18, and 21 are categorized as growing.

Proposition 2

Seventeen dyads were categorized above as being in the growing, troubled, or static development states. Mean values were calculated for various measures of the relationship dimensions:

formalization, standardization, reciprocity, intensity, and conflict,*
on a development states basis. In view of the small number of dyads
involved, these mean values are not subjected to tests of statistical
significance. The differences between the mean values are summarized in Table 15.1 and are regarded as being suggestive only.

Contrasting manufacturer-overseas distributor relations are
found for each of the three middle period development states. When
growing state dyads are considered, these are found to generally
exhibit more commitment and adaptation, as well as less conflict
between the two parties. Troubled state dyads present almost the
opposite set of characteristics; generally less commitment and adaptation is suggested, together with more conflict. Dyads in the static
development state present a less sharply contrasting set of characteristics. In many ways these dyads show characteristics that are
consistent with "partial withdrawal" from the relationship. Thus,
on most counts companies falling into this category are less committed to each other but at the same time quite adaptive and free of
conflict. These points are discussed further in the next section.
The findings shown summarized in Table 15.1 suggest some tentative support for P2.

DISCUSSION

In this final section the results presented earlier are considered more fully and from a more managerial viewpoint.

Proposition 1

Two sets of findings are worth noting in relation to P1, where
dyads were categorized by development state. The first set of findings results from viewing the distribution of dyads across development states: new - 2, growing - 5, troubled - 7, static - 5, inert -
2. Only five dyads (or 23 percent) were categorized as being in the
development state labeled "growing." Why is this number so small?
One explanation might be that manufacturer-overseas distributor

---

*Distance is not considered here since this can be considered
relatively uniform, given that each dyad was involved in the same
Canada-U.K. trading.

## TABLE 15.1

### Characteristics of Relationships in Growing, Troubled, and Static Development States

| Relationship Dimensions | Development States | | |
|---|---|---|---|
| | Growing (n = 5 dyads) | Troubled (n = 7 dyads) | Static (n = 5 dyads) |
| **Commitment** | | | |
| Formalization | | | |
| Type of agreement | most formal | less formal | least formal |
| Contact intensity | | | |
| Number of letters | most letters | less letters | |
| Number of visits | less visits | | most visits |
| Other contact frequency | most frequent | less frequent | |
| | | | |
| Resource intensity | | | |
| Support materials[a] | less support | most support | less support |
| Stock carried[b] | most stock | least stock | less stock |
| Effort expended | most effort | less effort | least effort |
| **Adaptation** | | | |
| Standardization | | | |
| Stability of roles and routines | least stable | most stable | less stable |
| | | | |
| Reciprocity | | | |
| Extent of joint decision making | most joint | least joint | most joint |
| **Conflict** | | | |
| Conflict frequency | least frequent | most frequent | less frequent |

[a]Single response measure, that is, support materials provided by manufacturer to overseas distributor.

[b]Single response measure, that is, stock of manufacturer's products carried by overseas distributor.

relationships are intrinsically hard to manage and that, as a result, success is difficult to achieve. Another explanation relates to Robinson's (1973) thesis of stages of international business involvement. This states that exporting is often the method first used by most firms in international business. Good success in exporting, however, tends to be followed by more direct involvement overseas involving sales subsidiaries and sometimes overseas production. If this argument holds true, then it would seem unreasonable to expect to find a high proportion of very successful relationships in a sample such as this one.

The second set of findings concerns the distribution of dyads by development state and length of association and is shown in Table 15.2. This analysis brings a time dimension to the consideration of relationship development. Naturally, both new relationships in the sample fall into the under-two-years category, but it is in the two- to five-years category that an important finding is seen. Four of the six relationships in this category are troubled. This contrasts markedly with proportions in other length-of-relationship ranges. It seems that if relationships have a tendency for trouble, then the trouble will show up relatively early on in the association. This finding seems reasonable enough, for by the end of four years, enough time should have elapsed to permit evaluation of one dyad member by the other. Equally, it may be two years before companies are able to differentiate between what might be regarded as "teething" problems, and those that are more substantial. The seemingly high incidence of "trouble" in the two- to five-year association period is an interesting finding, but caution is urged here in view of the small sample size involved. The other point to make regarding the "troubled" state is that some dyads experience this state relatively late in their association. It seems that there is always the possibility of the dyad entering the "troubled" state, although there is a greater likelihood of the state in the first two to five years.

TABLE 15.2

Development State Groups and Length of Dyadic Association

| Length of Relationship | New | Growing | Troubled | Static | Inert |
|---|---|---|---|---|---|
| Less than 2 years | 2 | | | | |
| $\geq$ 2 years < 5 years | | 1 | 4 | 1 | |
| $\geq$ 5 years < 10 years | | 2 | 1 | 1 | 1 |
| $\geq$ 10 years < 20 years | | 1 | 1 | 1 | |
| 20 years or more | | 1 | 1 | 2 | 1 |

Turning to the growing and static states, it is evident that dyads may experience these states at almost any time. Sales may become static soon after the relationship is established. Then again, sales growth may begin or persist long into an established association. Clearly time is not an important determinant of performance, for many other factors have a more potent effect on sales, for example, selling efforts by D (distributor), M's (manufacturer) prices, U.K. competition.

Finally, the inert state is merely a residual one, in that the useful purpose once served by the association is past. Thus, both relationships in this state are somewhat older in years than more dynamic state dyads.

These points make it clear that the relationship development process is not necessarily orderly or progressive over time. This, in turn, implies that relationship management is crucial under this kind of export arrangement. How these relationships are managed and how they should be managed are matters that can be addressed from the P2 results.

## Proposition 2

The facts that various development states are found to exist in the 21-dyad study sample and that quite contrasting relationship characteristics were found suggest that these relationships are managed quite differently. (This point was certainly marked when the transcriptions of individual interviews were analyzed.) Interesting information on the range of actual management and what management might be recommended is provided by a description of troubled and static dyads and contrasting these to growing dyads.

Static state relationships were described earlier as exhibiting "partial withdrawal" characteristics. Sometimes this situation resulted from a long trading history where sales were considered difficult to expand. In other cases the association between manufacturer and overseas distributor was newer, but manufacturers were not very committed to exporting. In some instances a large home market absorbed the exporter's attention. In one case sales to other divisions within the conglomerate cushioned the firm from more competitive market realities. Along with this reduced commitment to export markets, there was also found either a reluctance to, or failure at, product adaptation to overseas market requirements. The lack of product adaptation was often matched by a lack of procedural adaptation. Thus, the distributor claimed that these exporters were often remiss in terms of replies to inquiries, delivery delays, and in matters of documentation. In this situation, distributors tended not to be very enamored of their relationship. Nevertheless, the exporters hoped for improved sales, however unrealistic this may have been. Overt conflict was not very frequent in these relationships, even though performance was not all that it might have been. This appeared to be due to the fact that the firms were not very intensely involved with each other.

Troubled state relationships involve two subcategories, that is, troubled-growing sales and troubled-sales in decline. As a result, somewhat differing situations prevail. For example, where sales are in decline, both parties seem ready to blame the other, whereas in the two cases where sales are growing, there appeared more agreement about the problems faced. Generally, distributors in these dyads regarded their export principals as being poor performers. This complaint was leveled at various facets of the manufacturer's operations, that is, product value-for-money, technical innovativeness, support offered to distributor. In some cases exporters were critical too. Sometimes the exporter's criticism was concerned with the scale and resource abilities of the distributor, and overall lack of sales aggression was cited in other instances. In these dyads, disagreements were more frequent and open conflict more apparent. Naturally, in these circumstances thought was more often being given to alternate trading arrangements.

Both static and troubled dyads show contrasting characteristics to those of growing state dyads. These differences were presented in Table 15.1 and are extended here. In simple terms, growing state dyads show more commitment to exporting/importing and to the arrangement they are currently involved in. Thus, these manufacturers display a commitment not only to the U.K. market but also to the distributor they have chosen to operate through in that market. As a result there is more likely to be a formal distributor agreement in these dyads than in others. In addition, contacts are more frequent between these firms, as are the resources exchanged, for example, stock, reports, promotional assistance. A willingness to modify products and routines is also found in these dyads. In this way (and often in response to distributor requests), the potential presented by the market can be tapped. This is not meant to imply that no problems are faced by these companies. Sometimes product modification is less than successful, and often the parties disagree on pricing matters. However, bargaining behavior on these and other points results in workable and mutually satisfactory solutions, whereas in other development states this is less often so. Naturally, conflict is less open or serious in these dyads.

The characteristics of growing, troubled, and static development state dyads have been pointed to above. While causal relations were not tested in this study, the contrasting relationship characteristics found suggest that a change in management may well lead to a change in development state. For example, it might be that the manufacturer that increases the frequency of contact with the distributor and/or takes a more adaptive view toward exporting would help his dyadic relationship out of the troubled category.

In general terms, the study findings reaffirm the view that manufacturer-overseas distributor relations are not always (or even often) harmonious or successful. The findings presented here are instructive in that they offer insight to the manufacturer and distributor that is considering becoming involved with an overseas trading partner. The extent to which the other party will make commitments and adaptations are important factors to explore at the establishment state in a relationship. The matter is also worth constant review during the life of the relationship, for numerous factors make success a particularly difficult objective to attain when exporting through overseas distributors.

## REFERENCES

Aldrich, H. E. (1976). "An Interorganizational Dependency Perspective on Relations between the Employment Service and Its Organization Set." In The Management or Organization Design, Vol. II, edited by R. H. Kilman, L. R. Pondy, and D. P. Slevin. New York: North-Holland, pp. 231-66.

Beeth, G. (1973). "Distributors—Finding and Keeping the Good Ones." In International Marketing Strategy, edited by H. B. Thorelli. Harmondsworth, Middlesex: Penguin.

Bickers, R. L. T. (1971). Export Marketing in Europe. London: Gower Press.

Brady, D. L., and W. O. Bearden (1979). "The Effect of Managerial Attitudes on Alternative Exporting Methods." Journal of International Business Studies 10 (Winter):79-84.

Business International (1970). Improving Foreign Distributor Performance. Management Monographs, No. 22. New York: Business International.

Cunningham, M. T., and R. I. Spigel (1971). "A Study in Successful Exporting." British Journal of Marketing 5 (Spring):2-12.

Daniels, J. D., E. W. Ogram, and L. H. Radebaugh (1976). International Business: Environments and Operations. Reading, Mass.: Addison-Wesley.

Duguid, A., and E. Jacques (1971). Case Studies in Export Organization. London: Her Majesty's Stationery Office.

Etgar, M. (1977). "Channel Environment and Channel Leadership." Journal of Marketing Research 14 (February):69-76.

Ford, I. D. (1978). "Stability Factors in Industrial Marketing Channels." Industrial Marketing Management 7:410-27.

Ford, I. D. (1980). "The Development of Buyer-Seller Relationships in Industrial Markets." European Journal of Marketing, in press.

Goodnow, J. D., and J. E. Hansz (1972). "Environmental Determinants of Overseas Market Entry Strategies." Journal of International Business Studies 3 (Spring):33-51.

Hallen, L., and F. Wiedersheim-Paul (1979). "Psychic Distance and Buyer-Seller Interaction." Organization Marknad och Samhälle 16, no. 5:308-24.

Heck, M. J. (1972). International Trade: A Management Guide. New York: American Management Association.

Hirsch, P. M. (1972). "Processing Fads and Fashions: An Organization-Set Analysis of Cultural Industry Systems." American Journal of Sociology 77 (January):639-59.

ITI Research (1975). Concentration on Key Markets: A Development Plan for Exports, Betro Trust Committee. London: Royal Society of Arts.

Johanson, J., and F. Wiedersheim-Paul (1975). "The Internationalization of the Firm—Four Swedish Cases." Journal of Management Studies 12 (October):307-22.

Keegan, W. K. (1969). "Multinational Product Planning: Strategic Alternatives." Journal of Marketing 33 (January):58-62.

Marrett, C. B. (1971). "On the Specification of Interorganizational Dimensions." Sociology and Social Research 56 (October):83-99.

McMillan, C., and S. Paulden (1974). Export Agents: A Complete Guide to Their Selection and Control. Epping, Essex: Gower Press.

Mechanical Engineering EDC (1968). Market—The World: A Study of Success in Exporting. London: National Economic Development Organization.

Miracle, G. E., and G. S. Albaum (1970). International Marketing Management. Homewood, Ill.: Irwin.

Robinson, R. D. (1973). International Business Management. New York: Dryden Press.

Rosenberg, L. J. (1969). "An Empirical Examination of the Causes, Level and Consequences of Conflict in a High-Stake Distribution Channel." Ph.D. dissertation, Ohio State University.

Ross, R. E. (1972). "Selection of the Overseas Distributor: An Empirical Framework." International Journal of Physical Distribution 3 (Autumn):83-90.

Rosson, P. J., and I. D. Ford (1980a). "Some Aspects of Manufacturer-Distributor Relations in Exporting." Paper presented at the 1980 Academy of International Business Conference, New Orleans.

Rosson, P. J., and I. D. Ford (1980b). "Stake, Conflict and Performance in Export Marketing Channels." Management International Review 20, no. 4:31-37.

Schmidt, S. M., and T. A. Kochan (1977). "Interorganizational Relationships: Patterns and Motivations." Administrative Science Quarterly 22 (June):220-34.

Stern, L. W., and T. Reve (1980). "Distribution Channels as Political Economies: A Framework for Comparative Analysis." Journal of Marketing 44 (Summer):52-64.

Terpstra, V. (1972). International Marketing. New York: Holt, Rinehart and Winston.

Tookey, D. A. (1964). "Factors Associated with Success in Exporting." Journal of Management Studies 1 (March):48-66.

Tookey, D. A. (1975). Export Marketing Decisions. Harmondsworth, Middlesex: Penguin.

Tookey, D. A., E. Lea, and C. M. H. McDougall (1967). The
Exporters: A Study of Organization, Staff and Training. Ashridge, Berkshire: Ashridge Management College.

Van de Ven, A. H. (1976). "On the Nature, Formation and Main-
tenance of Relations among Organizations." Academy of Management Review 1 (October):24-36.

Wilkinson, I. F. (1973). "Power and Influence Structures in Distribution Channels." European Journal of Marketing 7 (Summer):
125-30.

Williamson, O. E. (1975). Markets and Hierarchies: Analysis and
Antitrust Implications. New York: The Free Press.

Williamson, O. E. (1979). "Transaction Cost Economics: The
Governance of Contractual Relations." Journal of Law and Economics 22 (October):232-62.

# 16

# SOME OBSERVATIONS ON THE RELEVANCE OF CRITICAL VARIABLES FOR INTERNATIONALIZATION STAGES

## S. Tamer Cavusgil

There has been a renewed interest in export marketing in recent years in many Western nations. (For a review of the literature, see Bilkey [1978] or Cavusgil and Nevin [1981b]). One of the research themes in exporting has been the stages of the internationalization process—the process by which firms increase their involvement in international marketing activities. The purpose of this chapter is to elaborate on the firm's internationalization process and to offer some evidence on the critical firm characteristics that facilitate or hinder firms' progression over the internationalization path.

An exposition of the internationalization process and its sequential nature is presented first. Operational definitions for four stages are then developed using data from a mail survey of firms in two states. Statistically significant differences among the firms in the four stages are analyzed with respect to a battery of firm and management characteristics. Finally, the findings are contrasted to those of the earlier studies and a number of conclusions are offered.

## THE SEQUENTIAL NATURE OF THE INTERNATIONALIZATION PROCESS

In my previous writings I have argued that firms' involvement in international marketing, in general, and export marketing, in particular, is best understood as a sequential process (Cavusgil, 1980). The available empirical research suggests a gradual pattern of internationalization with several identifiable stages (for example, Johanson and Wiedersheim-Paul, 1975; Johanson and Vahlne, 1977; Wiedersheim-Paul, Olson, and Welch, 1978; Welch and Wiedersheim-Paul, 1980a and 1980b).

The majority of firms appear to approach export marketing in an experimental manner with their managements holding the amount of resources (including time) to be committed for exporting at any particular time to a minimum level. This cautious behavior is due partly to the fact that initial export marketing decisions will be made in an environment of greater uncertainty and lesser familiarity. Confidence of managers will be low, thus adding to the perceived risk associated with decision making. Coupled with a certain amount of uncertainty associated with the profitability of initial exporting, these circumstances will create a cautious type of management, one that is likely to proceed with decision making in an incremental manner. Such a management would acquire some experience before deciding on further involvement and avoid making large, spectacular strides.

An additional explanation for the sequential nature of the internationalization process may be provided by the decision-making dynamics of especially smaller firms. Typically, it will be very difficult to divert management attention from the usual and routine activities of the firm. It will take some time before export marketing opportunities are incorporated into the company goals and the planning system. Managers may go through a long process of learning and becoming sufficiently motivated before opportunities in foreign markets are made an integral part of the firm operations.

My conceptualization of the internationalization process and various stages along the process are illustrated in Figure 16.1. The basis for distinguishing among the firms in various stages includes: management's level of awareness of foreign market opportunities, the nature of search processes for information, decision-making mode of management, typical decision-making skills utilized, and the nature of international marketing involvement. The five stages that are identified should be regarded as tentative characterizations. The essential proposition, however, is that firms do differ in terms of the manner in which they exploit export marketing opportunities. The extent and the nature of involvement in export marketing will vary from one firm to another. This is because the opportunities that are encountered by the firm, and the way in which the management responds to those opportunities, are different among firms. An implication of this proposition is that there can be meaningful differences among exporting firms and that the characterization of a "typical" exporting firm would be erroneous (see Cavusgil, Bilkey, and Tesar, 1979, for empirical evidence). A related implication is that firms may travel through several stages on the way to becoming truly internationalized.

# FIGURE 16.1

Characterization of the Stages in the Internationalization Process

| | STAGE 1 | STAGE 2 | STAGE 3 | STAGE 4 | STAGE 5 |
|---|---|---|---|---|---|
| STAGES IN THE INTERNATIONALIZATION PROCESS | PRE-INVOLVEMENT STAGE | REACTIVE INVOLVEMENT (Response to unsolicited opportunities) | LIMITED EXPERIMENTAL INVOLVEMENT | ACTIVE INVOLVEMENT | COMMITTED INVOLVEMENT (Full-fledged and perpetual) |
| AWARENESS OF OPPORTUNITIES | Low | Sporadic | Moderate | High | Intense |
| NATURE OF SEARCH PROCESSES | Limited and selective | | | Intensive venture search | |
| DOMINANT DECISION-MAKING MODE | Disjointed and incremental | | | Formal and structured | |
| TYPICAL DECISION-MAKING SKILLS UTILIZED | Passive | Reactive | Intuitive and Problem-solving oriented | Proactive and Entrepreneurial | Highly systematic and informed |

Source: Adapted from Cavusgil (1980).

## AN OPERATIONALIZATION OF THE
## INTERNATIONALIZATION STAGES

For the purpose of partially operationalizing the above conceptualization, data obtained from a mail survey of firms were used. The survey was conducted among a systematically selected group of manufacturing firms in Maine and New Mexico. It sought a variety of information from the responding top executives.

In operationalizing the internationalization framework, two stages were created for exporting firms and two for nonexporting firms. Interest in gathering export-related information served to distinguish the two types of nonexporters, and the level of export activity was used as the basis for differentiating the two types of exporters. More specifically, the firms in each of the four stages were defined in the following way:

Stage One:    Nonexporting firms. Not interested in gathering export-related information.

Stage Two:    Nonexporting firms. Interested in gathering export-related information. (These correspond roughly to "preinvolvement stage" in the conceptualization.)

Stage Three:    Exporting firms. Export less than 10 percent of their output. (Correspond to "limited, experimental involvement stage" in the conceptualization.)

Stage Four:    Exporting firms. Export more than 10 percent of their output. (Correspond to "active involvement stage" in the conceptualization.)

While these operational definitions are not totally satisfactory, they do provide a way of classifying firms into one of the stages and subsequently searching for meaningful distinctions among them.

## EXPLANATORY VARIABLES OF THE
## INTERNATIONALIZATION PROCESS

Once the firms were classified into one of the four stages, it was desirable to test for meaningful and statistically significant differences among them. Firms were contrasted in terms of a battery of variables identified by previous research as critical determinants of international marketing activity. The reader may be referred to Bilkey (1978) or Cavusgil and Nevin (1981a) for an elaboration of the variables that are hypothesized to influence firms' exporting behavior.

Four groups of variables were delineated and then used in the empirical analysis. Similar to the Cavusgil and Nevin (1981a) categorization, the groups are identified as differential firm advantages, level of commitment to export marketing, personal characteristics of the decision makers, and management's perceptions of profits and risks in exporting. Differential firm advantages are derived from the nature of the firm's products, markets, technological orientation, and resources. As examples of these advantages we have included the following: management expertise in finance, management expertise in marketing, perceived company strengths (quality of products, new product development capability, patents, and national network of middlemen), technology intensiveness, local versus national market orientation, and firm size.

Level of commitment to export marketing was measured by the management's information-seeking behavior. Responding executives had indicated whether or not their firm has sought information on exporting from external sources in the preceding five years. These information sources include the U.S. Department of Commerce, the state government, executives of other firms, and export agents. The two personal decision-maker characteristics that were included in the study were age and educational background. Finally, managers' perceptions of how profitable and risky export marketing is, compared to domestic marketing, were included as the fourth group of critical variables hypothesized to explain firms' progression over the internationalization process.

## THE EMPIRICAL ANALYSIS

Table 16.1 presents the results of the univariate tests (F-test) of differences among the firms in the four stages in terms of the four sets of critical variables discussed above. Levels of significance (p-values) are given for those differences that are statistically significant.

In explaining the progression from Stage One to Stage Two the following variables seem to be useful. First, new product development capability and product quality are two differential advantages possessed to a greater degree by the Stage Two firms. These advantages may serve as initial motivation for managements to be interested in exporting. Wiedersheim-Paul, Olson, and Welch (1978) labeled these "attention evokers." Second, Stage Two firms appear to be more active in gathering export-related information than Stage One firms. Personal sources—executives of other firms and export agents—rather than impersonal sources account for the differences. Third, both personal characteristics are useful in

TABLE 16.1

Significance of the Variables That Account for the Firm's Progression over the Internationalization Process

| Explanatory Variables | From Stage One to Stage Two | From Stage Two to Stage Three | From Stage Three to Stage Four |
|---|---|---|---|
| Firm size (number of full-time employees) | — | — | — |
| Local market orientation (state's share of firm's sales) | — | .00 | .03 |
| Technology intensiveness | — | .08 | .00 |
| Quality of products as a perceived strength | .02 | — | — |
| Capability to develop new products | .00 | — | — |
| Patents held as a perceived strength | — | .07 | — |
| National network of middlemen | — | .00 | — |
| Management expertise in marketing | — | .00 | — |
| Management expertise in finance | — | .00 | — |
| Seek information from U.S. Department of Commerce | .03 | .00 | — |
| Seek information from a state agency | — | .04 | — |
| Seek information from executives of other firms | .00 | .00 | — |
| Seek information from an export agent | .00 | .07 | — |
| Respondent's age | .00 | — | — |
| Respondent's education | .00 | — | .05 |
| Perceived risks of exporting | — | .03 | .00 |
| Perceived profits from exporting | — | .08 | .08 |

Note: The figures are the p values for univariate F-ratios. Only those results that are significant beyond the 0.10 level are shown.

distinguishing Stage Two firms from Stage One firms. Managers of Stage Two firms are more likely to be younger and more educated.

It is interesting to note that neither profit nor risk perceptions discriminate between the Stage One and Stage Two firms. This finding, then, would add credibility to the hypothesis that, during the firm's initial preparation for or the actual involvement in export marketing, profit motivation does not play a significant role. Nonprofit or noneconomic motives, such as desire to exploit excess capacity or an obsolete product, may be more dominant.

A larger number of statistically significant differences are detected between Stage Two and Stage Three firms. Progression to Stage Three appears to be, among other things, the result of an expansion in the national market and the possession of a national network of middlemen. This finding concerning the importance of national rather than local-market orientation is reinforced by the "extraregional expansion" argument put forth by Welch and Wiedersheim-Paul (1980b). According to this argument, firms need to go through an internationalization process in the domestic market itself. Domestic expansion provides a training ground for future exporters and "represents the beginnings of the internationalization process, merely circumscribed within national borders" (p. 2).

Stage Three firms are more likely than Stage Two firms to enjoy management expertise in marketing and finance. This may be because of the substantial learning involved in export starts. A technologically intensive product is also a characteristic of the Stage Three firms. In addition, Stage Three firms have been more active in gathering information on exporting from all four sources.

It will be noted that the risk and profit perceptions of managers are significantly different between Stage Two and Stage Three firms. Interestingly, Stage Three firms (exporters) perceived greater risks and lesser profits in exporting. This is possibly because these firms are relatively new to exporting, finding themselves confronted with a number of unexpected hurdles. This finding can also be explained with the previously discussed argument that the initial involvement is less likely to be brought about by purely economic motivations.

Progression of the firm to Stage Four seems to be facilitated by the presence of a technologically intensive product. A national market orientation continues to be critical. Perceived profits and risks are also important. This time, however, the perceptions are as expected: Stage Four firms are more optimistic about exporting than Stage Three firms. Surprisingly, information gathering from external sources does not help to explain progression to Stage Four. This is possibly because the Stage Four firm, by now, has developed its own marketing intelligence system and does not have to rely on an outside source of information.

## COMPARISON OF THE FINDINGS WITH EARLIER STUDIES

Two other studies have been reported that are similar to the present investigation in its attempt to classify firms into internationalization stages for subsequent analysis. Bilkey and Tesar (1977) identified at least six stages along the export development process and provided analysis for three of these. Their findings bear surprising similarities to ours.

In searching for correlates of having explored the feasibility of exporting (their Stage Three), they found the following variables useful: whether or not management plans for exporting (indication of commitment), and perceptions of competitive advantages. They found no meaningful correlations with management's profit or other expectations regarding the effect of exporting on the firm. They concluded that "Stage Three of the export development process seems to be much more nearly a function of managements' general images of exporting and foreign lands than of immediate economic considerations" (Bilkey and Tesar 1977, p. 94). Quality and dynamism of the management was found to be an important determinant of exporting experimentally (their Stage Four). Finally, expectations and perceived barriers were overwhelmingly important among experienced exporters (their Stage Five), suggesting a more rational decision making at this stage.

Both our results and those of Bilkey and Tesar suggest that size of firm does not have an impact on the firm's progression over the internationalization path. Relative to commitment, differential advantage, personal, and perception variables, size does not seem to matter. An inference can be drawn from this finding stating that both small and large firms can travel the internationalization path. However, one needs to be cautious about this conclusion since firm size is usually correlated with the availability of resources, quality and dynamism of management, and other variables. Hence, size is likely to have an indirect effect on export behavior causing, perhaps, small and large firms to travel the internationalization path at varying speeds.

The second study, reported by Czinkota and Johnston (1981), employed a richer basis for classifying firms into stages. The classification criteria included export sales volume, length of export experience, types of countries exported to, number of export customers and transactions, personnel committed to exporting, management attitudes, firm size, and service orientation of the firm.

Firms were classified into the following stages: the unwilling firm, the uninterested firm, the interested firm, the experimenting exporter, the semiexperienced small exporter, and the experienced large exporter. After experimenting with four alternative ways of segmenting firms, Czinkota and Johnston concluded that differentiation based on the internationalization stages provides the best approach. They noted, however, that differentiation of firms according to size requires the least amount of information and may be the best approach to use for identifying firms for unilateral assistance programs.

## CONCLUSIONS

This investigation sought to provide empirical support for the argument that the internationalization of the firm tends to take place in sequential stages and that the critical variables that influence firms' progression from one stage to the next tend to vary by stage. Though they remain tentative, the following conclusions are warranted. During the "preinvolvement" or "preparation for export start" stage, a number of differential advantages—serving as initiating forces—and the appropriate change agents appear to be critical. During the "experimental involvement stage" a broad-based marketing experience and active commitment of resources seem to make a difference. It is doubtful that the firm ventures into export marketing with purely economic considerations in mind. Favorable expectations of profits, on the other hand, appear to be responsible in converting the experimental exporter into one that is more active, committed, and serious about exporting.

In sum, along with the Bilkey and Tesar (1977) and Czinkota and Johnston (1981) contributions, our findings suggest that different variables are at work in facilitating or hindering firms' progression over the internationalization path. Future investigations should follow up on this research avenue and, it is hoped, further refine the internationalization stages and develop a more comprehensive battery of critical variables that affect those stages. A better understanding of the export behavior of firms and a better targeting of the stimulation efforts are bound to emerge from such research.

## REFERENCES

Bilkey, Warren J. (1978). "An Attempted Integration of the Literature on Export Behavior of Firms." Journal of International Business Studies, Spring/Summer, pp. 33-46.

Bilkey, Warren J., and George Tesar (1977). "The Export Behavior of Smaller Sized Wisconsin Manufacturing Firms." Journal of International Business Studies, Spring/Summer, pp. 93-98.

Cavusgil, S. Tamer (1980). "On the Internationalization Process of Firms." European Research 8, no. 6:273-81.

Cavusgil, S. Tamer, W. J. Bilkey, and G. Tesar (1979). "A Note on the Export Behavior of Firms: Exporter Profiles." Journal of International Business Studies 10:91-97.

Cavusgil, S. Tamer, and John R. Nevin (1981a). "Internal Determinants of Export Marketing Behavior: An Empirical Investigation." Journal of Marketing Research 28, no. 1:114-19.

Cavusgil, S. Tamer, and John R. Nevin (1981b). "State-of-the-Art in International Marketing: An Assessment." In Review of Marketing 1981, edited by Ben Enis and Ken Roering. Chicago: American Marketing Association.

Czinkota, Michael R., and W. J. Johnston (1981). "Segmenting U.S. Firms for Export Development." Journal of Business Research 9, no. 4.

Johanson, J., and F. Wiedersheim-Paul (1975). "The Internationalization of the Firm—Four Swedish Case Studies." The Journal of Management Studies, October:305-22.

Johanson, J., and J. Vahlne (1977). "The Internationalization Process of the Firm: A Model of Knowledge Development and Increasing Foreign Commitments." Journal of International Business Studies, Spring/Summer, pp. 23-32.

Welch, Lawrence S., and Finn Wiedersheim-Paul (1979). "Export Promotion Policy: A New Approach." Australian Journal of Management 4, no. 2 (October):165-76.

Welch, Lawrence S., and Finn Wiedersheim-Paul (1980a). "Initial Exports—A Marketing Failure?" The Journal of Management Studies, October, pp. 333-44.

Welch, Lawrence S., and Finn Wiedersheim-Paul (1980b). "Domestic Expansion: Internationalization At Home." Essays in International Business, No. 2 (December), The University of South Carolina.

Wiedersheim-Paul, Finn, H. C. Olson, and L. S. Welch (1978). "Pre-Export Activity: The First Step in Internationalization." Journal of International Business Studies, Spring/Summer, pp. 47-58.

# PART IV
## CONCLUSIONS
Michael R. Czinkota

At the end of the International Symposium on Exporting, from which the contributions to this volume result, the participants discussed their impressions of export management and responded to a questionnaire. The purpose of this discussion was to arrive at a consensus of the current state of the art of export management operations and research. Since the chapters in this volume detail the findings of the individual researchers, only general issues are presented here.

The discussions about the export activities of the firm focused on two main issues. The first one dealt with the question: What makes a firm export? Various factors were suggested that, either individually or jointly, were thought to account for export activities. The two major ones were the motivation of top management and the firm's need for expansion. The latter factor was seen to be a result of continuous growth requirements on the part of owners/ stockholders, pressures of survival, and cyclical demand at home. The high profitability of export operations was seen as a factor of slightly lesser importance with many participants voicing the opinion that this perceived profitability was frequently not obtained in the short run. Other factors that were thought to play a role were unsolicited orders, special knowledge about opportunities, and the prestige of international operations.

The second main issue concerned the problems that firms encountered in beginning their export operations. A lack of information on the part of firms about foreign markets, customers, and middlemen was seen as a major problem. The firm's lack of ability to finance export activities was seen as being almost of equal importance together with the scarcity of personnel trained in export operations. Of major import were also logistic issues such as the movement and handling, packaging, and servicing of goods. Other problems mentioned were the lack of management time and commitment, the failure of firms to reorganize internally for market expansion, the identification of appropriate marketing strategies, and government red tape.

Another major area of discussions centered on issues of export management research. When trying to identify research findings that could be globally accepted to form the basic building blocks of an export management theory, only very few issues emerged. Apart from the aforementioned factors that motivate the export activities of firms, and those that present obstacles to the exporting effort, only few statements could be agreed upon:

- Exporting can be beneficial to firms over the long run.
- Many firms perceive export activities as difficult and not worthwhile.

- Many firms are too shortsighted in their planning for exporting.
- In order for export efforts to be successful, management must be committed to the undertaking.

Judging from these few issues, it appears that at this time it would be inappropriate to speak of the existence of a coherent export management theory. Three major reasons were thought to account for this situation. One was the apparent lack of rigor of many studies carried out in the area of international business in general. Although the great methodological difficulties of carrying out international research were recognized, some fear was expressed that current research in international business sometimes does not have the quality of work carried out in economics or other functional areas of business.

A second major reason was seen to lie in the frequent national and regional constraints of research. It was felt that truly international research, for example, taking not only exporters and their concerns but also their foreign counterparts into account, is not carried out sufficiently. A clear need for more awareness of the international literature on the part of researchers was also felt, which could eliminate some of the attempts to reinvent the wheel in different parts of the world.

Lack of systematic longitudinal research was seen as a third reason. Although funding problems were viewed as representing part of the difficulty, the short-term orientation and quantity pressures of academia were also cited. While these time pressures were mentioned particularly in context with the research environment in the United States, it appears that similar circumstances tend to exist also in Europe.[1]

Some research areas were suggested for further fruitful pursuit. Most participants felt that more research into the internationalization process of the firm, particularly into the beginning exporting stages is warranted. Currently conflicting findings and the importance of understanding this process in order to initiate change, were seen as incentives for such work. The motivational factors and attitudes of management also should be researched further, focusing on the identification of factors that are determinant rather than salient. Another major research thrust should concentrate on an evaluation of the cost and benefits of exporting as compared to alternative expansion strategies and the identification of growth/performance links. More attention should also be given to the organizational restructuring process in the exporting firm, to the issue of firm size and its effect on export capabilities, and to the interaction between exporting firms and governments.

Export management is fraught with many problems that for some firms and researchers will turn into opportunities. The International Symposium on Exporting provided a forum to discuss and define these opportunities more clearly. By taking into account the international interdependencies that impact the export operations of the firm, and by carrying out international research in more of a structured and interactive fashion, these opportunities can be turned into results.

NOTE

1. Peter Wapnewski, "Die Republik und ihre Elite" (The Republic and Its Elite), Die Zeit 36, 41, October 9, 1981, p. 12.

# INDEX

# ABOUT THE EDITORS
# AND CONTRIBUTORS

MICHAEL R. CZINKOTA is an Assistant Professor of Marketing in the School of Business Administration at Georgetown University and a Fellow of the Center for Strategic and International Studies. He studied Law and Business Administration at the University of Erlangen-Nuernberg in Germany, and was a partner in an export-import firm. In 1975 Dr. Czinkota won a Fulbright Award and studied at The Ohio State University from where he received his MBA in 1976 and his Ph.D. in 1980.

Dr. Czinkota has written extensively on the subject of exporting in publications such as the Columbia Journal of World Business, the Journal of Business Research, the International Journal of Physical Distribution and Materials Management, and has published a book with Praeger on U.S. export promotion entitled Export Development Strategies.

GEORGE TESAR is Professor of Marketing at the University of Wisconsin, Whitewater. He has a Ph.D. from the University of Wisconsin, Madison and an MBA from Michigan State University. He was a faculty associate at the Center for Strategic and International Studies in Washington, D.C. Dr. Tesar was a Fulbright Lecturer in Marketing at the Central School of Planning and Statistics in Warsaw, Poland. Currently he serves on the editorial board of the Journal of International Business Studies and on the Wisconsin Governor's Committee on International Trade. He has taught at the University of Wisconsin, Madison and Georgetown University. His area of research is in export development and export stimulation among small- and medium-sized firms. He also works with industry in the areas of product development and internationalization of corporate operations.

MARY R. BROOKS is Assistant Professor of Marketing, School of Business Administration, Dalhousie University, Halifax, Nova Scotia.

PETER J. BUCKLEY is Senior Lecturer in International Business, University of Bradford Management Centre, United Kingdom.

S. TAMER CAVUSGIL is Associate Professor of Marketing at the University of Wisconsin, Whitewater.

DAVID FORD is Visiting Associate Professor of Marketing in the Graduate School of Business, University of Texas at Austin, Austin, Texas, while on leave from the University of Bath in England.

GÉRARD GARNIER is Professor of International Business, Faculty of Administration, University of Sherbrooke, Quebec.

CHARLES H. GREEN is Senior Associate, Management Analysis Center, Inc., Cambridge, Massachusetts.

RONALD E. HOYT is a member of the Faculty of Sciences Administration, University Laval, Quebec.

WESLEY J. JOHNSTON is Assistant Professor, Academic Faculty of Marketing, the Ohio State University, Columbus, Ohio.

PAT JOYNT is a Professor at the Norwegian School of Management, Norway.

ERDENER KAYNAK is Associate Professor of Marketing and Chairman, Department of Business Administration, Mount Saint Vincent University, Halifax, Nova Scotia.

ANNA LAWSON is a faculty member at the University of Bath, England.

J. F. NICHOLLS is a faculty member at the University of Bath, England.

ERNEST W. OGRAM, Jr. is Professor of International Business at Georgia State University, Atlanta.

STAN REID is Assistant Professor in the School of Management, Syracuse University.

PHILIP J. ROSSON is Associate Professor of Marketing, School of Business Administration, Dalhousie University, Halifax, Nova Scotia.

RAVI SARATHY is Assistant Professor in the College of Business, Northeastern University.

LOIS STEVENSON holds an MBA and is a Lecturer in Marketing, Department of Business Administration, Mount Saint Vincent University, Halifax, Nova Scotia.

JESSE S. TARLETON is Associate Professor, School of Business Administration, College of William and Mary, Williamsburg.

DANIEL VAN DEN BULCKE is Professor at the Economische Hogeschool Limburg (Diepenbeek). He also teaches at the College of Europe (Bruges) and ICHEC (Brussels) and is vice-president of the International Trade Invest Institute (Brussels).